MAKING PEACE
IN YOUR
STEPFAMILY

MAKING PEACE
IN YOUR
STEPFAMILY

*Surviving and Thriving as
Parents and Stepparents*

HAROLD H. BLOOMFIELD, M.D.

with Robert B. Kory

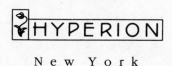

HYPERION

New York

Anyone with a history of mental disorder, or who is in an emotionally unstable stepfamily situation, should not do the exercises in this book without first consulting a qualified mental health professional.

Copyright © 1993 Harold H. Bloomfield and Robert B. Kory

Library of Congress Cataloging-in-Publication Data
Bloomfield, Harold H.
    Making peace in your stepfamily: surviving and thriving as parents and stepparents / Harold H. Bloomfield with Robert B. Kory. — 1st ed.
        p.   cm.
    Includes bibliographical references (p.   )
    ISBN 1-56282-885-1
    1. Stepparents—United States. 2. Stepfamilies—United States. I. Kory, Robert B. II. Title. III. Title: Making peace in your stepfamily.
HQ759.92.B56 1993
306.874—dc20   93-35074
                                                                             CIP

Book design by Richard Oriolo

First Edition

10 9 8 7 6 5 4 3 2 1

To dearest Sirah, Shazara,
Damien, and Michael,
with love and appreciation

C o n t e n t s

Chapter 3 HOW TO BE A GOOD STEPPARENT

Chapter 4 SHARING DISCIPLINE, FAMILY ROLES, RULES AND RITES

Chapter 7 MONEY MATTERS; LOVE MATTERS MORE

MAKING PEACE
IN YOUR
STEPFAMILY

Chapter 1

STEPFAMILY
CRISIS

B y the year 2000 the stepfamily will be the predominant family form, more than nuclear or single-parent families. Half of all Americans are already a member of a stepfamily (when you include grandparents, uncles, half-siblings and other extended family). Yet, tragically about 70 percent of all stepfamilies will end in divorce in less than ten years' duration. Learning to make peace is essential to survive and thrive as a stepfamily.

The modern family is in turmoil, and nowhere more so than in the stepfamily. The breakdown of the nuclear family, which began with the rising divorce rates of the early 1970s, has accelerated to become a virtual chain reaction. Since the early 1970s, over one million children annually have watched their parents separate and divorce.

Over half of these children have also watched at least one of their parents remarry, creating the new dominant U.S. family structure—the stepfamily. Seven million children are now stepchildren; one-third of all children will live in a stepfamily household before age eighteen. There are over twenty million stepparents in the U.S. Yet, stepparenting is still a role for which there is either no script or, at best, a poor one.

There is an enormous amount of pain and a great need for practical guidance about how to alleviate family conflict. There is also a strong nostalgia for the past and a desire to return to what seem to be the idyllic days of the "Leave It to Beaver" nuclear family. The time has come to let go of an idealized past and instead learn how to embrace the stepfamily, so that this new family structure can support the emotional well-being of parents and children alike.

"Step-": From Shame to Pride

In my research on the stepfamily, I have been intrigued by the negative connotations of the word. In our culture, there is a sometimes subtle and sometimes not so subtle shame associated with stepfamilies. People in stepfamilies often feel unsafe, enraged, pressured, wicked, rejected and cheated—and so isolated that they are ashamed of these feelings. The word "stepfamily" is associated with broken homes and deprivation. In fact, *stepchild* is defined by the Random House Dictionary not only as "a child of a husband or wife by a previous marriage," but also as "any person, organization, affiliate or project that is not properly treated, supported, or appreciated."

Our society has been in denial about the guilt and shame associated with stepfamily life. Fortunately, brave people are coming out of the closet to talk about the pain and loss sometimes associated with stepfamily living. President Bill Clinton, a stepson, has talked extensively about the intense conflicts in the stepfamily in which he grew up and the ambivalence he had in taking on the last name of his stepfather. Interestingly, George Washington, the "Father of Our Country," was also a stepfather.

If this book succeeds at nothing else, I am hopeful that it will enable remarried couples and their children to declare their pride in being part of a stepfamily. You are the new wave of what family is all about in America, and you are the ones saving the family as an institution from the dire consequences of divorce and postdivorce hostility and further breakdown.

Steps to Becoming a Family

I have chosen to interpret *step* in "stepfamily" in its literal meaning. A stepfamily is a remarried couple with children who are taking *steps* toward becoming a family. A wedding makes remarried couples with children into an instant family from a legal point of view. From an emotional and spiritual vantage point, however, becoming a family takes time. You have to take many steps, one step at a time, but as long as you remain on the right path, you will arrive at a wonderful goal.

What makes stepparenting so difficult and stepfamilies so complex are the conflicting emotions that almost always develop when two families merge. Most stepparents report they are troubled by frustration, guilt, and resentment in their new families. Remarried parents typically feel caught in a crossfire between their children and a new spouse, while the postdivorce animosity toward an ex-spouse continues to cause conflict. So, too, stepchildren are typically driven by unacknowledged fear, remorse, and rage. These feelings have complex origins, but the good news is that these conflicts can be effectively resolved with a little insight and a lot of commitment.

Almost every day in my office, I see parents, stepparents, and their children struggling with divided loyalties, guilt, and disappointment. I also see stepfamilies learning about the causes of their family turmoil and specific ways to make peace. For those stepfamilies committed to survive, everyone involved—parent, stepparent, children, stepchildren—discovers the miracle of the stepfamily. The new bonds of love, trust, and respect forged through the resolution of stepfamily conflict are often stronger and more rewarding than any family bond they have known before. In many cases the children find themselves growing closer both to their stepparents *and* to their natural parents, while ex-spouses learn how to stop fighting and start cooperating with each other as parents.

Most couples remarry with high expectations and a certain wisdom gained from a previous marriage and a walk through the valley of the shadow of divorce. These new couples' high hopes are often dashed by the harsh realities of stepfamily life. That was my experience when I remarried and became a stepfather to my wife's two sons. At first, I honestly doubted our stepfamily would survive. You may be feeling the same. Fortunately, life in a stepfamily doesn't have to be a nightmare. You and your spouse *can* learn the specific skills that lead to loving, accepting, intimate relationships within your stepfamily. Your stepfamily can provide joyous, fulfilling family experiences, if you understand the new rules of the game. For every hour you invest in reading, exploring, and working with the exercises in this book, you will save a hundred hours of unnecessary conflict, anger, and misery. You can make peace in your stepfamily.

That's why I wrote this book. You see, my wife and I learned how to survive as a stepfamily the hard way. When we first became a stepfamily, our marriage almost fell apart because we hadn't yet learned to cope with many of the challenges parents and stepparents must face every day. We found ourselves ill-prepared for the rivalries and resentments that can arise and fester in a stepfamily. Surprisingly, my psychiatric expertise and my wife's psychological training were of limited value. We had to learn why each of us in our new family was so fraught with turmoil, and then we had to develop specific strategies and techniques—some simple enough to use with our youngest child—to enable our stepfamily to make peace and become a true family. This is the book I wish someone had handed me.

My Stepfamily

My wife Sirah and I have each been married before. We have one child together and two boys from her previous marriage. Today, the quality of love and mutual support within our family nurtures us all. Not so obvious, however, is the intense emotional turmoil we went through or the work it took to create the quality of family life we now cherish. My personal story illustrates what it takes not only to survive but to make peace in your stepfamily.

When Sirah and I married, her former husband had insisted on retaining custody of her two boys. Rather than fight that battle, Sirah reluctantly agreed. We then had our own daughter, and I did relatively well with Sirah's sons during summer and holiday visits. My role as stepparent was very limited, and I naively thought of myself as having mastered stepparenting. All that changed when Damien, Sirah's then thirteen-year-old son, asked to move in with us.

The telephone call came in the middle of my nationwide lecture tour several years ago. Damien surprised us by asking to leave his father's house in Toronto and come to live with us in California before the start of the new school year. This innocent request—made out of love—turned out to be an emotional spark that gradually grew into a major family conflict. None of us were prepared for the intensity of antagonistic feelings or the turmoil of competing needs that eventually surfaced.

Damien's telephone call caught us by surprise. When we got off the phone, Sirah and I soon found ourselves arguing. It is difficult and embarrassing for me to admit that Damien's request represented a complication and an intrusion. For me the custody issue had long since been resolved; I had no plans to be the father of two teenage boys nor to engage in a protracted battle with their father. As a result, when Damien's call came, I was alarmed and defensive.

Sirah, on the other hand, heard Damien's plea for her love and support, and she responded with a mother's immediate desire to do anything possible for her son. She saw Damien's request as an opportunity to enrich all of our lives. What came to mind for me were more responsibility, financial burdens, and new challenges in dealing with a troubled adolescent boy. The prospect of these fundamental changes in my life did not seem appealing. What I saw as rational concerns, Sirah saw as my insensitivity both to her feelings as a mother and to Damien's needs as her son. We went to bed that night feeling hurt and misunderstood.

At that point in our relationship, we had been married for four years and, this major argument notwithstanding, we were a reasonably happy couple. Having worked through some of the communication problems that arose early in our relationship, we felt confident in our marriage. The year before, Sirah had given birth to our first child, and I thought our family was made in heaven. I wanted another baby; instead, Sirah now wanted Damien to live with us.

What neither of us appreciated at the time, however, was the enormous difference between meeting the emotional demands of marriage and meeting the more complex emotional demands necessary to make peace in a blended family. We thought the skills we had developed to support our intimate communication would be sufficient for us to create a family environment with high-quality communication and emotional nurturance. The fact is, however, that we felt suddenly overwhelmed by this crisis. Without the necessary peacemaking skills, stepfamily conflicts can threaten an otherwise satisfying marriage.

After Damien's initial request, we couldn't agree. Damien's father initially was adamant that Damien remain in Toronto. Whenever the issue arose with Sirah, I emphasized how Damien's relationship with his father and stepmother appeared strong, and that Damien had the benefit of four parents who loved him. I believed that any decision involving Damien moving to California should first require approval by Damien's father and stepmother as well. Soon I assumed the whole issue was closed.

In retrospect, I now recognize that much of my attitude was an emotional defense. My resistance to becoming a full-time stepfather was symptomatic of an unresolved personal conflict. Having organized most of my adult life on my own terms and having been raised as the "only son" by "Old World" European parents, I was not eager to have a stepson in my life on a full-time basis.

The conflict intensified over the next few years. Sirah asked that both of her boys spend more time with us, and I reluctantly agreed. When both Damien and his younger brother, Michael, visited us during the holidays and long summer vacations, I felt many of my old psychological "buttons" being pushed. I began resenting my stepsons for their "intrusion into my space," and I grew increasingly impatient with them. Economic questions as to what to provide for our daughter, as opposed to the boys, also arose. I avoided the real parenting issues by contributing toward Damien's education at a private school, while I kept my emotional distance.

I grew increasingly frustrated because Damien would not drop the issue of moving to California, despite my agreeing to long summer visits. Meanwhile, Damien felt I was hostile and only going through the motions as a stepfather to appease his mother. Intimidated by my attitude, Damien grew hurt, frustrated, and able to confide his feelings only to Sirah, who would take his side and later take it out on me. Here we were caught in one of the fundamental traps of family miscommunication—an emotional triangle—where the two people who most needed to make peace would not talk to each other directly. As tensions grew, quarreling and spiteful comments became common.

Each long summer visit now threw the household into turmoil. I became emotionally withdrawn, and got upset with the boys at the slightest provocation. They would come crying to Sirah about how they were treated. "How could you marry him?" the youngest would ask, while Damien would threaten, "I'm not going to take it." Sirah kept trying to make peace, with little success. When I became jealous of Sirah's attention, the boys became even more upset and protective of their mother. Some visits were better than others; we certainly had many good times. Yet Sirah felt increasingly unable to make her boys part of our family, and hoped for improvements that never really came.

Family Breakdown or Breakthrough

The growing tension in our family eventually started to erode my confidence in our marriage. After all that we had achieved in opening up to each other as a couple, here I was in deep turmoil about how my stepchildren would fit into my life, love relationship, and career.

To compound matters, I felt more strongly than ever that I wanted another baby. Sirah, on the other hand, wanted to balance her career with her responsibilities as a mother to the children already in our lives. I felt trapped and rejected by Sirah's refusal to have another child; Sirah felt unappreciated and resentful due to my pressure to have another child and my problems with my stepsons.

The growing conflict in our family finally erupted. Damien started acting out his frustrations in Toronto. Although Damien had been signaling his personal distress through angry outbursts, no one in the family had paid enough attention. Finally, he made his turmoil clear to all by getting into trouble with the police.

Sirah was devastated, and blamed herself. She also blamed both her ex-husband and me for failing to hear Damien's cries for help. As a result, Sirah began vehemently expressing her wish that Damien live with us. Damien's father and stepmother began to support the idea, in part because they felt Damien was out of control. I felt cornered, still hurt by Sirah's refusal to have another child with me.

For Sirah, the intensity of the emotional conflict became particularly acute. Having reluctantly consented to her boys' living with their father as a condition of her divorce, she carried both the pain of losing them and the guilt of not being available to them. The last straw came when Damien told her about a dream he'd had, in which he was living in California and arguing with her in the kitchen about the sprout-filled sandwich she had made him for lunch. When Damien told her that the dream ended in their laughter and hugs, Sirah cried. Damien had painted the picture Sirah longed for, and she became adamant that she had the right to have it.

Faced with a rapidly deteriorating home environment, Sirah and I decided to take a weekend alone together for heart-to-heart communication. Our own case illustrates how firmly entrenched family members can become in their roles, and how rigid the emotional positions can become. Away from the family, we were able to discuss and accept our hurt feelings, including our anger, fear, and grief. We also recognized that the tension in our family would not heal on its own. We needed to take specific steps, both in dealing with our own feelings and in working with our children, to make peace. Our weekend led to a year-long effort to heal our stepfamily.

In a family situation that isn't working, each person feels like "poor me." We all resist acknowledging our own mistakes, negative feelings, and petty selfishness. Aware of my resistances, I became determined to look honestly at my resentment, heated arguments and refusal to listen. If our marriage and family were to survive, I had to make peace in a way that acknowledged each member's point of view and integrated conflicting needs.

With Sirah's help, I began to focus specifically on the changes that we needed to make as individuals and the changes we needed to make as a stepfamily. I began examining what was behind my resentment toward Sirah's boys. We encouraged the boys to look into what was underneath their hostility. We all learned to acknowledge and heal emotional losses that we had unconsciously tried to avoid.

Sirah and I also started asking ourselves some difficult questions: Were we creating a family atmosphere where everyone felt enough safety, trust, and love to express feelings without fear? Were we communicating to each of our children that we valued them as individuals, or were we making assumptions about what we were communicating to our children?

It also became apparent that we had to find ways to help family members understand and transcend rigid roles and rules. Our family system was sclerotic, that is, each of us was locked into rigid roles and perceptions. Sirah's feedback, plus some painful self-examination, made it clear that I was stuck in the roles of "stepfather knows best" and "the family revolves around me." I was demanding and impatient with family members who challenged my plans. As long as I remained in that controlling, authoritarian role, change was impossible. Only after I stepped back from those roles could I begin to understand Damien as an individual. These rigid roles were supported by unspoken rules. For instance, Damien and I only talked to each other about sports or schoolwork, and never about how he missed Sirah or wanted to move to California. It was long overdue that Damien and I communicate directly with each other, one-on-one, in a heartfelt way.

Sirah and I also began to recognize unresolved feelings of loss that undermined all of our abilities to create a caring stepfamily. I was still struggling with my desire for another child of my own. Sirah was burdened by deep sadness and guilt about earlier having given up custody of her two sons. Damien was still dealing with unresolved grief and anger about his parents' divorce. By acknowledging these feelings, we allowed healing to occur. We stopped acting out our own personal resentments and instead began recognizing how much each of us had to offer.

Using the tools described in this book, we were able to break through the pain and conflict in our stepfamily. Many of these exercises were simple enough for even our six-year-old to practice. Rather than trying to force each other to change, Damien and I began to appreciate and affirm our individuality. As a result, the animosity not only faded but Damien and I wholeheartedly agreed, independently of Sirah, that he should live with us! A few years later, Sirah's son, Michael, also moved in with us full time.

Our family today is far more peaceful and loving than we ever would have anticipated during the dark days when our conflict was at its peak. We all feel more able to be ourselves, and more loving and bonded to one another. Whereas family discussions were once tense, we now find honest, supportive communication to be the norm. In a strange way, we are thankful for all that we have been through. In learning to make peace in our stepfamily, we have all grown in ways we might otherwise have missed. We have also learned more about family life than we would ever have imagined.

Stepfamily Survival Guide

I have written this book as a practical guide for stepparents and their spouses to recognize, understand and heal the principal conflicts that trouble stepfamilies. Each stepfamily is unique, but certain conflicts are common to all stepfamilies. I have found in my practice as a psychiatrist and family therapist that stepparents and parents are relieved to learn that their feelings and conflicts in their new families are normal and, indeed, to be expected. The emotional distress in most stepfamilies persists in large part due to lack of information about these expected emotions and strategies to resolve the inevitable conflicts.

I know how busy you are as a stepparent or parent. As a result, I have tried to keep this book focused on the practical techniques and insights you need to make peace in your stepfamily. The key to success is to pick out those exercises that seem most appropriate to solving your family's conflicts. Once you work with one exercise and see the results, you will find the others easier.

The goals of this book are ambitious, but you can achieve them if you take each chapter step by step. The process of making peace in your stepfamily need not be complicated. This guide presents practical, and simple, exercises to:

- Recognize the differences between a stepfamily and a first-marriage family
- Discard unrealistic expectations of "instant" love and develop a realistic nurturing and supportive relationship with your stepchildren;
- Recognize and successfully embrace the new roles required of you as a stepparent
- Help your children deal with the often difficult adjustment to a new parent

- Keep lines of communication open among all family members
- Turn stepfamily conflict into an opportunity for your own personal growth
- Recognize, mourn, and heal the losses that continue to trouble each member of the stepfamily
- Resolve conflicts with your spouse and your ex about money, discipline, and visitation
- Reduce jealousy and competition while encouraging love and cooperation
- Enforce discipline without creating more animosity toward the stepparent
- Lessen feelings of rejection, insecurity, and guilt among all stepfamily members
- bond together to experience the profound joys of family

In addition to useful and effective exercises, this guide provides realistic answers to the many challenges of stepfamily life. You will learn:

- The single most dangerous assumption you can ever make about your relationship with your stepchildren
- How to tell the difference between realistic expectations and potentially destabilizing family ideals
- How to stop pushing your partner away because you're upset with the kids
- Why it's important to make peace with your ex-spouse—and how unresolved issues from your previous relationships can poison your new family
- How to resolve the "hidden" emotional pain of stepparenting
- How to strengthen your remarriage
- Why your stepchildren may initially be hostile towards your new (biological) child—and how to handle it effectively
- How to avoid destructive emotional triangles—and encourage heart-to-heart communication between all family members
- How to resolve the intense power struggles that often occur in blended families
- What to do when a new in-law acts like you don't exist
- Why it's natural to feel jealous of your stepchildren's relationship with your spouse—and what to do about it

- How to avoid conflict when "shuttle" stepchildren come to visit for the weekend, the holidays, or the summer

Insight into the cause of a stepfamily conflict can be enough to reverse escalating emotional distress and begin the peacemaking process. For example, Joanne, stepmother to her husband's two daughters, Nancy, aged nine, and Julie, aged eleven, had been trying sincerely to be a good stepparent—taking the girls on outings, driving them to extracurricular activities, encouraging their relationship with their mother, shopping for new clothes, making special family meals, minimizing the girls' chores, and otherwise trying to be a supermom. No matter how hard Joanne tried, however, the girls seemed to go out of their way to be cruel. Nancy's favorite retort was "You're not my mother," and Julie regularly belittled Joanne.

When Joanne came to my office, she was considering a divorce. She had almost given up on her stepfamily and she was convinced that she was a failure. What Joanne needed most was insight into the emotional dynamics of the stepmother-stepdaughter relationship. When I explained that it is among the most difficult of all stepfamily relationships, Joanne's face visibly lightened. I further explained that issues of territory (Joanne had moved into the single-parent home of her husband and stepdaughters) compounded her problems. Once Joanne recognized that she was not a failure and that her stepdaughter's responses were normal, Joanne stopped taking their criticism personally. She stopped trying to be a supermom. Joanne asked for and got emotional support from her husband to implement the strategies and insights in this book. After two years, her relationship with her stepdaughters has steadily grown into one of mutual care and respect.

How Much Pain and Conflict Is in Your Stepfamily?

The place to begin making peace in your stepfamily is with a self-assessment to identify the degree of hurt and conflict that is present.

This quiz will enable you to determine where you and your family need help and to measure progress after you have worked with the exercises in the book. Consider each of the following statements and mark the degree to which each statement applies to you:

1—OFTEN   2—SOMETIMES   3—RARELY

1. React to stepfamily struggles by becoming depressed, withdrawn, or enraged.

2. Feel left out, unappreciated, taken for granted.

3. Our family atmosphere is marked by criticism and disapproval.

4. Stepsiblings get bogged down in fights, competition, and jealousy.

5. Family upsets drive me to drink alcohol to excess, abuse drugs, or overeat.

6. Have difficulty being myself, revealing my innermost feelings in my family.

7. Feel intimidated, bullied, or manipulated by a stepfamily member.

8. Find myself poking fun at or making spiteful comments toward or behind the back of someone in my stepfamily.

9. Weekends, holidays, and summers are a strain because the children shuttle back and forth between two homes.

10. Lose my temper or get depressed when dealing with my ex.

11. I'm straining to make stepfamily life work, and getting too little in return.

12. Find myself becoming overly meek, "nice," or compliant to cope with the pressures in our stepfamily.

13. Feel the quality of my marriage is threatened by stepfamily difficulties.

14. Feel that my self-esteem, health, or well-being has suffered because of stepfamily conflicts.

15. Regret that I'm a member of this stepfamily.

16. Stepfamily life seems to bring out the worst in me.

17. Feel burdened by financial obligations and money worries.

_____ 18. Feel jealous; feel like I need to compete for attention.

_____ 19. Feel guilty when my spouse, stepchild, or child feels disappointed or upset.

_____ 20. Have not been able to forgive an abusive or traumatic incident.

_____ 21. Resent that I have a stepchild.

_____ 22. Feel guilty or angry about not being able to spend time with my children who live with my ex.

_____ 23. Feel rejected or irritated when a stepchild declares, "You're not my real [mom, dad]!"

_____ 24. Feel stuck, in the middle of an emotional tug of war.

_____ 25. Spend too much time bickering or trying to settle disputes.

_____ 26. Get angry that my in-laws (or parents) don't treat all the children equally.

_____ 27. Am upset about our problems with child support.

_____ 28. Resent that we cannot afford to have another child of our own.

_____ 29. Feel discouraged about the future of this family.

_____ 30. Feel that my spouse doesn't really support me in disciplining the kids.

_____ 31. Feel that my spouse and I never have any intimate time to ourselves.

_____ 32. Think about getting another divorce; regret having remarried.

_____ 33. Feel restricted in expressing love for my spouse and family.

Now add up your score. Here is a summary to help you interpret your results:

85–99 In general, your stepfamily is in great shape. You trust and respect one another and you accept each others' strengths and weaknesses. Your emotional exchange is excellent; you are comfortable expressing your thoughts and feelings.

70–84 Your stepfamily relationships are in good shape. In some family situations you may be afraid to express your feelings; in others you may feel unsupported. You can easily develop a home atmosphere of more love, intimacy, and openness by applying the stepfamily peacemaking skills found in this book.

50–69 Most stepparents and parents score in this range. Your family is significantly troubled by emotional pain and conflict. You can't count on your current home life "getting by" without making significant improvements. You and your spouse should work with this book together. Choose several exercises that seem most appropriate to your needs. If you make progress, keep working with this book. If not, you should consider getting help from a family counselor. A few sessions may make a great deal of difference.

33–49 Stepfamily crisis, serious stress and resentment. Family relationship(s) have deteriorated to the point where it is unlikely you can solve the problems you face on your own. In addition to working with this book, find a good therapist or family counselor to assist you.

Some people find this quiz painful and discouraging. If the quiz raised unpleasant issues, I certainly appreciate how you feel. In the darkest days of my own stepfamily, my score would have been low, indeed.

What you must keep in mind is that the first step to making peace in your stepfamily is to acknowledge exactly where you are. You will find throughout this book that the key to making peace is accepting your own feelings and those of other stepfamily members. To do this, you must acknowledge the feelings you have, even if they are quite painful. Only then can you take the next steps of communicating your feelings, empathizing with others, and finally finding ways to make peace. With your commitment, this book will help.

It can be very useful if your spouse takes this quiz as well. One of the big problems in stepfamilies is that spouses do not communicate openly and often enough about their feelings. Each of you taking this quiz and then discussing your answers is a first step toward better communication that can significantly improve your relationship. If you both acknowledge conflict in your stepfamily, take heart. You have begun the process of making peace.

Steps to Making Peace

Family peace is not a fixed goal or a steady state of tranquility. How boring that would be! The emotional climate of any home changes daily, sometimes hourly, and that is healthy. Conflicting needs among people sharing the same household, as well as the vicissitudes of life, guarantee that every family will go through periods of conflict, pain, and frustration. The issue is whether these conflicts get resolved promptly and amicably, or whether stepfamily members argue destructively, hold on to resentments, become emotionally distant, and/or leave.

I suggest that you think of the remaining chapters as counseling sessions that address critical issues of stepfamily conflict. With each new exercise, I ask you to go through a three-step process as follows:

1. Examine a conflict in your stepfamily and explore its various possible causes, especially the role of your own attitudes and behavior in fueling the conflict.
2. Consider alternate ways you can respond to this specific family conflict. For example, modifying an assumption, understanding your spouse or stepchild's point of view, or letting go of an old resentment can each be a major step towards making peace.
3. Practice a specific exercise to help resolve the conflict and promote better communication and mutual respect.

I have written this book primarily for parents and stepparents who are struggling with the myriad conflicts that emerge in blending two families. My goal is to help you not only resolve conflicts involving your children, stepchildren, or ex-spouse, but also to strengthen your remarriage. The emotional foundation of every stepfamily is the love between the remarried couple, and the stresses of stepfamily living mean that your relationship with your spouse requires special care.

I have also written this book for remarried couples who want to reexamine the emotional status quo in their stepfamilies. In some cases where the remarriage has already survived for many years, stepfamily tensions continue to simmer just below the surface and emotions boil over periodically. This book is intended to provide the insights and the communication tools for you and your spouse to reexamine chronic stepfamily conflicts and find new ways to make peace, even if those conflicts have persisted for a decade or more.

While this book addresses current and chronic stepfamily conflicts, it is also intended as a manual for couples contemplating remarriage. If you are about to step across the threshold into a stepfamily, I applaud you and offer this book as an aid to guide you through what is likely to be rough emotional terrain. Throughout this book, I try to tell it like it is. One of the biggest mistakes made by remarrieds is to proceed with eyes closed to the unique emotional pressures of stepfamilies. Do not be disheartened by the fact that emotional conflicts can be intense during the early years of a stepfamily. Rather, you would be better served to anticipate a one- to two-year adjustment period during which the stepfamily begins to move into the loving bonds of family. This book will show you how to handle the inevitable conflicts as they arise. The book will also show you that the ultimate rewards are worth the effort.

I have also written this book for adult stepchildren who remain troubled by unresolved conflicts. When the divorce and remarriage rate began to rise in the early 1970s, the mental health profession presumed, somewhat overoptimistically, that divorce and remarriage left relatively few emotional scars on the children of divorce. The theory was that children would do better away from the constant emotional battles of married parents. Now, we recognize that children suffer trauma from divorce and remarriage. The children of the 1970s divorce wave are now adults, and many are struggling with feelings they do not understand about their stepfamilies. This book can help clarify those conflicted feelings and heal old emotional wounds. Understanding the origins of those feelings and how to resolve a legacy of conflict are essential to the emotional integration of adult stepchildren.

This book is intended to help ex-spouses lessen postdivorce hostilities, if not for their own sakes, then for their children's. One of the greatest dangers to a stepfamily is continuing conflict with an ex-spouse. One of the greatest gifts to a child of divorce is to demonstrate that a family can split up and later reemerge in the extended form of a stepfamily. For this process to have the greatest healing power for the children, the divorced parents must reestablish a parenting coalition where they treat each other with consideration and cooperate on parenting tasks.

Finally, this book is intended to be an informative and practical guide to therapists not familiar with stepfamily dynamics. I view the stepfamily as essentially resourceful and only sometimes and temporarily in need of therapy. I encourage the therapist to search for and use the stepfamily's own strengths and resources rather than viewing the family as deficient, less than, or in need of extensive repair. *Making Peace in Your Stepfamily* provides strategies and exercises that can also be used in a collaborative effort between family and therapist.

This book is not a panacea. Each person, couple, divorce, and remarriage is unique. I have tried to identify the conflicts which I have seen recur time and again in my practice. I have also provided exercises which I give to my clients as "homework." To illustrate the myriad variations and convey the dynamics of the peacemaking process, I have relied on as many case histories as possible. I am relying on you to share the insights you gain from this book with your spouse, ex-spouse, stepchildren, children, parents, and in-laws as appropriate, and to modify the exercises to suit your needs.

Making Peace Is a Personal Challenge

In an ideal world, you and your spouse work with this book together to make peace in your stepfamily. In the real world, you may be the one most concerned, and it may take considerable time to enlist your spouse's full support. It is important to recognize at this early stage in your efforts to heal stepfamily conflict that you do have the power alone to make a significant difference. You can initiate profound change that will accelerate positively if you take the first steps. My confidence in your ability is not a matter of mere conjecture, but is rather based on the most recent research on conflict resolution. If you doubt your ability to make a difference, here are some ideas to keep in mind.

Other people's behavior depends as much or more on the emotional environment you generate as on their personality traits. How often have you complained about another family member: "There he/she goes again, [criticizing, arguing, fighting, complaining]"; "She always acts that way"; "He/she is [a grouch, irritable, cold]"; "I can't get through to him/her"; "we just can't talk"; "He/she never wants to spend time with the family because he/she's always too busy, wants to be with friends, or gets upset."

Most of us perceive other family members as having fixed personality characteristics that show up time and again in our interactions. As a result, family members tend to engage one another in little dramas that they replay day after day, month after month, year after year. By expecting a family member to respond as he or she has in the past tends to reinforce old behaviors and keep the relationship stuck in conflict. Stepfamily conflict is reinforced by your perceptions that family members will always feel or behave as in the past.

Shattering this assumption is critical to stepfamily peacemaking. What psychologists now recognize is that people will exhibit very different responses if they are in an environment of conflict and mistrust, as opposed to an emotional environment of safety and peace. Your willingness to "source," or take 100 percent responsibility to create a state of safety, trust, respect, empathy, acceptance, and warmth, will allow both you and other stepfamily members to communicate openly, begin healing conflicts, and start responding to one another's needs, desires, and different viewpoints in new and positive ways.

Making peace in your stepfamily begins within you. One of the most common sources of stepfamily conflict is the misguided effort that family members sometimes expend trying to change one another. "I'm telling you this for your own good." "Can't you see that I'm trying to help?" "Won't you just try what I'm telling you?" These are the often heard refrains of one stepfamily member trying to change another. Such efforts are the antithesis of making peace. Every time you try to change another family member, you are invalidating that person's basic sense of self-worth. Fundamental to creating family is first recognizing each family member's need to feel appreciated and accepted exactly as that person is.

Psychologists have recently developed the concept of the *family change agent*—the person who identifies a problem and inspires constructive change. The most effective family change agent is not the person who can recite all of the stepfamily conflicts in detail, but rather the person who is a positive role model and helps bring out the best in each stepfamily member.

The process is to step back, take a good—at times, difficult— honest look at yourself, your intention to love under difficult circumstances, and your desire to use resolving stepfamily conflicts as opportunities for the growth of love. As long as you do that, you will find yourself very satisfied with the results. If, however, you still believe it is somehow up to your stepchildren alone to change, your spouse alone to make concessions, or something "out there" to shift before you can operate with greater personal happiness and family love, then you can expect to remain stuck.

You choose the family life you want. There is a common expression, "You choose your friends, but you cannot choose your family." In reality, you choose your family every day, by how you choose to communicate with them. When you communicate your feelings with compassion, understanding and love, you create a stepfamily where those essential qualities predominate. If you communicate resentment and anger, then you create an angry and resentful stepfamily atmosphere. So too, when you become so involved with your career that you have little time for your stepfamily, you choose to create a stepfamily with little exchanges of love, strong feelings of alienation, neglect and bitterness. On the other hand, when you spend time with each stepfamily member, keep in touch by phone or letter, and make your commitment tangible, then you create a stepfamily of warmth, mutual respect, and love.

My point here is so simple that it can easily be misunderstood or trivialized. How you treat other stepfamily members is your choice, and therefore, you have the power to create the stepfamily you desire through your choices. I understand the difficulties. Stepfamily conflicts have a life of their own. It can seem impossible to get through to your spouse, stepchild, parent, or child. Jealousies, resentments, and blind assumptions all get in the way. Nevertheless, this book gives you the skills to overcome those barriers to family communication and to begin choosing successfully to create a happy and close stepfamily environment.

You need not be a prisoner of a painful past. So much of recent psychology has been based on the premise that "you are a product of your past": If your parents divorced, then you are more likely to divorce. If you grew up with a good deal of fear and conflict surrounding your intimate relationships, then you are more likely to have difficulties in your own adult intimate relationships. But there is a difference between "likely" and "inevitably."

Psychology developed the stimulus-response model of human behavior by studying pigeons. The sad truth is that human beings often behave just as automatically and thoughtlessly as pigeons, particularly in emotionally difficult situations. We all develop emotional habits that take over when we are stressed, threatened, or upset. Nowhere do these automatic responses tend to occur most often than among family members. Close proximity, repeated contact, common emotional history, and intensity of the relationship all contribute to the predominance of emotional habits over well-intentioned choices in stepfamily conflicts. This book presents techniques to help you break the cycle of automatic emotional responses that impede genuine understanding and fuel further conflict.

Give Peace a Chance

So now what? A sense of humor helps, as does a willingness to experiment with some of the strategies that you resist at first. You have pessimism to lose, peace and love to gain.

A word of caution: psychological growth always takes place in a spiral, not in a straight line. At times, you and your stepfamily may take two steps forward and one step back. Instead of criticizing yourself when a struggle reappears, remember that *all families fight, and no family is perfect.* These are the times to give yourself and your family added support and guidance.

Creating a stepfamily is a special adventure in learning more about yourself and those closest to you. At times, this book will ask you to step outside a desire to "win," and to open up your heart. Making peace may require you to move beyond your annoyances, your self-righteousness, and your desire to punish. You may even need to accept someone in your stepfamily whom you resent or reject. The reason to persevere is not primarily for your stepfamily, but for you. Your peace of mind, your remarriage, and your own personal growth are at stake. The tools for making a shift in your family life—and in yourself—are now available to you.

"Is it really worth it?" you may ask. I know firsthand how much turmoil you may be experiencing. I also know firsthand the enormous rewards of working through the conflicts and ultimately making peace in your stepfamily. The remainder of this book provides the specific tools to help you succeed in this task.

No matter how discouraged you may be feeling right now, re-m ember that when stepfamilies make peace, they often work better and provide greater rewards than any other type of family. Children can truly thrive with the love and support of two sets of parents. Stepfathers and stepmothers can play invaluable roles as mentor and guide, and they can develop a loving relationship with their stepsons and stepdaughters, based on deep trust and mutual respect. The rewards to the parents and stepparents in personal growth, expanded capacity to love, and resolution of their own emotional limitations are equally great.

No doubt, making peace in your stepfamily is an enormous personal challenge. I assure you it is a challenge that can bring you lasting satisfaction and great personal rewards. The place to begin is with you, because ultimately, the only way to make peace in your stepfamily is through you.

Chapter 2

A STEPFAMILY
IS BORN OF
LOSS

S orrow, grief, remorse—these painful feelings are often the hidden causes of lingering conflicts within stepfamilies. In some cases, the pain persists from an unresolved emotional wound from the past. "My daughters haven't forgiven me for leaving their father," one mother feared. "They blame me, and I feel so guilty because I see the hurt in their eyes." In other stepfamilies, the pain results from repeated separations. "My son has visited three times," a recently remarried father explained. "Every time I put him on an airplane, he breaks down crying. It tears me apart, and makes me furious at the same time." Still, in other families, the pain results from the deep disappointment of shattered dreams and expectations. "I had hoped to be a real mother to my husband's children," confided one stepmother. "I wasn't prepared for how much I would be hurt by their rejection."

When a stepfamily in conflict comes to me for help, the first task is usually to assist a parent, stepparent, or child in acknowledging and healing the heartache associated with loss. Each stepfamily member—parents and children alike—has been touched by the tragedy of death or divorce. A stepfamily is also a crucible for loss. Parents and children must become accustomed to the anguish of long separations, repeated good-byes, and frequent disappointments.

Because loss in its many forms is so painful, the human psyche tends to protect itself by burying the resulting sorrow and grief. The benefit of this self-protective unconscious process is that we continue to function. The problem is that buried pain eventually reemerges as anger, depression, resentment, and guilt—destructive emotions that can tear a stepfamily apart. Repressed grief is one of the reasons why stepfamilies are so often troubled by angry outbursts and frequent bickering. In most stepfamilies there is a reluctance to confront the heartache for fear of making it worse and creating another divorce. A conspiracy of silence may overtake the stepfamily where members try to deny conflict by avoiding contact—stepfather and stepson may stop talking, stepmother and stepdaughter may retreat into themselves, father and stepmother may treat the father's ex as a taboo subject—but the pain does not disappear. More likely, it intensifies until it explodes.

To make peace in your stepfamily, it is essential to begin by asking yourself whether you or another stepfamily member might be struggling with repressed heartache from the past, intense disappointment due to shattered expectations, or the anguish of repeated separations and good-byes. This chapter will help you explore these painful feelings personally, and assist other family members to as well.

How Emotional Wounds Heal

Just as the body goes through distinct stages in healing a physical wound, so the mind must pass through three recognizable stages in the recovery from loss. First comes shock, denial and numbness. Unable to cope with a sudden emotional blow, the mind blocks it temporarily. We say things to ourselves such as "I can't believe it!" "He wouldn't have done such a thing!" "This isn't happening!" After a major loss, there may be complete emotional paralysis lasting from a few moments to a few months.

When the shock begins to wear off, the second stage gradually unfolds. This is the period of fear, anger and depression. Whenever you're hurt by someone you love, anger is an automatic and completely natural response, as is depression. You may find that you're crying a lot; this may last up to a year. The key to moving on from this stage is fully to experience your pain, and to express your anger without guilt. This is where the healing often gets stuck.

The final stage of recovery is understanding and acceptance. This is the point where the pain of loss can turn into a new opportunity for growth. Once the pain is fully felt and the anger vented, the loss can be accepted and understood. With time, it ceases to be so devastating that it must be blocked out. It is still a painful event, but you have survived. Energy and strength return often, in greater measure than before. Albert Camus summed up the crowning insight that marks the completion of this stage when he wrote: "In the midst of winter, I finally learned that there was in me an invincible summer."

One basic psychological principle is the key to healing the heartache of loss: *What you resist persists, what you accept lightens.* The more you try to deny your painful feelings, the more troubling they are likely to become. Paradoxically, by allowing painful feelings to surface, the emotional wound heals as you work through the stages of shock and denial, anger and depression, and finally understanding and acceptance. Even when it comes to the anguish of periodic separation, healing flows from feeling. It's better to embrace the pain of a tearful good-bye than pretend it doesn't exist and wind up depressed.

Recognizing Stepfamily Losses

Blake, a senior manager at a manufacturing plant, father of two boys, and stepfather to his new wife's son, Ian, and daughter, Claudia, sat impassively in my office with his arms folded. "Look, I'm only here because Sharon, my new wife, insisted," he stated flatly. "There's nothing you can do to help."

"Please, let's talk about it," Sharon implored. "Ever since Judy (his first wife) moved to San Francisco with your boys, you've changed.

Ian and Claudia are asking why you don't like them any more."

Blake and Sharon were stuck. Blake's former wife had taken his sons 500 miles north, despite his efforts to stop her. Now, he was unprepared for the pain welling up within. His posture was closed, his voice flat, his expression determined. In fact, he was the personification of stoic resignation. Little did he appreciate, however, that his internal defenses against his sense of loss were costing him his capacity to feel, love, and create a new family. Blake was in denial, and the first task in saving this stepfamily was helping him drop his defenses so he could feel both his intense anger and hurt.

Denial is common in stepfamilies. Look for hidden grief and disappointments in the following statements (ones I have frequently heard in my work with stepfamilies):

- "I try to be nice to my stepkids, but they do things spitefully to upset me."
- "Sure I want to love them, but at the same time, they're not my own kids."
- "No matter how hard I try, I will never be able to make up to my kids the pain of the divorce."
- "Why can't you be like my real father/mother?"
- "My mom is so busy with the new baby, she never has time for me."
- "My stepdad just can't accept that I'm different from what he wants me to be."
- "I can't stand going back and forth between two households; I'm constantly leaving my friends and missing out on special events."

In many stepfamilies, these complaints persist because the underlying loss remains unrecognized and unresolved. The result is miscommunication.

Loss is deeply personal. Each member of your stepfamily is likely to perceive his or her loss from a unique point of view. To heal your own losses and to help others in your stepfamily, it is important to appreciate the many losses that various members may feel. Here are some typical losses:

Parents. The divorce or death of a spouse means the end of a significant chapter in a parent's life. There is the loss of the marriage partner, as well as the hopes and ideals invested in the marriage. Divorce usually creates a loss of self-esteem, and there is often a financial loss or loss of economic status that accompanies single parenting. If custody of the children is shared, there is the additional pain of frequent separations as the children move back and forth between households. There can also be a deep sense of failure or regret for having dragged the children through a divorce. If the parent marries someone with children and the parent does not have custody of his or her own child(ren), then responsibilities and interactions with the stepchildren further deepen the pain surrounding loss of contact with the parent's own child(ren).

The parent is also likely to suffer significant losses from shattered expectations. The parent desperately wants the two halves of his/her life to come together—children and new spouse. Some parents hope that their stepfamily will instantly blend as smoothly as the Brady Bunch. But enormous work is required before that is possible. The process may take years. In the meantime, the parent has daily feelings of loss as long as the parent's dream of a new happy family goes unrealized.

Stepparents. If previously single or married without children, a stepparent must cope with the realities of an instant family, which means loss of privacy and freedom. In addition, the stepparent faces a loss of self-esteem if the stepchildren predictably remain distant from or outwardly reject him or her. Few stepparents are prepared for the rapid loss of romance with their new spouses. "Instant family" usually means "no honeymoon." Quite often, a stepparent suffers disappointment when a spouse seems to side with the child(ren) in an argument, or fails to insist that the children treat the stepparent respectfully.

The stepparent may also be the victim of unrealistic expectations. It is not uncommon for a stepparent to harbor a rescue fantasy— saving the formerly single parent and his/her children from the trauma of a failed marriage. Instead, the new stepfamily is fraught with tension. Competition with a spouse's ex is another emotional trap for the stepparent. No matter how hard the stepparent tries, he or she can never replace a child's biological parent. The stepparent usually loses by trying and must deal with daily feelings of inadequacy as long as the relationship with the stepchildren remains strained. Most stepparents come to the marriage ready to love their new stepchildren. These stepparents are totally unprepared for the rejection of their good intentions and are deeply hurt in the loss of their own dream of an instant loving family. No wonder stepparents soon begin to resent their stepchildren, or at least feel deeply troubled by guilt about their resentment.

Children. Loss is more difficult for children than for anyone else in the stepfamily. Children often feel responsible for their parents' divorce and harbor considerable guilt. When the custodial parent remarries, children typically feel abandoned by that parent. Having little or no role in the decision making, children feel helpless and vulnerable. Instead of welcoming the stepparent, the children often feel rejected, and bait the stepparent or emotionally withdraw.

The remarriage is difficult for the children for several reasons. Children of divorced parents carry divided loyalties. Most children harbor a strong reunion fantasy—"If only Mom and Dad would get back together." The appearance of the stepparent both challenges the stepchild's loyalty to at least one of his or her parents, and at the same time shatters the reunion fantasy. Divorce usually causes the stepchild to bond even more intensely with the custodial parent. Therefore, when the child sees his parent remarry, the stepparent may appear to be interfering with that bond. For all these reasons, stepchildren see the stepparent as an intruder. This rejection response is almost biological, as in the way that the body attempts to reject a foreign substance.

Where the divorced parents have joint custody, the continual back and forth between households compounds the children's sense of loss. Each time there is a visitation difficulty, an upsetting phone call between the divorced parents, a broken promise or a late arrival, the child's insecurities and feelings of loss are exacerbated. Sometimes, the more overtly loving the stepparent, the more the stepchildren seem troubled by divided loyalties. Stepparents can wind up in a no-win situation until the children learn that they can care for more than two adults in parental roles.

Stepchildren face other losses as well. Divorce and remarriage often mean a family move, in which case the children lose their old home, close friends, teachers, and familiar neighborhood surroundings. The children also notice the financial impact of divorce. If a nonworking custodial parent goes back to work, the children lose attention from that parent as well. Moving back and forth between parents also undermines the child's sense of belonging. Visiting children usually feel awkward, particularly if the noncustodial parent has remarried. All of these elements contribute to the stepchild's sense of fear, anger, and insecurity.

No matter how badly you may be feeling about your stepfamily or how much you have been hurt, there is good reason for hope. Healing from an emotional wound is just as natural as healing a physical wound. If you break a leg, you need to create the conditions for healing to occur—set the break, rest and keep weight off the leg. So, too, when you incur an emotional wound, the key is to create the conditions that allow natural healing.

What You Feel You Can Heal

The remainder of this chapter consists of the exercises to help you and your stepfamily move emotionally from denial of your losses, through pain, anxiety, and anger, to understanding, acceptance, and a renewed vision of your stepfamily's future. Three conditions are necessary for each of the exercises that follow.

First, you need to be able to address your feelings without interruption or interference. As a stepfather in my own household, I know how difficult that can be. Nevertheless, if you want to make peace in your stepfamily, you must make time to address the unresolved emotional issues. As you work through the various exercises, find a room where you can be alone and put a Do NOT DISTURB sign on the door. Tell your spouse that you are working with this book, and invite him/her to read it as well. Be assertive with your children about your need for uninterrupted time. Everyone will thank you in the long run.

Second, you need to create an atmosphere of safety and trust in your stepfamily. One of the best ways to do this is to have a talk with your spouse and children or stepchildren about your desire to help everyone feel better. Say that you are hoping to learn how to make your stepfamily work better and how to reduce bickering and conflict. Explain that you are hoping to find ways to make it easier for everyone to talk about their feelings and to work out their differences. DO NOT indicate at this early stage that you are expecting anyone in the stepfamily to change! Instead, acknowledge that you do not have all the answers and that you want to be more open to everyone's feelings.

Third, make a commitment to honesty and openness to the feelings of others. Stop trying to impress the neighbors or your spouse with how happy you are or what a wonderful stepfamily you have. Also, stop trying to convince yourself that your spouse and children or stepchildren are happy, when they are not. It is critically important to recognize that when it comes to feelings, no one is wrong. There is no reason for anyone in your stepfamily to feel ashamed, embarrassed, or afraid of his/her feelings. Rather, feelings must be accepted as *information* about needs, and whether those needs are being met, ignored, or frustrated. The only way to get this information is to be honest, and to avoid making yourself or anyone else in your stepfamily defensive.

REMEMBER, *What you feel, you can heal.*

Breaking Through Denial

"I honestly don't know what is happening to me," confessed Michelle, a thirty-two-year-old graphic designer and stepmother of an eleven-year-old boy, Oren, and a seven-year-old girl, Sandra. "Ever since Drew took custody of Oren and Sandra, our marriage has been falling apart. We fight constantly . . . the children hate me . . . and I don't see any way out."

"First of all, the kids don't hate Michelle," interrupted Drew, "and second of all, Michelle agreed that she wanted me to have custody when Evelyn decided to run off with her deadbeat lover. Michelle even told me she looked forward to being a real mother to Oren and Sandra."

Michelle and Drew continued to *talk about* each other without *listening to* one another's feelings, until I intervened. It was apparent that Michelle and Drew loved each other and had a good relationship prior to the arrival of Oren and Sandra. It was also apparent that neither Drew nor Michelle was prepared for all the challenges of creating a full-time stepfamily.

I suggested to Michelle and Drew that their bickering and the breakdown of their communication might be the result of unacknowl-edged pain they were both suffering as a result of the recent changes in their family. At first, Michelle and Drew both protested that taking custody of Oren and Sandra couldn't be a loss. We talked about the many types of losses experienced by stepfamilies. As we talked, both Michelle and Drew began to acknowledge the ways in which they were hurting.

I asked Michelle and Drew to write down the loss that each person in their stepfamily had suffered. Here are the losses they con-fided:

Michelle's Losses
- Lost my exclusive relationship with Drew
- Lost my privacy
- Lost my ability to take off with Drew whenever we want
- Lost the feeling that my home is my own
- Lost my self-control
- Lost confidence in myself as a loving person
- Lost my dream that the children would love me

Drew's Losses
- Lost my close relationship with Michelle
- Lost my ability to blame Evelyn for the kids' misbehavior
- Lost my financial freedom
- Lost my privacy
- Lost ability to make spontaneous plans
- Lost my hope that we would quickly be one big happy family

Oren and Sandra's Losses
- Lost their mother
- Lost their familiar home
- Lost their friends
- Lost hope that their mother and father would someday reunite
- Lost faith in adults as safe and reliable
- Lost their neighborhood and school
- Lost their privacy (they now have to share a room)

This simple exercise initiated a breakthrough in Michelle and Drew's relationship. Suddenly, they stopped blaming each other for their conflicts, and instead began to appreciate how each was hurting.

Take time now to examine losses in your own stepfamily. You need a pencil and paper and twenty minutes of uninterrupted time alone. Use the following questions as your guide:

- What are some of the specific losses you, your spouse, and your child/stepchild have suffered?
- What unfinished business do you still have concerning your previous marriage?
- Which of these losses have had the greatest impact on stepfamily life?

If you are having trouble with this exercise, go back to the summary of losses experienced by typical stepfamilies (see pages •–•). Give yourself a chance to break through any of your own natural denial.

The Heart Letter

Acknowledging your losses and disappointments is the first step in healing. The next step is to give yourself permission to express all the hurt, anger, and frustration associated with those losses and disappointments.

One effective technique to release painful feelings is to write what I call a "Heart Letter." You write a letter to your spouse, child or stepchild, in which you vent the unresolved hurt, anger, and pain. At first you may resist this process, because most people are hesitant to express negative emotion, especially if their feelings are intense. In this case, you are writing the letter for yourself, not to send to anyone, so you can let your feelings go without fear of hurting anyone.

Writing this letter is safe. Most clients report that a Heart Letter reduces the sense of chaos and frustration that is so often a part of stepfamily life. It will also help you feel more in control. Being honest with yourself is liberating; you feel less like a victim and more in touch with your feelings.

To try this exercise, you need paper, a pen, and a quiet place to write uninterrupted. Now is the time to stop resisting your feelings about your stepchildren or your spouse. Remember:

1. Be honest and don't intellectualize.
2. Don't edit your thoughts or worry about looking good. Your feelings are enough in their raw form.
3. Don't spend your time blaming or criticizing, these too are defenses against feeling. Simply express your hurt, anger, frustration, and pain.
4. Don't try to defend yourself or try to change anyone.

When you write your Heart Letter, draw from the following list of phrases. These suggestions will help you to express your buried feelings.

Stage I of the Heart Letter—overcoming shock and denial

1. Express your grief, disappointment, and pain. For example:
    "I feel miserable because . . ."
    "I feel I have failed because . . ."
    "I feel cheated that . . ."
    "I have lost . . ."
    "I feel trapped when . . ."
    "I miss . . ."
    "I am pained because . . ."
    "I expected . . ."

2. Express your sadness, remorse, and doubt. For example:
    "I feel guilty because . . ."
    "I feel burdened by . . ."
    "I feel inadequate as a stepparent because . . ."
    "I feel sad that . . ."
    "I feel disloyal when . . ."
    "I am doubtful that . . ."
    "I am ashamed that . . ."

3. Express your feelings of incompetence and ambivalence. For example:
    "I feel like I'm bumbling when . . ."
    "I feel like a hypocrite when . . ."
    "I agonize over . . ."
    "I have serious misgivings about . . ."
    "I feel emotionally drained because . . ."

"I feel unappreciated when . . ."
"I wonder why . . ."

Stage II of the Heart Letter—healing hurt, fear and anger

4. Express your anger, resentment, and annoyance. For example:
   "I hate it when . . ."
   "It makes me furious when . . ."
   "I'm disgusted with . . ."
   "I resent that . . ."
   "I feel like the mean stepparent when . . ."

5. Express your hurt, rejection, and jealousy. For example:
   "It hurts me when . . ."
   "I feel rejected when . . ."
   "I am embarrassed to admit . . ."
   "I feel jealous when you . . ."
   "I feel nervous about . . ."

6. Express your fear, anxiety, and insecurity. For example:
   "I feel scared when . . ."
   "I dread having to . . ."
   "I become upset when . . ."
   "I feel insecure about . . ."
   "My worst fears for our marriage/family are . . ."
   "I feel trapped when . . ."

Stage III of the Heart Letter—understanding, acceptance and growth

7. Express your understanding and what you are learning. For example:
   "I see myself as a courageous person because . . ."
   "I am starting to gain some serenity and peace of mind because . . ."
   "My stepfamily is very unique because . . ."
   "As I look upon my history with my stepfamily, I am reassured that . . ."
   "I feel deeply moved and touched by . . ."

8. Express your growth, appreciation, and love. For example:
   "Positive changes I have noted in myself/my spouse/my stepkids are . . ."

"Areas of growth in family life that I am excited by . . ."
"Advantages of being in this family are . . ."
"I am fortunate because . . ."
"I feel increasingly affectionate toward . . ."

Toward Making Peace with Stepchildren

Here is Michelle's letter to Drew, Oren, and Sandra. She wrote this letter after a major fight with Drew. Note that she addresses her letter to both her spouse and her stepchildren. This letter was not meant to be read or delivered to them, but rather strictly to help Michelle release her pentup feelings.

Dear Drew, Oren, and Sandra,

As a stepmother I feel like I can never do enough. In this home I feel frozen out like a second-class citizen. I am expected to cook and clean, and yet I feel treated with contempt. I have not been able to become a mother to children of my own, and I suppose I miss that too. But still, the most painful experiences I've had in my life to date were that of being rejected by you two children as a stepmother. I felt devastated when you compared me so unfavorably to your mother. I also feel like this isn't at all what I planned for. I've never been around children so I don't know what is normal for an eleven-year-old and a seven-year-old, but I do know that when I ask you to put your clothes away and all I get is anger, I have a sense of frustration and panic.

As to you, my dear husband, I sometimes feel like you abandoned me when your children moved in, and now all you want to do is work and bring home the paycheck. You are so self-centered. I feel like you put your relationship with your kids first, your work second, and I'm a distant third. It really hurts me when I feel you don't appreciate how hard I am working to love you and to make your two children my own. It hurts me when you get mad at me for not getting along better with your children. I feel like I need your support. I feel frustrated and sad that we don't have more time alone together. I feel rejected sometimes by both the children and you, and that turns me into feeling like the "wicked stepmother," which I hate.

I am afraid that being in a stepfamily and raising these children will never allow our marriage to grow close again. I am terrified that our conflicts will destroy our marriage. I am afraid that you will hold me accountable for any problems or complaints that your children have with me. I am terrified of you taking their side. I am afraid to show you how much I need support from you as a wife and as a mother. I feel guilty for not being a "good enough mother." I feel guilt for always seeming to nag at you and the kids. I am sorry that I get cranky and lose my temper. I feel terrible when I yell and scream. I am sorry I called you names last night. I didn't mean it. I truly want to get closer to the children, and I want us to be as close as we were. I want us to have more time as a family, as well as to have more time for us.

Though this has been very hard for me, I feel like I am starting to gain some deeper understanding of myself and what it takes to really love and be loved. I am proud of myself for doing pretty well with becoming an instant parent. I forgive you for not giving me all the support and attention I need, because I know how much strain you are under. The times when we can be together and be close make a real difference to me. I want to learn to be a better stepparent and I'm excited that we are talking more about what we need and want, both for ourselves and the children.

> I love you,
> Michelle

In most instances, a Heart Letter is a private matter. You may find, however, that the letter expresses your feelings in a coherent and noncritical way. As a result, you may be inclined to share it.

Here is a Heart Letter that Allison, a stepmother, decided to share with her stepdaughter, Melissa.

Dear Melissa,

I'm sorry that your parents divorced, but I am tired of you taking out your anger and resentment on me. I'm sorry you have to spend so much time commuting between two households, but I feel like I'm your scapegoat. I did not split up your parents. Being a stepmother is a very difficult role for me. I can't stand it when you say "My real mother would never say that." Can't you give me an honest chance for a quality relationship? What is the matter with you? If you're so unsatisfied with the meals that I make, why don't you start fixing some meals and get your dad to help? I hate your complaining. I want you to appreciate all that I'm trying to do for you and not put me down all the time, especially to your father. I feel like you get in the way of our marriage really working. Sometimes I feel like you even want to split us up.

It hurts so much to feel that no matter what I do it isn't good enough; you're constantly pointing out my mistakes. It hurts me when you say you don't want me to be your mother. It hurts when you talk behind my back to your father. It makes me feel sad when you raise your voice to me and call me a bitch.

I feel guilty that I was seeing your father before the divorce between your parents was over. But I want you to know that they did not divorce on account of me. I am remorseful that your father has not talked to you honestly about this himself. The three of us must sit down.

I am afraid that the tension between us is going to continue to make our home life miserable, and cause further problems in my marriage to your dad. I'm afraid that I am becoming too strained and working too hard to please you, to please your father and do my career. I'm afraid that you will continue to see me as a lousy stepmother you begrudgingly have to live with. I want to have more time to play together and not just work, work, work. I'm confused because while I find myself angry with you a lot, I feel guilty about it. I'm sorry because the truth is that I don't want to take out my frustrations on you. I'm sorry when I lose my temper. I'm sorry when I yell at you. I'm confused and ashamed when I take out my frustrations on you.

You are a really terrific young lady, and despite all our frustrations I love living with you. The lessons that we are learning are tough ones, but I still remember some of the great times, like when you and I made brunch for your grandparents last weekend. I love how bright you are and how much other people admire you. And I know that you would like to see my relationship with your dad work. I want to be not only a stepmother but more importantly, a friend and companion to you. I want to be proud of you and want you to be proud of me.

> I love you and want you to be happy,
> Allison

Allison shared her Heart Letter with Melissa one Saturday afternoon after explaining that she was trying to find ways to get along better. For Allison, sharing the Heart Letter was a breakthrough. Melissa was moved by Allison's pain, so much so that she began to cry. Allison joined her in what she later described "as one of the most wonderful weeping sessions of my life."

Helping Children to Understand and Grow

Your children or stepchildren are also likely to be troubled by unresolved feelings of loss, and writing a Heart Letter can help if the child writes easily and is old enough to understand the task. One way to encourage a child to write a Heart Letter is to explain that you are writing one yourself, and why. Assure the child that a Heart Letter is a private exercise, and he or she need not fear expressing true feelings.

Pamela, thirteen, was constantly at odds with her stepdad, Ryan. Here is Pamela's letter:

Dear Ryan,

I feel like you hate me. You've never wanted me in your life. You've never liked me or supported me. I hate you for treating your kids so special and being so cold to me all these years. I'm angry when you are so mean to me. I feel like all you do is get pissed off and complain. I feel like you've never really wanted to be a father to me, and I don't like the way you treat my mother. I get so angry when you yell at Mom. I'm afraid that no one has ever wanted me, not my real Dad or you. I want to forgive you but I'm afraid I can't. I'm sorry that I am always such a burden to you. I want you to stop drinking. I'm sorry you are so miserable.

I wish I could help you. I think you're a nice person when you're not drinking—then you treat my Mom and me much better. I know that you try. I know that being a stepfather has been hard on you. Your treating me special sometimes would mean a lot to me. You are an important person in my life.

Love,
Pamela

John, a fourteen-year-old boy, had become very depressed since his natural father had stopped visiting regularly. His mother had tried to communicate with her ex to explain how badly John was feeling, but he eventually lost contact. John's mother finally recognized that she had to help her son accept the loss of his father. Here is one of John's letters:

Dad,

It hurts me that you never cared for me. I feel like I never really had a father. I never even really knew you and that makes me want to cry. I hate when you don't want to come and visit me. I feel sad that you live so far away. I'm afraid you don't really love me. I wish you would become a part of my life again and not feel so threatened by Mom or her husband. It makes me very sad that you don't love yourself enough. It's sad you don't feel closer to your own flesh and blood. I want you to come visit me more. I want you to be more generous with your time, but if you can't, then I am sorry for you and for me because a Dad shouldn't run out on a son.

John

When John wrote this letter, he began to cry, and his crying soon became intense sobbing. Be available to your children or stepchildren during this exercise to provide contact and comfort as needed. It is extremely important to assure children that the feelings expressed in their Heart Letters are normal. Explain that they are a not bad person because they have feelings of anger, guilt, resentment, or fear, and that when it comes to feelings, no one is wrong. Provide comfort and understanding by assuring them that it's OK to cry and that you appreciate how much it hurts.

Helping children acknowledge and express their feelings without fear, guilt, or shame is a great service to their long-term growth.

Healing Through Poetry

A Heart Letter is only one way to cleanse yourself of painful feelings. Poetry is another approach which I have found exceedingly effective for many people. A poem is a simple clear expression of a fully felt experience. What makes a poem powerful as a therapeutic tool is the necessity to focus intensely on your own feelings and put them into words.

A colleague, Dr. Natasha Josefowitz, wrote a poem to describe feelings about her stepchild:

Their Father's Wife

Mine, but not really mine
his, but not his alone
not of my flesh,
but part of my family
sharing no genes
not sharing a name

Wanting to love
unconditionally
not always able to

Not quite a mother
not quite a friend
not an aunt
or a cousin

No title fits:
I am their father's wife.

Remember that poetry need not rhyme. The point is that it identify words or phrases that capture your feelings. Children can also benefit by writing poetry.

For inspiration, you might consider reading poetry. I have used it extensively in two of my previous books, *How to Survive the Loss of a Love,* and *Love Secrets for a Lasting Relationship.* Many of the great poets will help you because loss is a universal subject for poetry.

Grieving for a Lost Parent

If remarriage occurs in a short space of time after the death of a parent, most children are not prepared to accept a new adult into their lives. The children, particularly teenagers, see their parent's remarriage as a betrayal of the former parent who has died. If the new partner is presented as a replacement for the lost parent, a child's grief is especially acute.

After the death of a parent, the children, and also sometimes the remaining parent, idealize the memory of the dead parent. When a widow(er) remarries, the loyalty issues for children can be even more difficult than after a divorce.

Such was the case for Nathan, who was referred to me by his father and new stepmother after twice being arrested for shoplifting and truancy from school. Nathan's mother had died in a head-on car accident two years previously. His father had made the well-intentioned but terrible mistake of introducing Louis to his new wife-to-be by saying, "This is going to be your new mother."

Sitting in my office, Nathan looked as though his mother's death could have been yesterday. There were dark circles under his eyes. His expression still reflected shock and disbelief. When he spoke about his mother and their relationship, he became visibly more animated, but soon found himself struggling against tears.

"There is no one like her," he said of his mother, as if she were still living. "She always knew what I was thinking. She is the only one who understands me." The boy idolized her: "It just isn't the same. No one else can be my mom." The tears began to flow. The death of a mother may be one of the most painful emotional experiences a child can endure.

Following the death of a parent, there is a normal period of emotional turmoil that often persists for up to a year. Depression, reduced interest in other people, crying spells, and reduced vitality are natural parts of the healing process during recovery from such a loss. Normally, the process goes through stages, but for Nathan, the healing process had gotten stuck.

Two years later he still exhibited delinquent behavior and depression. He was filled with bitterness that his mother had died and left him. He had turned his anger inward and felt guilty for not doing more for her when she was still living. He thought of her constantly and resented his new stepmother. Unwilling to let go of mourning, Nathan treated his misery as a way of honoring his mom. He had little energy or enthusiasm for school. He seemed to care little about his arrests.

Nathan needed help in dealing with his feelings of regret, betrayal, and guilt. The little child in Nathan could not admit his rage toward his mother for so suddenly—and permanently—leaving him. His stepmother was a convenient scapegoat. He could not admit his anger toward his deceased mother, because his anger made him feel guilty. He had no idea that anger following a loss, especially of a mother you love deeply, isn't rational. It simply *is*. It must be resolved if it is to heal.

Healing Regrets and "If Onlys"

The death of a spouse or a parent often results in immobilizing regrets. Thoughts recur about "what might have been"—what might have been done, written, or given. Each regret is followed by painful feelings of remorse, because the thought of what might have been is quickly followed by the realization that it is too late.

One of the ways to heal regrets is with the "If only" exercise. As if writing a letter to a lost parent, you list your regrets by using the phrase, "If only . . .". For many people, regrets come easily to mind. For others, the memories are deeply submerged and take time to be released. It is very helpful to have a photograph of the deceased parent or spouse to prompt repressed feelings of regret. Try this exercise several times and on different occasions.

Here is Nathan's letter to his mother:

Dear Mom,

> If only I hadn't been so busy the last couple of weeks you were alive.
>
> If only I could have prevented the accident.
>
> If only you'd been less hung up on cleaning the house, we'd have had more good times together.
>
> If only we hadn't had that stupid quarrel about the party the day before you died.
>
> If only you had lived and Dad hadn't remarried.
>
> I regret not being there when you died.
>
> I regret those worries I caused you all those nights in high school when I didn't come home and didn't bother to call.
>
> I regret that time I forgot to remember your birthday.

With the gradual release of his guilt, Nathan's depression began to lift. No longer did he need to hold on to an idealized memory of his mother. He could begin to appreciate his mother as she truly was: wonderful in many ways, but not perfect. Remaining distraught was no longer proof of how much he loved her. He could accept the tragedy for what it was, and see that the greatest testimony to his mom was to pick up the pieces and accept his new stepfamily. Although Nathan knew it would take time before he was ready to accept his new stepmother, he now felt more ready to move forward.

Regrets may trouble young children as much as they do older ones. While written exercises may not be age-appropriate, you may be able to break through an emotional wall by asking a young child to draw a picture of what the loss (parents no longer living together, a parent's death, going back and forth between two homes) looks and feels like. Provide crayons, colored pens and large sheets of paper. Once the child has drawn a picture, ask the child to talk about the feelings expressed in the picture. You may be surprised by the intense anger, fear and loss that emerge. Listen attentively, and ask gentle questions to encourage the child to express his/her feelings fully.

In addition to talking about feelings of loss, it is also helpful to provide healthy outlets and distractions from their distress. Encouraging a child to join a soccer team or a gymnastics group can help them take their minds off past losses, raise self-esteem, and provide a safe outlet to yell, run, and blow off steam. Extra effort on the part of the parent and/or stepparent can mend a hundred previous slights. The new stepfamily provides these children with an opportunity to have their faith in adults and family life reaffirmed. To help the children, as well as you and your spouse, to avoid suffering more unnecessary loss, this faith in the possibilities of stepfamily life must be realistic and not based on fantasy.

Most children receive little or no warning of an impending death or divorce. A child is often better prepared by a parent for a tonsillectomy or vaccination than for death or divorce. The child probably woke up one morning to find one parent suddenly moved out or "gone." In the turmoil that follows, the child's emotional trauma gets little attention or support. Often, it is only after stepfamily life has begun that a child's painful losses can be addressed. If your children or stepchildren are still reeling from postdivorce trauma, it is important to take time to help them heal.

Calming Children's Fears

Having suffered the trauma of divorce, many children hold back from participation in a new stepfamily because they have lost trust in the adult world. The children fear another painful loss and instinctively protect themselves. Sometimes children fear that they were the cause of the previous divorce and that getting too close to a stepparent will risk discovery. To assist your children in opening their hearts, you must provide repeated reassurances that they will not be abandoned.

- Explain to your children that both you and your spouse will always love them, and that you will always be there to protect them no matter what happens.

   Acknowledge that the breakup of one family and the creation of another has created mixed emotions for everyone. It is OK, even natural, to feel happy, sad, confused, angry, and afraid from time to time. Assure them that "everything will be all right" and that their lives will get back to normal.
- Discuss the separation and divorce openly. Let them know that they still have two parents, and a stepparent as a bonus.

- Tell them that their Mom and Dad still love them. Reassure them that the divorce was Mom and Dad's decision, and they were not a cause.
- Provide as much physical affection as possible. Hold them when you nap, hold hands on walks, hug often. Words of love are definitely not enough reassurance for children of divorce.
- Expect displays of emotion—crying, angry outbursts, depression. These are part of the process of healing.

Expect your children's fears to persist for up to two years following the separation. You will need to repeat all the above suggestions many times to help your children through this difficult period. By providing them the necessary reassurance, you enable them to open their hearts to a new stepfamily.

Stepfamily Beginnings Are No Honeymoon

Couples usually remarry with great hopes for their own and their children's futures. These hopes often develop into unrealistic expectations that become broken dreams when the reality of stepfamily life sets in. When the children rebel soon after the wedding ceremony, it is easy to feel confused and betrayed. It can also be difficult to let go of the fantasy that the children will be delighted with the remarriage. Letting go of a lost hope requires acknowledging and healing a loss.

Most parents are wise enough to spend some time introducing their children to a prospective stepparent before announcing the engagement. During the courtship, it is very easy for the parent and future stepparent to imagine that the children will wholeheartedly welcome the marriage.

Eleanor had a boy, aged fourteen, and a girl, aged nine; her second husband, Kameron, had an eleven-year-old son. When Eleanor and Kameron started getting serious, they made a point of planning some family outings so everyone could get to know one another. "Before we got married, we all got along great," Kameron recalls. "I couldn't believe the upheaval after we got married and moved in together."

When Kameron and his son moved in with Eleanor and her children, open hostility broke out. The children seemed to conspire in an effort to break up the marriage. Tony, Eleanor's oldest, tried his best to sow seeds of distrust about Kameron's fidelity. Phoebe, Eleanor's seven-year-old girl, took another tack. She decided she wouldn't let her mother have time alone with Kameron. If they wanted to sleep late on Saturday, Phoebe was knocking on the door. If they went to bed early, Phoebe had to have several drinks of water. Edward, Kameron's son, refused to have anything to do with Eleanor.

Though their tactics may seem Machiavellian, such children feel betrayed by the parent who, by remarrying, forever crushes their reunion fantasy. Most children respond with barely suppressed rage that spills out either in rejection of the stepparent or in overt efforts to sabotage the remarriage.

When you and your spouse realize that certain hopes—such as your children easily welcoming your remarriage—are unrealistic, you can help each other enormously just by *acknowledging* the lost hope. Don't try to hide your disappointment, and don't defend yourself from your own disappointment by blaming your spouse or her children. It is time simply to accept the fact that the children are unlikely to welcome the remarriage. If your stepchildren reject you, accept that their feelings are normal. You must avoid taking their rejection personally.

By acknowledging your mutual disappointment, you and your spouse can accept the pain and let it go. Now you better understand the realities of the stepfamily.

You Can't Hurry Love

Almost every prospective stepparent marries with the hope and expectation of quickly establishing a loving relationship with stepchildren. When this fails to develop, everyone is disappointed, and resentments follow.

"I tried to love Gabrielle," one stepmother told me about her six-year-old stepdaughter. "When I first met her, I thought she was adorable, and I knew how much Ben wanted us to be close. *I* wanted to be close! But after two years of visits every other weekend, her father doting on her, and her treating me like the maid, I'm fed up. I don't really like the way this child is being raised, and I've got to establish my own relationship. Sometimes I feel like I'm being forced to be the wicked stepmother, but someone has to set limits."

Ben dejectedly replies, "It has been hard for me to face the fact that Joanna does not love Gabrielle. It's a big disappointment. I'm angry and frustrated; I don't know what to do."

Both Joanna and Ben got caught up in the instant love fantasy. They set themselves up to fail by imposing an unrealistic expectation on themselves. They then began punishing themselves for their failure.

Take some time to separate the myth from the reality of love in a stepfamily.

- You do not have to love your stepchild.
- Your stepchild does not have to love you.
- Your stepchild can grow up to be a healthy, happy person without your love.
- Love between stepparent and stepchild almost always develops slowly over a period of years, if at all.
- You can have a wonderful stepfamily without the kind of love you think you "should" have.

Stop worrying about whether or not you love your stepchild, and instead focus on establishing a relationship of caring, open communication where each of you listens and respects the other. In this environment, love can grow.

Accepting Your Stepfamily

The next exercise, "Accepting Your Stepfamily," is straightforward. Take a sheet of paper and draw two columns. In the left column you write your affirmation, or positive statement, that you want to reinforce. In the right column you write your response. Each time you write an affirmation, picture your stepfamily—children, stepchildren, and spouse. Then notice your feelings. Don't edit; don't judge. Perhaps you notice a desire to exclude someone from the family, to send one of your stepchildren to live with his or her other biological parent.

Look for anything sarcastic, doubting, or bitter that contradicts your intention to make peace. *Whatever comes up, write it down.* Then repeat your affirmation by writing it again in the left column, and give yourself another opportunity to respond honestly. Repeat. This exercise allows the affirmation to take root in your psyche and also brings forth suppressed feelings and resistances.

Here is one of Joanna's affirmations:

I accept my stepfamily.   No I don't.

I accept my stepfamily.   Gabrielle drives me crazy.

I accept my stepfamily.   I prefer my own child.

I accept my stepfamily.   I wish Ben didn't have kids.

I accept my stepfamily.   It's not what I dreamed of.

I accept my stepfamily.   We had a great time at the fair.

I accept my stepfamily.   Why should I?

I accept my stepfamily.   Ben could help more.

I accept my stepfamily.   I want to love Gabrielle.

I accept my stepfamily.   We have had some great times.

I accept my stepfamily.   But we've also been miserable.

I accept my stepfamily.   Maybe we can learn to make it better.

I accept my stepfamily.   I got it. This is my family.

Repetition is the key to making affirmations work. When you have written "I accept my stepfamily" ten to twenty times, you may begin to feel that all your resistances have emerged. You may need to do the exercise several more times. When you can easily and comfortably write "I accept my family" (leaving out *step*) a few times without resistance, you have completed the exercise.

You can modify the affirmation to target a particular problem. One of my clients was having great difficulty with her two stepdaughters. She found herself constantly at odds and unable to get through to them. She used the affirmation "I love Julie and Ann" to discover how she might be contributing to the problem. By allowing these feelings to emerge, this stepmother found that many of her resistances began to melt away.

AGAIN, *what you resist persists, what you accept lightens.*

Here are some affirmations you might find useful:

"I am a good stepparent."

"I am creating a place in my stepfamily."

"My spouse respects me."

"I am a patient listener with my stepchildren."

"I deserve respect from my stepchildren."

Try a few of these self-esteem affirmations, particularly if you are feeling unappreciated. Talk about your feelings with your spouse. Your disappointment will gradually lift, and a more caring stepfamily will be possible.

You can also use affirmations to support your stepfamily as a whole. Here are several examples:

"We are making peace."

"We are treating one another with respect and kindness."

"We are surviving the chaos."

"We are all healing from loss."

"We are family."

In addition to using these affirmations, try writing one or two on notecards and placing them on a refrigerator. The message is valuable for everyone in the stepfamily, and it might promote good discussion. You may even try making an audio tape of some of these affirmations. Listening to them in a quiet room, breathing deeply and relaxing each body part, can help you find inner peace. The goal of this exercise is to remain clearheaded and at peace even when you are confronted by conflict-inducing thoughts. Only after you have heard each statement at least three or four times and have continued to feel relaxed should you then slowly open your eyes. It is helpful to repeat this exercise a number of times, especially before a visit with your stepchildren, or take a time-out when conflicts arise.

You may at times fall back into old patterns and feel yourself starting to react automatically to your stepchild. During those moments, remember to stop, relax, and choose a more appropriate response. By breathing slowly and recalling the warmth and relaxation you achieved in this exercise, you will be more likely to respond with an open heart.

"Shuttle" Children: Easing the Heartache of Good-byes

In my therapy practice I frequently find myself explaining that there are two constants in life—love and loss. One of life's greatest challenges is to learn how to cope with loss in ways that deepen your capacity for love. Nowhere is this more true than in the stepfamily.

One mother came for help because she suffered overwhelming grief each time she returned her two daughters, aged five and eight, to their father's home every other weekend. "When the time comes to drive the girls back to their father's house, I try very hard to get myself together so I don't make them feel bad about leaving," she explained. "But when I come home, I start sobbing and usually can't stop for hours. I know that the girls only live only twenty miles away, and I also know I'll see them in two weeks, but being rational doesn't help. I'm angry at the judge for giving Rick custody. . . . I'm angry at myself for the divorce. It just never gets any easier."

Saying good-bye over and over again is not any easier for the children. A ten-year-old boy, whose mother had remarried, and whose father saw him one weekend a month, found saying good-bye to his father to be terribly painful. "When I come home to my Mom's house," this boy explained, "no one understands how I feel. I really love my Dad, even if my Mom doesn't. I have a great time with him, because he really understands me; we talk about stuff and he really listens. It's not like with my stepdad, who never listens. When my Dad puts me on the train, he tries to make jokes, but I can see what he's doing; he's just trying to make us both feel better. But I'm afraid that with my Mom remarried and all, he's not gonna see me much. My Mom sure wouldn't care, and that really hurts."

There is no way to escape the poignancy of separation in step-families. The only way to ease the heartache of good-byes is to look even more deeply into your heart to find ways to express your love for your children. Here are some practical suggestions that my clients have found helpful:

- Give yourself and your children permission to talk about how much it hurts to say good-bye. Explain that the painful feelings are natural and that you all share them. Also explain that the feelings will pass and its OK to let them go.
- Create little ceremonies or traditions for saying good-bye. A good-bye meal, a walk in the park, even something as simple as a secret handshake can provide you and your children with a sense of continuity and connection, even as you are letting go.
- Make sure that you preserve your child's presence in your home and that your child knows it. Keep a special drawer for his or her toys and a closet, or space, for clothes so that your child knows he or she remains part of your home.
- Make plans about when you and your child will see each other again. Keep matching calendars in which you can write down anticipated visits. Keep a running list of fun things you want to do when you see each other again.
- Try to make the trip back and forth as neutral as possible. Say your good-byes before you leave the house and avoid emotional upsets in the car, at the train station, or at the airport. Better to create a feeling of a happy send-off once you have left the house. If you find this impossible, then have your spouse drive the child to his other parent or take your child to the train or airport.
- Make sure that you and your child get extra rest as the moment of departure approaches. Don't try to jam activities into the last few days and wind up exhausted. Fatigue makes you and your child much more emotionally vulnerable.
- When your child is leaving, avoid any criticism of your ex, anger about the divorce, or messages to deliver. All these actions complicate your child's ability to deal with his or her own feelings of saying good-bye.
- After your child departs, send a postcard or write a letter that

will arrive a few days later. Your child can start a collection of cards and letters as a reminder of your presence.

- Give yourself and your child permission to mourn, even if you see each other every other weekend. Every separation is a loss which requires healing. The cycle of shock/denial, anger/depression, and understanding/acceptance will inevitably recur. Give yourself time to let your feelings unfold. Soon enough you may find yourself completing the mourning cycle in a day or even a few hours, but above all, don't pretend your painful feelings aren't there. Let yourself feel so that you heal naturally.
- Develop a parenting coalition so that you and your child feel part of an extended family where children naturally move back and forth between the two homes and derive all of the benefit of two mothers, two fathers, stepsiblings, grandparents, and step-grandparents. If, however, your ex-spouse is hostile or abusive, you must set appropriate limits and seek professional assistance. (See Chapter 9.)

These suggestions can help you ease the heartache of good-byes. They can also help you avoid taking anyone in your stepfamily for granted, and they can help you to nourish love even when you and your child are parting.

What You Believe Becomes True: Your Stepfamily Vision and Mission

---

Imagery—the movie of your mind—is very powerful. Your inner pictures of the "perfect" family may be the standard against which you compare the family you are in. Most likely, the idealized family of your childhood or romantic dreams did not include stepchildren.

Your frustration and disappointment with your stepfamily may point to a need to examine and change your mental pictures. Accepting your stepfamily means putting aside the quiet, polite images of family life represented in television commercials or children's books. If you never have been married before, you may have an overly romanticized image of marriage and children. Idealized images become a prison; accepting reality frees you.

Take a few moments right now to sit quietly and relax as you do the following process:

Imagine your stepfamily sometime in the future. The family has successfully dealt with its conflicts and resolved its key problems. Each member is treated with dignity, care, and respect. Each person feels support to grow to his or her full potential.

What would your stepfamily be like if this were so? Picture a family gathering, one-on-one conversations, sharing a meal. Draw in your vision with as much detail as you can.

Imagine holidays, celebrations, and traditions evolving—that which makes this family special. Picture open, genuine expressions of care and concern among stepfamily members. There is emotional support and assistance among stepfamily members. There is respect for each person needing private space and individuality within the stepfamily. There are well-defined interpersonal boundaries and communication skills involving a third person; no one gets caught in the middle.

What your mind can picture is the beginning of what you can create in your life. If you can picture your stepfamily as a happy group where each member offers love and support, you are on the way to transforming that picture into reality. The point is not to create a Pollyanna vision that serves to deny your loss or resistances, but to support your ability to realize your goal.

A family photo session is a very simple means of furthering this vision in a simple, natural way. Ask a friend or hire a professional photographer so that all of you can be in the pictures. Take a picture of your stepfamily in a circle or group with arms interlocking, or otherwise showing mutual support. Once you have a good family photo, place copies in strategic places—by your bedside, in the living room, and on your desk at work. Put snapshots in your wallet, on the dashboard of your car, and on the refrigerator door. Make a point of looking at these photos at least once a day and saying to yourself, "This is my family." The very simplicity of this exercise is its strength.

Family Life Purpose and Goals

You are reading this book for a purpose—to make peace in your stepfamily. A purpose is like the North Star, a guiding light that sets you on a course and helps to keep you fixed on it.

Here is an exercise to help further explore and expand upon what your purpose in family life may be. Pick five qualities from the list below that best complete the following statement:

My purpose in family life is to ——— people.

- guide
- inspire
- rescue
- stimulate
- control
- be loved by
- empower
- please
- have blood ties
- free
- serve
- support
- understand
- nurture
- be served by
- enable
- educate
- push away
- see my genes in
- influence

This is a terrific exercise to share with your spouse and children. Each of you write down on a separate sheet of paper the five qualities that best express your family life purpose. Then, as a team, write down five qualities that your entire family agrees upon as its collective purpose.

Once you write these down individually and as a family, they can become your goals. Goals are like magnets; they pull you towards them. They are commitments to meet. Keep your family life purpose and goals sheets where they can inspire you daily.

Now, enroll stepfamily members in developing a "Family Mission Statement" to express your family purpose and core values. Quality mission statements take a few drafts, with lots of discussion and notes in between. A mission statement should be brief, less than fifty words. The prime purpose of a mission statement is to inspire. Here is an example from a stepfamily I saw in therapy:

> We want to provide a secure, safe home base for each member to grow in and contribute to. Each person is proud of who he or

she is, and all of us are proud of our family. Love, health, humor, play, and service permeate our family atmosphere.

If children refuse participation in a family photo or a mission statement (are shy, for example) don't give up, but try again later.

From Loss to Gain

During the darkest periods of stepfamily life, making peace can seem to be a hopeless endeavor. That is the time when you need confidence, resolve, and a message of hope. Here is one such message from a fifteen-year-old who has survived two divorces and now thrives in her extended stepfamily:

> Let me introduce you to my family. I have three moms and three dads, twelve grandparents, and too many brothers, sisters, and cousins to count. I now truly believe that my Mom's divorces are a blessing, not a burden.
>
> It definitely wasn't always easy. I have seen the good, bad, and ugly part of divorce, but I survived and prevailed, and now I couldn't have a better family.
>
> Our family went through many discussions for me to feel this way about my mother's and father's decisions. I know at times I felt rejection and fear, and I got really mad. I'm sure I blocked out some of the pain for a while, but I have learned so much, especially that underneath it all, my stepparents—all of them—truly love me. I couldn't recommend a better way to learn these things than through our discussions. If I hadn't, my feelings would have been suppressed when I needed to talk the most. Now, I'm very grateful to my Mom and all my parents because they are so loving and supporting. I know all these people want the best for me.

Making peace in your stepfamily *is* possible. You only need to proceed one step at a time. As you proceed, you might keep several simple points in mind:

1. *Acknowledge your growth.* Stand back periodically and give yourself credit. You are learning to handle very complex stepfamily issues. If you remain calm after a stepchild gets upset

with you, or if you don't fight when your ex makes vacation scheduling seemingly impossible, you deserve a pat on the back.

2. *Treat yourself and your spouse kindly.* No one person is responsible for the conflict in a stepfamily, and no one person can make peace for the whole family. Do what you can and take the time you need to rejuvenate. Working in harmony with your mate, you can achieve your family goals.

3. *Proceed systematically.* You will get best results if you discuss the strategies in this book with your spouse. Modify the exercises to suit your family needs. Difficulties and challenges will always arise. Use any setback as a new opportunity to solidify and further growth.

4. *Everybody "blows it" sometimes.* Making peace in your stepfamily is not some idealized concept. Do not become disillusioned or cynical when you make "emotional mistakes." You will; count on it. Rather, acknowledge your error as quickly as possible, perhaps with a simple heartfelt apology. Your spouse and stepchildren will benefit from your humility and vulnerability.

As one remarried couple so aptly put it, "The art of stepfamily living is learning how to enjoy plan B."

Chapter 3

How to Be a Good Stepparent

When I became an instant parent to Sirah's sons, I felt strangely uneasy and alone. The problem was not lack of support from Sirah, who was and is a terrific wife and mother. In retrospect, I realize that my anxiety was rooted in deep uncertainty about my role as stepdad. I wanted to support Sirah's desire to create a close family, yet I felt an enormous emotional gap between her sons and me. The boys already had a good father, and it wasn't at all clear how I could fit into their lives or if they could fit into mine.

In my years of counseling stepfamilies, I have come to recognize this uncertainty as the rule rather than the exception. Most adults today grew up in the traditional nuclear family, and few of us know anything about the unique emotional dynamics of a stepfamily. Trying to understand your stepfamily in terms of a traditional nuclear family is like trying to fit a square peg into a round hole. Even worse, trying to model your role as a stepparent on your memories or expectations of your own parents in a nuclear family is usually a formula for disaster.

Frustrated stepparents frequently come to my office complaining that they don't seem to know how to be a good stepparent. They often feel as if the abuse from stepchildren and lack of support from a spouse are forcing them into the archetype of the wicked stepmother or the cruel stepfather. Stepparents usually come to their new families ready to love their stepchildren, but often meet rejection instead. The ensuing conflicts baffle parents and stepparents alike. What most remarrieds fail to understand, however, is that the stepparent's role in the stepfamily evolves slowly along a reasonably predictable path. The secret to effective stepparenting is understanding the stages of the evolving stepparent-stepchild relationship and how to facilitate growth from one stage to the next.

The Hidden Shame of Feeling Second Class

Even though the stepfamily is rapidly supplanting the nuclear family, and much has been written about stepfamilies over the past decade, appreciation of the stepparent is sorely lacking. Engagement, marriage, and birth are occasions for celebrations, gifts, and warm congratulations. Not so when you become a stepparent. Have you ever heard of a "stepchild shower" for a new stepmother? What about a day for stepmothers or stepfathers?

Regrettably, stepparents assume their roles not in an atmosphere of celebration but in one of uncertainty, isolation, and for some, even a sense of shame. When a child is born, grandparents and friends are eager to provide advice and support. Not so for the stepparent. In fact, most parents respond with concern if their own sons or daughters announce an engagement to a future spouse with children from a previous marriage, and to a large extent, this concern is justified. Our society treats stepparents as second class.

Many stepparents are troubled by feelings of being second-class parents. Angela, a stepmother to her husband Guy's nine-year-old and six-year-old, is typical.

"After I've put the kids to bed and gone to bed myself with Guy, I sometimes lie awake thinking I've missed out," Angela confided at our first session. "Sean and Cassie will never love me like they love their mother."

Angela came to me hurt, disappointed, and on the verge of divorce. After eighteen months of marriage, she still had trouble with her stepchildren, who persisted in rejecting her attention and seemed intent on breaking up her marriage to their father. One of Angela's deepest fears was that she had "made a huge mistake" and would forever be a "second-class mother." She dreaded the prospect of caring for Guy's children but never feeling any real joy or satisfaction as a mother.

Angela's fears are common among stepparents, but often remain suppressed. The result in many second marriages is the gradual growth of frustration, until the stepparent finally gives up and asks for a divorce. In most stepfamilies, this tragedy can be avoided.

Angela's case is a perfect example. After several months in my program for stepparents, she had small breakthroughs with each of her stepchildren. On his own, Sean asked for her help with homework; later that same week, Cassie brought home a drawing as a gift. Through patience, understanding, and a new sensitivity to her stepchildren's emotional needs, Angela began to recognize that stepparents are not second class. To the contrary, she started to realize that her role as the stepmother holds opportunities for joys and satisfactions equal to, and perhaps even greater than, those available for her stepchildren's biological mother. This discovery changed Angela's life and saved her marriage.

Stepping Up to First-Class Parenting

The first step in becoming a good stepparent is banishing once and for all any lingering feelings that you are a second-class parent. The stigma associated with stepparenting stems from this ignorance and, as with all beliefs rooted in misunderstanding, can be difficult to overcome.

Let's look at the reality of stepparenting. Today, stepparents are rapidly growing in numbers equal to biological parents. Over 30 million adults now live in stepfamilies, and with the current rates of divorce and remarriage, over one million new stepfamilies form each year. Nevertheless, a stigma remains.

One of my stepfather clients summarized the problem well: "Whenever I introduce my stepsons, who still have their father's name, there is always a puzzled look. Then I explain, and inevitably there is some sort of ill-at-ease or embarrassed response like, 'Oh, I didn't know.' I then feel a twinge of shame. Rationally, I know it doesn't make sense."

Your choice to create a stepfamily should be a matter of pride, rather than one of guilt or shame. With all my psychiatric training, I allowed myself to be a victim of antiquated feelings of shame about being a stepfather. I always felt uncomfortable explaining to my stepsons' teachers that I was their stepfather, and I harbored feelings that I needed a biological son of my own.

A breakthrough occurred for me, however, when Damien's grades began to improve after I started working with him on his study habits. I realized that I had become a parent to Damien in the fullest sense of the word. It didn't matter whether we were biologically related or not; I had invested myself in him so that he could grow toward becoming a self-sufficient and responsible adult. It is strange how a report card can result in an epiphany. Damien's report card helped me let go of my own self-doubt associated with the word *step* and to embrace my role as one of Damien's parents.

What Is a "Real Parent"?

Take a moment to understand what the word *parent* means to you. Few words are more emotionally loaded. Perhaps you recall your own parents. You may feel love, anger, appreciation, fear, shame, guilt, or any number of emotions depending upon your relationship with your parents. No doubt, you also associate the word with your own role as parent. Webster's defines a parent as one who "begets or brings forth offspring," yet biological parenting is hardly the defining characteristic of a parent. Equally, if not more, important is bringing the child forth into adulthood, and the person who assumes that role is just as much, and in some cases even more, a parent than the biological parent. It is noteworthy that courts have begun defending the rights of stepparents against claims made by natural parents who have abandoned their children for years, and suddenly seek to regain custody.

I frequently ask stepparents to write down what *parenting* means to them, emphasizing that *to parent* is a verb. Here are some notable responses to the following sentence completion:

Parenting means ————.
- caring for children as they grow up
- giving children love and support to become adults
- helping children grow into autonomous individuals
- being there for children when they need you, providing guidance, nurturing, and instilling a sense of values

These are but a few client responses. Try this exercise yourself. I would be surprised if you thought the defining characteristics of parenting were conception and birth alone. There is no reason why stepparents cannot parent just as effectively as biological parents. Stepparents can do an extraordinary job of parenting and reap all the emotional rewards of a close, loving family.

Emotional Forces in Stepfamily Bonding

Complex emotional forces are at work in the formation of a stepfamily. Its members are drawn by intense feelings that alternately push them together and drive them apart. Few are prepared for the power of these emotions.

To appreciate the intensity of emotional forces in the formation of a stepfamily, I find it helpful to use an analogy from physics. It is perhaps not by chance that we describe the modern family of mother-father-children as a nuclear family. The mother-father relationship is a nucleus around which the children orbit. When the mother-father bond explodes in divorce, the whole family can spin out of control, even though a strong pull remains between the children and each natural parent.

When one parent remarries, the new parent-stepparent bond replaces the divorced parents as the nucleus of the new family. This new nucleus exerts a strong pull on the children who also remain emotionally bound to each natural parent now living apart. Children orbiting in this new emotional environment find themselves pulled in three directions simultaneously—toward each natural parent and toward the nucleus of the new stepfamily. The emotionally charged atmosphere of the new stepfamily is ripe for conflict, misunderstanding, rejection, hurt, and anger. Stepfamilies are easily polarized between the angry stepparents and the unruly stepchildren.

Does the existence of intense emotional bonds between a child and both of its biological parents mean that a stepparent can never be a "real" parent? Most emphatically not. The parent-stepparent bond can become the nucleus of a new, stable and joyful family; children can form close emotional bonds with more than two adults in a parental role. It is possible to form a parenting coalition with bonds between new nuclear families, where children enjoy the extraordinary nurturance and guidance of three or four loving parents, two biological parents and one or two stepparents. The key to achieving this new and wonderfully supportive extended family structure is understanding and working with, rather than against, the emotional forces in the original nuclear family.

The core issue in stepparenting is respecting the child's preexisting emotional bond to his or her noncustodial biological parent, while nurturing your own emotional bond with the child. Parents encounter their own conflicting emotions when introducing their children to their new marriage partners. On the more conscious level, parents want the children and new spouse to like and appreciate each other. On the more unconscious level, the parent wants to preserve a primary bond with his or her children. As a result, parents often feel pulled in two directions as soon as the marriage ceremony is consummated. Parents tend to bury this internal conflict, hoping for one big happy family.

Strong psychological forces also drive most stepparents to attempt to bond too quickly with their stepchildren. First, there are our own ego needs. We want to be acknowledged as likable. The marriage validates that we are worthy of love; most of us instinctively look for more validation in our spouse's children, and we fear rejection. Second, there is our need to reinforce the marriage. We know that a loving relationship with the stepchildren will reinforce the marriage, while a conflict will inevitably undermine it.

Equally strong psychological forces compel stepchildren initially to reject their stepparents. Stepchildren almost always resent the new stepparent because he or she has dashed hopes that mom and dad will get back together. Having lived through the trauma of a divorce once, children are also reluctant to get too close to someone who might also let them down by walking out of their lives. Children may feel that liking a stepparent means they are being disloyal to their absent, biological parent. Finally, the parent's attraction to a new mate may be perceived by the children as a loss of his or her love and attention; now their parents must be shared with a "stranger."

This is the first paradox of stepparenting. While strong psychological forces push stepparents to bond with their stepchildren, equally strong unconscious forces drive stepchildren to reject their stepparents. Parents often wind up caught in the middle.

Stages of Bonding with Your Stepchild

The solution to this fundamental stepfamily paradox is refreshingly simple. Give up the "instant love" myth, and *give your stepchildren the emotional freedom and the opportunity to develop a relationship with you at their own pace and on their own terms.* As a stepparent, you have an enormous amount to offer your stepchildren, who have enormous needs. Try to remain confident that the potential for a warm and loving relationship is there. In order for you to build that relationship, you must allow it to evolve through normal stages of parent-child bonding.

Think for a moment about how biological parents bond with their children. First, the parents care for the infant in an atmosphere of pure love and play. There are no issues of discipline because the infant's needs are food, sleep, warmth, and stimulation. When the child begins to talk and crawl, a new stage unfolds. The parents begin providing elementary guidance as the child develops fundamental trust and confidence. Soon the parent teaches the child and the child looks to the parents to learn about the world. As the toddler develops his or her own sense of autonomy, the parent exerts more authority, and the child first begins to recognize the parent as a teacher of values and authority on rules of behavior.

The healthy stepparent-stepchild bond evolves through similar stages. The first stage is establishing a simple friendship. It may be helpful to them to think of this stage as analogous to the initial bonding between a parent and an infant. The primary task is simply to learn to enjoy your stepchild, and for your stepchild to learn to enjoy you. *Fun* is the operative word. This doesn't mean you disregard your adult role or responsibilities, but it does mean that you rely on your spouse to handle primary responsibility for discipline (more on this issue in Chapter 4).

The second stage in bonding with your stepchild is establishing basic trust. You must become skilled in dealing with difficult emotions. The child needs help in dealing with his or her own feelings of divided loyalties, and that he or she can become angry without losing your friendship and love. Further, it is also important for the child to feel you accept him or her, and that you can share mutual appreciation.

The third stage in your evolving relationship leads to mentoring. At this point, your stepchild enjoys and trusts you. It is quite natural for him or her to begin looking to you for help in solving problems: a conflict with a teacher, or even a concern about one or both of his natural parents. The fact that you lack a blood tie may elevate you in the child's eyes as an objective observer. At this stage, you begin to influence the child in profound ways by building self-esteem and teaching values. The challenge of this stage is to start accepting the mantle of codisciplinarian.

Finally, your role may evolve to what I call the "parental guide." At this stage, you and your stepchild share a deep and enduring love. Neither you nor your stepchild is concerned that you may be competing with your stepchild's natural parents, because you have developed your own special relationship. Your stepchild knows that you are committed to his or her development and well-being, and appreciates and loves you for that commitment.

When stepparents and stepchildren allow their relationship to evolve through these stages, they usually develop a bond that is deeply loving and rewarding. In contrast, problems in the stepparent-stepchild relationship often occur when the natural evolution of the relationship is arrested. For example, when the stepparent either tries too hard too soon or ignores the stepchild, elementary friendship may never develop, and the relationship may be doomed to conflict. In other cases, the stepparent may establish basic friendship, but a deeper trust may remain elusive because the stepchild is troubled by difficult emotions such as resentment. The new stepparent may get caught up in reacting to rather than resolving the emotional conflict.

For the stepparent's role to expand from trusted friend to mentor, the stepparent must invest substantial time in becoming part of the stepchild's life. Persistence is critical in the face of institutions such as schools, which still harbor a bias against stepparents. With patience and determination, a stepparent may finally emerge in the role of parental guide, but only with the full support of the spouse. Sometimes that support is lacking and the whole stepfamily remains troubled by conflicts concerning discipline and money.

Trying Too Hard

When Angela, mentioned earlier in this chapter, sought my help, she revealed in her first session a series of misunderstandings and mistakes that blocked the initial bonding she so desperately hoped to achieve with her stepson and stepdaughter. Angela put so much pressure on herself to be a good stepmother that she did not realize how she was pressuring her stepchildren. The more she described how hard she had tried—cooking, cleaning, buying the children new clothes, planning family outings, trying to teach better manners—the more apparent it became that her stepchildren rejected her. Angela's mistakes are instructive because they are so common among new stepparents.

First, Angela felt overly sorry for Sean and his sister, Cassie. The children had been through a custody battle, and Angela's husband won because Candace, the children's mother, had a drug problem. Although Angela's sympathy for the children was understandable, she worried too much about how they had been damaged by the divorce. Angela indulged the children with excessive pampering and gift giving to make up for the past. Instead of getting to know Angela as a person, they saw her simply as Daddy's new wife who was at their beck and call.

Second, Angela thought she could be a better mother than Candace. In effect, Angela wanted to replace Candace not only in her husband's heart but also in the hearts of her stepchildren. The children saw her efforts as extremely threatening.

Third, Angela pushed herself to be a supermom. In addition to her homemaking tasks, she enrolled her stepdaughter in ballet and her stepson in piano lessons. She arranged visits with her in-laws, and soon found herself the principal disciplinarian because she had convinced Guy and herself that she was a supermom. She also became obsessive about maintaining what she perceived as family harmony. She thought well-planned family outings—whether to the movies, the lake, or a picnic—would break down the barriers with her stepchildren. While her efforts created the semblance of a family, her stepchildren grew increasingly abusive. Angela soon became bitter because her stepchildren did not appreciate her efforts. She failed to realize that they perceived her efforts as coercion.

Forcing Love Creates Rejection

The irony of Angela's story is that the breakthrough she sought was just around the corner. All she had to do was stop trying so hard. What Angela had failed to do was give her stepchildren the chance to get to know and like her as a friend, on their own terms. I advised Angela to slow down, stop trying to create her Norman Rockwell ideal of family harmony, and give herself and her stepchildren the chance to get to know one another. This was the turning point in their relationship.

Are you trying too hard with your stepchildren? Here are some questions to ask yourself:

- Do you frequently change your schedule to accommodate your stepchildren?
- Do you frequently sacrifice time with your spouse to meet your stepchildren's needs?

- Do you put up with your stepchildren's misbehavior with a polite smile to mask your anger?
- Are you trying to make your stepchildren love you?

If you answered "yes" to two or more of these questions, you probably are trying too hard. Slow down and give yourself a chance to make friends without pressure.

Becoming Friends: The Power of One-on-One Time

The best way to make friends with your stepchild is by spending time together one-on-one. Stepfamilies are often so hectic that there always seems to be other family members around. In such an atmosphere, some stepparents find it difficult to carve out time for each of their stepchildren. Balance between family activities and one-on-one activities is important, just as balance is necessary in spending time with each of your stepchildren.

There is nothing more important for a stepparent and stepchild than positive, fun, one-on-one time. I often advise setting aside one evening of fun time (playing sports or cards, going out for dinner) per week, for just the two of you. It need not be anything extravagant. View it as a definite commitment. You must have an extremely valid reason to cancel or postpone it. Have as much fun as possible; this is a time for mutual enjoyment and support. Both the anticipation and the sharing of memories will enrich your stepfamily immeasurably. You might take photographs of these activities to build a shared family history.

Some activities are appropriate for teenagers, others for younger children. I am sure you have many skills and interests that provide an opportunity for bonding. Whether it's gardening, jogging, baking, car maintenance, carpentry, or sewing, kids are usually receptive to joining these activities if you make it a point to involve them one-on-one.

Remember the old adage, "You can't buy friendship"? That is only partially true! Money alone certainly won't do it, and may even cause resentment. Your time and attention count most. Stepkids know if you are merely trying to "bribe" them for affection. But in our culture, money and what it buys *do* signify love and being part of a family. It is good for stepkids to know that a stepparent is contributing to their support. When a stepparent becomes the one to give the weekly allowance or movie money, the kids are often genuinely appreciative. Have your child make up a list of three wishes for gifts, presents or toys, each under $25. Use this list for special treats.

If your stepchild is very young, you can create poems or artwork together. Make a collage from magazines and photographs taken since you became a stepfamily. You might design a stepfamily flag, or crest. Be sure to display these works of art, and proudly share them with extended family and friends.

One of the great ways to bond with young children is to read aloud to them. When you read to a child, you create intimacy by focusing all your attention on sharing a story with the child. This focus of your attention coupled with the mutual sharing of images generated by the spoken word is enormously powerful in bonding.

A commitment to spend regular one-on-one fun time with your stepchild can help break down barriers, even when those barriers have persisted for months or years. Angela asked Sean and Cassie what they would like to do most. Sean picked having a dinner at McDonald's; Cassie wanted to play with Angela's jewelry. Instead of worrying about whether these activities were "good" for the children, Angela accepted the opportunity to play with and enjoy them on their own terms. In the process, they all began to relax as well. It was not the specific activity that Angela shared with each of the children but rather the devotion of her time and attention to each of them separately for a few hours that worked. The simple experience of bonding without any pressure whatsoever was a turning point. The children's resistance, which had persisted for eighteen months, began to melt.

One-on-one time may be even more important for men than women in establishing a friendship with their stepchildren. Studies show that most women tend to respond favorably to the sight of a child, whether their own or someone else's. In contrast, men tend to exhibit loving parental feelings only to their own children. Stepdads probably need more time than stepmoms to begin enjoying truly loving feelings toward their stepchildren, and one-on-one time is very effective.

Problem Kids Are Promises
Waiting to Be Fulfilled

If there is substantial antagonism with your stepchildren, creating one-on-one time may require special effort. Stan and his wife, Jennifer, sought my help because Stan and his two stepsons were at each other's throats. On further investigation, it became clear that Stan had prematurely assumed the role of disciplinarian. Jennifer had divorced four years earlier, and the boys had relatively little contact with their father. Stan thought they were out of control, and Jennifer encouraged him to assert a firm hand. The boys rebelled. "I'm not going to have him telling me what to do all the time," wailed Tommy. "I'll stay up as late as I want, and nobody's gonna make me not watch TV when I want."

I explained to Stan and Jennifer that force would never result in the boys' respect for Stan's parental authority, and that failing to develop a primary bond would make parenting difficult at best. I suggested that Stan have a talk with each of the boys and explain his desire to know each of them. I also suggested that he acknowledge that he had come on too strong with new rules. I advised Stan to propose that he and each of the boys arrange some time just to have fun.

"The boys were suspicious when I sat down and told them that I was bearing down too hard," Stan later reported. "They were surprised when I asked them what they would like to do, as long as we could do it together. Tommy eventually said he'd enjoy a pro basketball game. Jeremy wanted sailing lessons. They certainly knew how to take advantage of an opening."

Stan bought season basketball tickets and signed up for sailing lessons. But more importantly, he followed through on the commitment, even when it was difficult to make the time. In a matter of months, he had achieved a breakthrough.

"I don't know whether the boys saw me as buying them off, or if spending the time together was what worked," Stan explained, "but since I made the commitment to the games and lessons, our whole relationship has turned around. One of the best parts is how we talk in the car. I'm really starting to like these boys."

Avoiding Competition with the Natural Parent

One of the most difficult issues posed for stepparents in initial bonding with stepchildren is avoiding competition, real or imagined, with the absent natural parent. Since stepchildren tend to remain loyal to both natural parents, they can perceive a stepparent's efforts to become friends as a demand that they give up their love for their other parent, as well as their hope that mom and dad will reunite.

Natalie and her second husband, Marshall, sought help because his two sons, Peter, aged twelve, and Russell, aged nine, had become withdrawn since her remarriage. Only a few months after the remarriage, Natalie's ex-husband, Nolan, had accepted a job in Chicago. Natalie was concerned because the boys' attitude toward Marshall had changed dramatically. "Peter and Russell are very close to their Dad," Natalie maintained. "I knew that the move would be hard on the boys, but Nolan and I talked to them at length. We assured them that they would stay in close touch with their Dad. Peter seemed especially proud of his Dad's promotion. The boys don't seem to be depressed. It's just that they don't want to have anything to do with Marshall."

"Before the marriage, I thought the boys and I were getting along very well," Marshall added. "I thought they loved staying over at my house with the big pool and their own rooms. Now that they've moved in, they seem to be hiding behind a wall. I try to make conversation, but I can't get anywhere."

Natalie and Marshall were hoping that I would have some special insight about what had changed in Peter and Russell's perceptions. I explained that we had two choices. Either Natalie could arrange for the boys to come in and talk to me, or Marshall might consider "leveling" with the boys himself. I suggested to Marshall that he raise the issue of whether the boys thought he was supposed to be a replacement for their Dad. I told Marshall to tell the boys they needed to be honest with one another, and emphasized the need to assure them that when people are "on the level," they accept what one another has to say and try to work out their differences.

Being "On the Level"

This issue is so emotionally charged that I recommend stepparents confront it early and directly. One helpful tool is a technique I call "leveling." Friendship is impossible without open communication, and there are few better ways to begin building open communication than by showing children that you are open to their feelings, and willing to share your own. Leveling is a technique to show your stepchildren that you can be "on the level" with them, as they can be with you.

It can be very helpful for you to establish some simple rituals to precede a leveling session. For example, you might choose a special place (i.e., the park, the family room) or a special time of day. Make it clear that your time is just for the two of you to talk honestly without interruption. It is essential to give your stepchild the sense that you respect his or her feelings, and you expect him or her to respect your own. Although leveling is most effective with children ten and over, it can be helpful with bright six- and seven-year-olds.

Marshall and Natalie came back amazed at how leveling could change Marshall's relationship with the boys. "I had a session with Peter and Russell, alone, and then a session with all three of us," Marshall reported. "They were clearly surprised when I asked each of them if we could have an 'on the level' talk. I told them right up front that I was committed to their mother and to the new family, and I also spent some time assuring them that they could be honest. I told them that I was feeling hurt about the way they were treating me. That seemed to break the ice. Each of the boys in his own way was feeling mixed up about their Dad moving away, and then moving into my house. Tuning me out was their way of saying 'I'm still loyal to my Dad.' Once I understood what was going on, we got through it very easily. I just told them that I respected their Dad very much and never intended to be a replacement. My offer to help with homework and to go to a game were my ways of being a friend, not stepping into their Dad's shoes. After our leveling session, the relief was written all over their faces."

Here are some suggestions to consider for your leveling sessions:

- Make it clear that you do not intend to replace the child's biological parent.

- Convey your desire to support a positive relationship between the child and both his/her natural parents.
- Acknowledge that you may be uncertain as to how you fit into the child's life but that you want to be a friend.
- Express how much you value an honest relationship and give permission to the child to ask for a leveling session.
- If your relationship has been rocky to date, acknowledge the conflict and explain your desire to make friends.
- Assure the child that leveling sessions are times to express feelings without fear of what will happen by being honest.

Your style and approach must be "on the level" too:

- Listen to what your child has to say and don't interrupt.
- Generate mutual respect by asking how your stepchild feels rather than assuming you know how he/she feels.
- Encourage mutual self-disclosure by sharing your feelings such as disappointment about conflict in the family.
- Give yourselves permission to laugh, make jokes, and not take it all too seriously.

By observing these guidelines, you may be able to establish a new level of communication with your stepchild and begin reversing months of conflict.

Addressing the Name Problem

Leveling can be very effective in addressing one of the most basic early problems: what does your stepchild call you? What last name does your child or stepchild use?

Mixed feelings are the norm when it comes to names in a step-family. Stepchildren frequently wish to reserve "Mom" and "Dad" for biological parents because to do otherwise would make them feel disloyal. Many stepparents, on the other hand, associate a child's use of a parent's first name as a sign of disrespect and lack of intimacy. Sometimes, the whole issue is ignored, and the stepparent winds up a "he" or "she" at home and "my mom's husband" or "my dad's wife" when introduced.

The name issue can be terribly troubling to a stepchild, particularly when both parents have children from a prior marriage. When a woman remarries, she may adopt her new husband's last name. She then has the same last name as her new husband's children, but her own children usually retain their biological father's name. Children in this circumstance often feel embarrassed, particularly at school or church where the difference becomes conspicuous. The child suddenly finds himself or herself having to explain why he or she has a different name than his or her own mother! Use leveling to discuss the problem:

- You must take the initiative. Children tend to mask their discomfort.
- Trust your instincts about your sense of discomfort. Your stepchild may be calling you by your first name, but that does not mean that he or she is comfortable with the arrangement.
- When you raise the issue, create trust by sharing your own feelings first. Explain that you have mixed feelings about what your stepchildren should call you, and assure them you want everyone to find names that make each family member feel comfortable.
- Reiterate your desire to be on the level, which means you and your stepchild share your real feelings.

In my own stepfamily, my stepsons, Damien and Michael, have become comfortable calling me "Harold" or their "other Dad," and when talking about their father in Toronto, the boys call him their "Father" or "other Dad." In this way, we all acknowledge that the boys have two Dads, both of whom are "real Dads," but each of whom has a special role in the boys' lives.

Building Trust by Resolving Anger

For many children of divorce, a quiet seething anger is a constant emotional companion. Most children of divorce are unaware of their rage because the psyche mercifully represses their intense feelings so that the children are not emotionally overwhelmed. Instead, the anger seeps to the surface slowly through acting out, rebellion, and sour moods. One of the great challenges for any stepparent is assisting the stepchild to express and resolve this anger.

Coping with a stepchild's anger is particularly difficult for stepparents and parents alike, because the stepparent is often the target for the anger. In most instances, children harbor repressed anger toward one or both of their parents. They perceive one or another of the divorcing parents as breaking up the family and abandoning them. The children are deeply hurt, and their anger toward their parents is normal. Rarely, however, are the children capable of coping with these feelings on their own, because the anger is also clouded by guilt ("Daddy is leaving Mommy because he's angry at me") and fear ("Mommy and Daddy might send us away—what will happen to me then?"). The stepparent often becomes a safe target for the child's anger.

Watching their children attack their new spouses, apparently without reason, leaves many parents horrified. A stepchild's unprovoked animosity is especially painful to a stepparent, who comes into the new family with the best intentions.

In the spirit of trying to create family harmony, many parents and their new spouses make the mistake of trying to suppress angry feelings. This strategy inevitably fails, since suppressed feelings won't go away. Open up to the children's anger so that healing and ultimately trust and respect can emerge.

Coping with a stepchild's hostility—or even suppressed rage—is not easy. The emotional dynamic is very complex and highly charged. I suspect that all the fairy tales about the wicked stepmother and cruel stepfather have their psychological origins in the enormous difficulty which stepparents have in coping with a stepchild's rage. However, knowledge, patience, and determination can work wonders.

Jackie and Mel had been married for a little more than a year when they came for counseling. Both had been married before; she had two children, Roger and Larry, aged eight and aged three. He had one child, Todd, eleven, who lived with his mother.

Jackie and Mel sought help because Roger had become unmanageable. "He's become almost sullen," Jackie said in describing her older son's moods. "He comes home from school and goes into his room. Since Mel moved in, he stopped inviting his friends over, and he won't do anything I ask without it becoming a battle. Everything is an argument—"

Mel and Roger had difficulty from the first day Jackie told her son that Mel would soon become his stepdad. Roger's response, recalled Jackie, was "I've got a dad, I don't need him." Mel's inclination was to go slowly and let Roger adapt, but Mel soon tired of being the butt of his stepson's outbursts.

"Last Saturday was the last straw," Mel declared with obvious regret. "Roger had his toys strewn all over the living room. We were having friends over, so I offered to play awhile and then help him clean up as his mother had asked. He looked up and said something like 'This is my house and I don't need you to play with me.' I became so furious I could have hit him. Instead, I yelled at him to start cleaning up immediately. He started crying and ran to his mother. It was a disaster."

In counseling with Roger, it became apparent why he was so difficult. He missed his natural father terribly, and he blamed his mother for "chasing Dad away." Roger was also not about to risk any disloyalty to his father by getting too close to Mel. I also discovered that Roger harbored a dark rage. He felt abandoned by his father who had taught him to play catch, and shoot a basket. When I was able to get Roger to recall some of these memories, he brightened visibly. He turned dark just as quickly when he talked about his recent visits with his Dad. "He's got his new wife Paula, now. Dad says she's nice— nicer than Mom—but I won't be nice to her. They're having a baby, and Dad doesn't have time for me anymore. We don't even play when I visit."

When people are hurt by someone they love, the natural response is anger. The deeper the love and hurt, the more intense the anger. Roger was deeply hurt by his father, and equally angry. Unable to cope with his anger, he rebelled against his mother and attacked his stepfather.

Games are often an effective way to help a child express repressed feelings. Roger liked basketball, so we played a little game which I call "slam dunk." I explained that we could have some fun getting out some feelings about people in his life. So we took an ordinary wastebasket to serve as the basket and we rolled up a piece of paper to serve as the ball. But before we crinkled up the paper, we wrote a name on it. I then pretended to guard Roger while he tried to get to the basket where he would slam-dunk the paper, and symbolically the person whose name was written on it. By making it just a little difficult to get to the basket, I provided a resistance for Roger to overcome and a measure of safety in his venting his feelings. In short order, Roger was slam-dunking Mel, his Mom, his Dad, and his new stepmother. As the game progressed, we took a little more time preparing each piece of paper by adding some reasons why Roger was mad.

Once Roger and I had played this game, we taught it to Mel and his mom. His Dad eventually played, as well. In one session with his mother and stepdad, Roger was able to ask me to write his mother's name along with the message "chased Dad away" and his stepdad's name along with "bosses me around." Roger then played first with his mom and then with his stepdad, each of whom offered appropriate resistance. This raucous session soon led to cheers and laughter as Roger acknowledged his anger and symbolically let it go through the slam dunk.

The result of several slam-dunk sessions was a breakthrough. Roger found a way to let his parents and stepparent know how much he was hurt and some of the reasons why. His parents and stepparents gained an insight into Roger's feelings, and were able to respond with support and patience. Roger's Dad learned how important it was to spend more time with his son. Roger learned at a very young age that he could love, be hurt, and rediscover love again.

Threats, Tantrums, and Tears

Monica and Bruce came for help because Bruce's daughters, Tricia and Ashley, ages 15 and 12, appeared determined to break up their marriage when they visited. Monica's son Al, who lived with her and Bruce, was a senior in high school. He welcomed the marriage because he and his mother had been on their own for seven years, but Al, too, was concerned that his stepsisters heaped endless abuse on his mother when they visited.

"They hate me," was Monica's tearful comment about her stepdaughters. "Ever since the wedding, these girls have gone out of their way to hurt me. They remind me that I'm not their mother at every opportunity, and if that's not enough, they do their best to cause problems. They visit mostly on weekends, and they know how important phone messages are when I'm showing houses in my real estate business, so they conveniently forget to write them down."

"I'm frustrated, and I'm furious" was Bruce's response. "I'm here because I don't know what to do. I love my girls, but they have turned into monsters. It's as if they won't be satisfied until they break us up. The last straw happened last weekend. I had to work late Friday night, and I wasn't home when the girls arrived. So what does Tricia say to Monica? 'I wonder if daddy is really working late!' That girl hears from her mother over and over again about my affair three years ago."

I discussed with Bruce and Monica a variety of reasons why Tricia and Ashley might be acting out. The good relationship between Bruce and Monica had shattered the girls' reunion fantasy. They may be jealous and want to have their Dad all to themselves, or may resent Monica's efforts to mother them. The girls may have felt abandoned because their parents had both remarried spouses with children of their own. I suggested that the best way to break through the emotional defenses was to encourage the obviously bright girls to talk about how they were feeling. Monica had reached her limit in coping with them and initially rejected the idea, saying, "I didn't do anything to deserve this treatment."

"You're probably right," I said. "But now let's talk about how you can be effective in helping the family heal."

When It Comes to Feelings No One Is Wrong

The "When It Comes to Feelings No One Is Wrong" exercise presumes that you can approach your children or stepchildren to have a frank discussion. Many parents and stepparents have been surprised at how insightful and capable of explaining feelings their children are. The key to this technique is creating an atmosphere of safety and trust so that a child can express his or her feelings without fear of retribution, abandonment, criticism, guilt, or shame. The "No One Is Wrong" exercise begins with an invitation to talk about conflict in the stepfamily. For example, I suggested to Bruce that he be direct with Tricia and say, "Tricia, I've noticed that you are tense when you visit. If you are angry at Monica or me, would you like to talk about it?"

Bruce's offer was enough to get Tricia started. In many cases, however, some additional coaxing and reassurances may be necessary. Acknowledge that everyone in the family has rough feelings, and give explicit permission to acknowledge feelings.

State explicitly that you will always love and be there to protect your child, no matter what. Tell them that you won't stop loving them because they get angry. Having watched the breakup of your marriage, your child might not trust these assurances at first. Explain that a husband and wife's relationship is different from a parent and child's. Parents can get divorced, but a parent can't divorce his or her child. With enough reassurances, your child may consent to talk.

The next step is choosing a time and place. Your goals should be twofold. First, involve your child in the decision, so that he or she can see that you really want to know how he or she feels. Demonstrate your desire to listen. Second, find a place of comfort and privacy where you will not be disturbed. Tricia liked the big couch in the den. Bruce unplugged the phone and put a DO NOT DISTURB sign on the door.

The third step is discovering your child's feelings. Here are some of Bruce's questions:

- Has Monica done anything to hurt you?
- Are you mad because your mom and I still fight?
- Are you mad because your mom and I have made your life difficult?
- Could it be me and your mom who really make you angry?
- Could you be taking your anger toward me and your mom out on Monica?
- Are you mad because your mom and I are not getting back together?

When you ask questions, it is critical that you neither interrupt nor pressure. If you want your child to expand upon an answer, the best thing to say is simply, "Could you tell me more?" The better you listen, the more your child is likely to disclose. Allow at least one hour for this exercise.

When Bruce finally got through to Tricia, he learned that she was deeply hurt by the constant fighting between Bruce and his ex-wife, Edith. Tricia felt "torn in half" every time she came to visit, because her

Mom was usually upset. Tricia also felt that Bruce didn't care about her feelings because he always tried to create such a happy family with Monica, but he didn't think about how unhappy his fighting was making Tricia at home. This information was a revelation for Bruce, who had no idea how his continuing conflict with Edith created tension for Tricia and for his new family. Bruce learned that the most important step to lessening conflict between Tricia and Monica was for him to work out a better relationship with Edith.

The "No One Is Wrong" exercise can be particularly healing if you try several sessions to see if any agreed upon changes in the family are working to help the child feel better. It can be helpful to include the stepparent. Bruce promised Tricia that he would work harder to have a better relationship with her mother. Several weeks later, he suggested to Tricia that she, Monica and he all have a "No One Is Wrong" session. Tricia had an opportunity to explain to Monica why she had been so angry. With the simple authentic statement, "Gee, Tricia, I can see how you feel," Monica melted Tricia's resistance. A stepmother-stepdaughter relationship was born.

Losing Your Temper Is Losing

Whether you are a parent or stepparent, you cannot become too skilled in learning to cope with anger. Anger is an integral part of stepfamily living. It is almost impossible to live in a stepfamily without hurting someone you love from time to time. You need to become skilled in accepting the answers (including your own), acknowledging the hurt, and healing the breach of love in the relationship.

Here are a few points to keep in mind:

- Try to avoid taking angry outbursts personally, particularly from stepchildren. Remember that anger usually stems from hurt, and the key to making peace is getting behind the anger to heal the hurt.
- Control your own tendency to become defensive when your stepchild becomes angry or upset. When you feel inclined to become defensive, you would be better served by using three simple words, "Tell me more."

- Avoid the trap of "win/lose" arguments. When a defiant step-child stakes out an emotional position such as "I don't want to study" or "You're not my mother," there is little to be gained by proving yourself right. The price of your victory is your step-child's resentment. I am not suggesting that you let your step-child trample upon house rules, but arguments about who's right are rarely helpful.

Try to model healthy interpersonal communication by listening with empathy rather than reacting defensively. You are listening em-pathetically when you:

- Invite discussion with openers such as "Can we talk?"
- Appreciate feelings behind the words
- Ask questions to understand another point of view
- Express warmth in eye contact, vocal tone, facial expressions
- Use phrases such as "I understand how you feel. . . ."; "I appreciate your saying. . . ."
- Remain relaxed even if you are attacked

In contrast, you are responding defensively when you:

- Interrupt your stepchild at every opportunity
- Judge, justify, and contradict
- Demonstrate impatience by using phrases such as "I know" and "I don't have time for this"
- Make your stepchild feel stupid, guilty, or incompetent with abrupt statements such as "That doesn't make sense" or "Don't be stupid."

Empathic listening has one great drawback: it takes time. When chaos reigns around your house, as it sometimes will, reminding yourself to slow down and listen can be difficult. Try to remember the old adage: Haste makes waste. Haste with your stepchild today is likely to cost you enormous anguish, conflict, and loss in the future if your new marriage fails, in part, because of problems with your step-children.

Mutual Acceptance: The "Lifeboat" Exercise

Another essential skill for stepparents is promoting mutual acceptance within the stepfamily. When families merge, a certain measure of culture shock is inevitable. Differences in the simplest habits of everyday living (Who makes the beds? Who uses the bathroom first? When are mealtimes?) can be irritating sources of conflict. I remember how unprepared I was for the changes in my routine that inevitably followed Damien and Michael moving in with us full-time. The challenges of mutual acceptance are even greater when both parents in a remarried family have children. Often, the "lifeboat" exercise can be helpful.

In the "Lifeboat" exercise, the whole family gets together to figure out how to make uncomfortable situations more comfortable. The parents begin by explaining that a stepfamily is something like a lifeboat for everyone involved. When a previous marriage breaks up, it is a tragedy, something like a sinking ship. But lifeboats allow people to not only escape the tragedy but survive and make their way to a better future. To make it in a lifeboat, however, everyone must learn to cooperate and get along. Lifeboats still face rough seas. Here, the parents must make it clear to all that they are committed to captain this new family to a happier future for all, and that they are hoping everyone will help.

Now, each stepfamily member writes down his or her pet peeves about the way the family is working. It is important for the parents to establish that feeling irritated or annoyed in a new living arrangement is natural. To illustrate, each of the parents should give an example—but beware of singling out your stepchild. It's better to use each other as examples.

After ten minutes, the "captain" collects the papers and shuffles them. One of the shipmates then takes the top paper and reads the pet peeve. With each complaint, the captain opens the floor to a discussion of how to resolve the issue.

This exercise helps diffuse irritation and creates an atmosphere of mutual acceptance and respect, not just solutions to specific conflicts. The process is very important to the children. Instead of feeling thrown together and told to share with a new sibling, the children feel supported in taking responsibility to work out new relationships on terms that respect their needs and feelings. The "Lifeboat" exercise can be useful whenever minor irritations seem to be undermining an atmosphere of acceptance in your stepfamily.

You May Be Criticizing a Stepchild for Qualities You Can't Accept in Yourself

---

Each of us has idiosyncratic traits, and most of us find certain behaviors of others to be particularly irksome. Quite often, what we find most bothersome in others is a trait found in our own character. For example, people who most hate to be interrupted when they speak are most often prone to interrupt others. No matter how hard you may try to work out accommodations with your stepchildren, you are likely to be irked by some of their idiosyncratic behaviors. Whenever you find yourself reacting intensely to a stepchild's behavior, consider asking yourself the following:

Am I reacting to a characteristic that I don't like in myself?

Am I reacting to my own sense of guilt or inadequacy?

Am I reacting to something in my own past?

If your negative reaction to a stepchild's behavior is particularly intense, it is likely that one of the above questions will yield insight into the source of your intense reaction. The challenge then is to learn from this insight and let go.

One of my clients, Leon, a stepfather to three boys, felt the boys were driving him crazy with their sloppiness around the house. When he proposed that everyone pitch in and clean up, he found himself becoming very angry and as a result, was very ineffective in this request. Through asking himself the above questions, it dawned on Leon that he was so upset with the mess at home because he harbored deep self-criticism and frustration about his chronically messy office at work. Recognizing his own problem allowed him to ease up on both himself and his stepsons.

While developing acceptance is very valuable, a stepparent must also be willing to set limits. Remember that it is possible to accommodate stepchildren to a fault.

Appreciation: What You Focus On Grows Stronger

Cultivating a culture of mutual appreciation is yet one more important step in strengthening the stepfamily. Fostering mutual appreciation not only develops trust but even more importantly builds a child's self-esteem.

One simple way to show your appreciation of stepchildren, particularly stepchildren who only visit periodically, is by displaying their photographs. One insensitive father was surprised when his second wife told him that his two daughters were hurt because there were no photographs of them in their father's new home, only photographs of the new baby. Then she made sure that the family portraits were prominently displayed. This stepmother overruled her husband's objections to family photographs that included the girl's mother. "You can't ban her from your life," this stepmother declared, "so why try at the expense of your daughters?"

Photographs at work can also be important. One mother recalled that her new husband displayed his own children's photos prominently on his desk, but he had no photos of his two stepsons. Only by accident did she overhear one of her sons informing their father that their stepfather must not like them because he didn't have their photos at work. This stepfather promptly corrected the oversight, and arranged for one of the boys to go pick up mail at his office one Saturday morning to "inadvertently" discover their photos prominently displayed.

Another excellent way to encourage mutual appreciation is to enroll children in family tasks. It is helpful at first for the parent to take the initiative, inviting the stepparent and all the children to join in. Consideration must also be given to age appropriate activities. Here are some ideas:

- Plan a family outing at the beach or a picnic, and ask everyone to help in assembling what you need.
- Get involved with a local charity and volunteer together.
- Sort through the attic and garage, then hold a garage sale together.

While these activities can involve the whole family, you can also create mutual appreciation through one-on-one tasks. For example you might:

- Ask a stepchild to help you wash the car
- Enlist a stepchild in helping you shovel snow or rake leaves
- Ask a stepchild to help you cook meals or rearrange the kitchen

Any of these activities can become the basis for you and your stepchild to accomplish tasks and enjoy the results together. You then have genuine basis for you to use words such as:

- You're a super kid.
- Thanks.
- You made my day.
- I knew you could do it.
- You're special.
- Way to go!

Children and teenagers alike are sensitive to insincerity. These words only have value when expressed genuinely.

Developing Empathy: *"Walk a Mile in My Shoes"*

Another excellent exercise to encourage mutual appreciation is called "Walk a Mile in My Shoes," for children aged ten and up. You can propose this activity to the whole family as a game in order to have fun and get to know one another better. Don't be surprised at how much everyone learns.

This exercise begins with each person in the stepfamily taking off a shoe and placing it in the middle of the circle. Then all the shoes are mixed together in one big pile. Everyone then closes their eyes, reaches in, and pulls out the first shoe they touch. Then open the eyes. Find the person whose shoe you picked and get the other shoe as well. Put on both shoes. Then take ten minutes to walk around in that person's shoes. While you do, take on the gait, gestures, and tone of voice of that person. Try to feel, perceive, and behave like that family member.

Now sit in a circle, still wearing those shoes, and take turns responding to these questions:

- What was it like to "walk a mile" in [name of person] shoes?
- How did you feel?
- Did you learn something new?

One further note about appreciation: don't let it become a one-way street. Stepchildren are notorious for taking advantage, particularly of stepmoms early in the life of the new stepfamily. If you feel underappreciated by your stepchildren when you are doing everything possible to accommodate their needs, talk it over with your spouse. Your spouse can then call a family circle meeting. There your spouse can express his or her disappointment at how you have been treated, and you can share how you feel openly. (More about a family circle is included in Chapter 6.)

Welcome Home: Creating Family for Visiting Stepchildren

When children only visit periodically, as is customary for the parent without primary custody, creating a sense of real family can be difficult. Part-time stepparents tend to regard their spouse's visiting children as either guests to be entertained or intruders to be endured. Because the parent sees the children so infrequently, there is often a tendency for the parent to spend time with the visiting children to the exclusion of the stepparent. For some part-time stepparents, this is a relief; for others, it is a source of disappointment. When visiting stepchildren join children already in the home, the visitors can easily be made to feel unwelcome and the resident children can feel put-upon. With a little planning, most of these pitfalls can be avoided.

The broad issues I have raised in this chapter apply equally to becoming a good stepparent for a child living with you full-time or part-time. Your parenting relationship still evolves in stages. It is necessary to go slowly at the beginning and to concentrate on establishing friendship as a first step. One-on-one time is perhaps even more important for visiting stepchildren than for those children who live with you, because you have so little time with a visiting stepchild. You need the same skills in dealing with a visiting stepchild as one who lives with you. Acceptance and appreciation are perhaps even more important to the visiting child, who can so easily feel like an outsider.

The challenge in becoming a stepparent to a visiting child is establishing emotional continuity. One of the best ways to establish a sense of continuity is to create a sense that the children have a permanent place in your home and are always welcome. One way to do this is to provide each child with a private place to keep toys, and personal items. Another way is to keep certain clothes, and other daily items in your home so that the children can arrive as family members rather than guests. Introducing the visiting children to other children in your neighborhood is also helpful.

It is also important to demonstrate to the visiting children that they are part of the family and not guests. This means that the visiting children need to be included in the range of family activities from household chores to a night out at the movies. If you treat the visitors as guests who are exempted from daily chores, you ensure jealousy from the children living in your home full-time. It is advisable to accommodate the visiting children with the least amount of change in the household routine as possible. The children should also spend quality alone time with the parent during their visit.

Mentoring Through Heart Talks

Stepparents have a unique opportunity to mentor their stepchildren. Because stepparents are not biological family, they represent to their stepchildren, in some sense, the "outside world" and "what other people think." This perceived objectivity can be especially valuable for a child who needs to build trust and self-esteem.

Children of divorce, more often than not, suffer wounds to their sense of self-worth. Guilt and shame about the divorce compound feelings of low self-worth for many stepchildren. Recent studies show that children of divorce do best when they establish a close bond with an adult who assists in rebuilding self-esteem.

Certainly honest appreciation is one tool. Don't worry about spoiling your stepchild with praise. Actually, the worse your stepchild may be behaving, the more your stepchild needs to hear sincere praise that can boost his or her self-worth. You needn't wait for your stepchildren to earn praise. It is better to make the effort to catch your stepchild doing something right.

But beyond praise and reassurance, you can also help your stepchild by creating opportunities for what I call Heart Talks. These opportunities won't appear until you have established and then moved beyond basic friendship, but eventually, your stepchild is likely to offer you openings into his or her insecurities, frustrations, and dreams. When you sense your stepchild reaching out, you can establish a connection that will allow your stepchild to confide in you about feelings that he or she may not share with anyone else.

Heart Talks evolve from the confidence you have built through leveling sessions. A stepchild who knows he can talk privately, away from the family, phones, and interruption—will have the sense of safety and trust to confide difficult feelings.

Mack, a forty-eight-year-old stepfather to his wife Holly's son, Jason, aged twelve, sought help. After two years as a stepfather, Mack had become deeply concerned about Jason. "His teachers say he has ability," Mack reported. "I've seen it when I can get him to talk about the news or about a movie he enjoyed, but he's getting nowhere in school."

Jason had no relationship with his father, Richard, whom Holly left in part because she felt Richard was emotionally abusive. Richard's most frequent comment to Jason was, "How can you be so stupid?"

Mack had investigated special summer camps that provide remedial education in a fun atmosphere and was eager to send Jason, but he felt correctly that this strategy would only work if Jason became committed to improvement.

I suggested Mack try to encourage Jason to open up through a Heart Talk about school and Jason's feelings about it. Mack was looking for openers, and a recent report card provided several. Here are some of the approaches considered:

- "Report cards can sure be a drag. You must be bummed. I know the feeling. My grades weren't always so good. I'd like to hear how you feel. Sometime it can help to talk about it."

- "Your mom showed me your report card. Let's go get some ice cream to kill the pain and talk about it. Worse things can happen, and there is no use getting down on yourself."

- "Jason, school can be discouraging. I've had some tough times myself. It might help if we talked about it."

For Mack, the ice-cream approach succeeded in helping Jason to open up. I had prepared Mack by explaining that the primary purpose of a Heart Talk is to find out how another person feels; not to reach an agreement, make a decision or change an attitude or behavior. For example, I had told Mack that if Jason said "I am stupid" or "I don't have any brains," Mack would get nowhere by saying "No, you're not." Rather, a Heart Talk progresses with assurances of supportive understanding. If Jason insisted that he could never do well because he was dumb, Mack was prepared to say "It's tough when you feel that way," or "I hadn't really appreciated how you felt before today." I also advised Mack to help Jason open up by listening with full attention, and as little interruption as possible.

Mack understood that Heart Talks with stepchildren take time and patience to be effective. The goal of the first Heart Talk was simply to encourage Jason to begin disclosing his feelings, and to feel better as a result. When Mack came back to discuss what happened, he was surprised at how much progress he had made. "Jason was aching inside for someone to talk to," Mack explained. "I was the safe person—family and not family, if you know what I mean."

I suggested that Mack propose that the two of them see if there might be a way for Jason to feel better about school and do better in class. Over a period of several weeks and several Heart Talks, Mack helped Jason come to three realizations. First, Jason began to see that his feelings of being dumb were only feelings and not necessarily facts about his ability. Second, he learned that many people—objective people including Mack and several teachers—thought Jason had much more ability than his grades showed. Third, Mack told him many stories about people who "came back from behind" once they identified a problem and focused on a plan to overcome it. Mack confided to Jason his own terror of math and how he overcame that terror with the help of a tutor.

Through Heart Talks, Mack literally touched and began to help Jason heal a deep wound to his self-esteem. Mack told Jason that his mother had said his Dad had been awfully tough on him; maybe too tough. Mack's reassurance began to counterbalance Richard's legacy of criticism. Once he began to feel that someone he trusted really believed he had ability, he began showing more interest in school. When Mack talked about a special camp that might help him discover how smart he really is, Jason jumped at the idea. One summer at an educational camp enabled Jason to create a string of successes in reading, math, and art. With this base of achievement, he moved from a D to a B student in one semester.

Take Pride in Becoming a Guide

When your stepchild needs support and guidance, you can play an important role. Here are a few pointers for a Heart Talk with your stepchild:

•*Create emotional safety.* Above all, your stepchild needs reassurances that you will not be judgmental. The key is to communicate "I understand" and not "How could you?" no matter what your stepchild might reveal. Just as important, your stepchild needs to know that you will keep confidences private.

•*Keep your promises.* Your word is an important bond to your stepchild. Therefore, it's better not to make a promise that you may not keep. It's OK to say "I'll try" rather than "I promise."

•*Reveal your own fears and strengths.* It can be a great help to a child to learn that you have shared the same feelings of fear, loneliness, or low self-worth. Your explanation of how you overcame those feelings is both an affirmation that these feelings can be overcome and a roadmap for doing so.

•*Offer confidence and support.* By communicating faith in your stepchild, you strengthen his or her self-esteem. If you have ever had anyone believe in you, then you are aware of how much that belief can mean to your energy, performance and perseverance. You can be the believer in your stepchild.

In the natural evolution of your relationship with your stepchild, the day will come when it begins to blossom. You probably will not notice the change until a specific event reveals how much your stepchild has grown to rely on you.

The mature stepparent-stepchild relationship has a unique quality of love, respect and mutual appreciation. A stepparent can become like the polestar, a readily available source for guidance. What makes the stepparent's guidance so valuable is the emotional closeness coupled with a certain detachment. A stepparent gets to know a child well, but usually retains a measure of objectivity that biological parents lack. Far from second-class parenting, the mature stepparent-stepchild relationship can be every bit as fulfilling and lasting as any parent-child bond.

"Good" Is More than Enough

Becoming a good stepparent is a learning process, a growth experience of the first order. Whether you succeed in making peace in your stepfamily or whether your remarriage becomes another divorce statistic depends in large measure on how open you are to this learning process. Will you regard stepparenting merely as a consequence of your love for your spouse, or will you accept your new role as a challenge of self-discovery?

To be a good stepparent requires you to keep your heart open—to feel the child's loss, your spouse's pain. Sometimes it is easier to shut out these painful feelings rather than care so much. The more you allow yourself to respond to your stepchild's pain, the more you open up to your own, and the more your capacity for compassion grows. Then you, your spouse, and your stepfamily can walk forward positively, learning from all of life's experiences.

To stepparent requires responsibility. You may be preoccupied with your career, earning a living, rushing through life. Who has the time to care? The members of your stepfamily need your help. Becoming a stepparent means embracing conflict, giving of yourself and then giving some more. Growth and growing pains are inevitable. Your reward is the joy of contributing to a young person's life in your own unique way. You don't have to, nor should you try, to do it all. *When it comes to stepparenting, "good" is more than enough.*

SHARING DISCIPLINE: STEPFAMILY ROLES, RULES, AND RITES

*E*arly in the life of any stepfamily, few problems loom as large as defining and enforcing parent and stepparent authority. The stepchild's strong emotions tend to find outlets in a wide range of misbehavior, from simple verbal abuse to dangerous or self-destructive acting out. Discipline is hard enough in the traditional nuclear family where parents and children have evolved a set of rules and expectations over a period of many years. In the stepfamily a clash of personalities coupled with a clash of values can turn family rule making into chaos.

Effective discipline in your stepfamily requires that you and your spouse create a well-thought-out plan which you both wholeheartedly support. This plan must address three basic questions:

- What are the values and expectations you want your children to internalize?
- What are the rules and limits you expect your children and stepchildren to respect?
- How do you teach values, enforce rules, and set limits when your child's behavior deviates from your expectations?

These are the questions any couple must address in coming to grips with disciplining children. In the nuclear family, parents work out their answers over a period of many years as the child grows from infancy to adulthood. In the remarried family, you and your spouse do not have the luxury of slowly evolving your answers. This chapter will help you to come to agreement on the difficult issues of discipline in your stepfamily.

Child-Rearing Values

Children understand rules best when they know what you desire for them as they grow and mature into adulthood. The focus should be on the "dos," not the "don'ts." Write down your basic child-rearing values: the fundamental hopes and expectations you have for each child. Here are some examples of healthy hopes, dreams, and goals:

- Be physically fit and healthy
- Have high self-worth and confidence
- Care about and become the most of who you are; discover and fulfill your talents and potential
- Develop an enjoyable career and be financially secure
- Be an aware and responsible global citizen
- Have an attitude of gratitude; spiritual values

The expectations you have for your children are powerful determinants of whether these hopes and dreams become realities in their lives. To a large degree, *what you expect of your children is what they come to expect of themselves.*

Rules, then, are specific family policies that you have determined will best support your children to realize their full potential. A parent and stepparent must come to agreement on the hopes, values, and expectations they have for the children, and then agree on the rules that best support each child's and the family's aspirations.

"Let's Talk About It Later"

One of the major causes of conflict in the stepfamily is an ad hoc approach to discipline. When Hollis met Bonnie, he had custody of his son, Jonathan. She had custody of her son Richard, and daughter, Marie. During their nine-month courtship, Hollis and Bonnie wisely made it a point to arrange outings together with all the children. After the engagement, Bonnie even invited Hollis and Jonathan to stay over in her home "to see how everyone would manage." There were enough bedrooms for all the children, who didn't seem to mind sharing a bath. Hollis later reported that he was delighted with the visit, although Bonnie recalls her first inkling that Jonathan might be more difficult than she expected.

As the wedding approached, Bonnie thought it would be helpful to talk about their parenting philosophies. They agreed on the big issues—encouraging independence, the importance of education, letting the kids take responsibility—but when it came to specific rules, they each had different ideas. Hollis came from a liberal home where he had been allowed great freedom as a child. He carried that philosophy over into his attitudes about raising Jonathan. Bonnie, on the other hand, grew up in a very strict household. She, too, carried those attitudes into the discipline of her children. Though aware of their differences, they didn't want to create conflict before the wedding. Instead, they both agreed to talk about it later.

After their marriage, they moved into Bonnie's home as planned, but discussion of their attitudes about discipline kept getting postponed. Bonnie began to become irritated with Jonathan, but Hollis preferred to take problems one at a time. "I thought we were doing fine," he later explained. "I didn't think it was necessary to sift through all my feelings about bringing up the kids." By repeatedly putting off the discussion of their disagreements, Bonnie and Hollis eventually allowed minor irritations to erupt into full-scale war, which brought them in for counseling.

Bonnie initially became concerned that Jonathan was having a bad influence on Richard and Marie. Jonathan watched TV whenever he liked, while Richard and Marie could only watch TV after homework and chores were finished. Jonathan's room was usually a mess, but Richard and Marie were expected to keep their rooms neat. Jonathan read comic books and played video games seemingly without end, and soon Richard and Marie were emulating him. The blowup began when Bonnie found Jonathan and Richard watching TV, and asked them whether their homework was done. Both said no, and Bonnie turned off the TV. Jonathan challenged her by asserting "Hey, Dad says TV is my business. I'll do my homework later. You can't make the rules." This, of course, set Richard off in a tirade of rebellious crying. "He always gets away with everything. It's not fair."

The problem grew worse when Bonnie, feeling that all the children were getting out of control, demanded Hollis's help in enforcing discipline. Bonnie insisted that Hollis step in to punish the children for talking back to her. When Hollis sat down with Jonathan, however, Hollis heard a tirade from Jonathan of about how Bonnie was treating him like a baby, that his grades were good, and that he wasn't going to let his stepmother run his life. When Hollis tried to back up Bonnie in disciplining Richard and Marie, all he heard was an outburst of protest about how unfair it was that Jonathan "got away with everything."

In most stepfamilies, discipline administered without a well-thought-out plan becomes a constant source of conflict. Hollis and Bonnie could not possibly make peace in their stepfamily until they had first come to grips with the significant differences (and even conflicts) between their respective expectations and values. Nor could they expect their children to learn appropriate self-discipline as long as the two adults were giving conflicting messages. Only by resolving their own practical and philosophical differences about child rearing and discipline could they establish family rules that made sense for them and their children.

Rescuing the Rescuer

One of the most common mistakes made by remarrieds is enrolling the stepparent in the role of disciplinarian too soon. Just as a stepparent bonds with a stepchild through evolving stages, so too, in most cases, should the stepparent's role as disciplinarian evolve at a gradual pace.

Prior to many remarriages, one of the parents has been living alone with custody of the children. The emotional and financial pressures of single parenting often force single mothers or fathers to allow their children more latitude than they might prefer. When a stepparent in these circumstances meets a new marriage partner, it is natural for the parent to feel joy in the new marriage and relief at having another strong person to share the parenting duties. In most cases, however, the unique emotional dynamics of the stepfamily preclude such an easy rescue.

However, in most families, once the bond of friendship begins to form with the stepchildren, the stepparent can become more active in setting limits and defending his or her own needs for privacy and consideration. It is very important to continue to talk about family rules, limits, and values with your partner and the children.

When a parent and stepparent maintain a strong consensus on family rules, the stepparent's authority naturally tends to grow. It is helpful for the stepparent to participate as early as possible in family discussions about family rules, and to remember not to try to rush things. When the children feel more comfortable with the stepparent as a parental figure, the stepparent can join the parent in enforcing limits. Eventually the stepparent assumes the full mantle of parental authority.

The Exception That Proves the Rule

For all rules, there is an exception, even to the rule that stepparents should not assume the role of disciplinarian too soon. Randy and Ellen are an exception. Ellen had two children, Kip and Laura, when they married. Ellen had been a single mother for seven years, and she acknowledged the children's need for strong discipline. Randy also felt strongly that the children needed more direction, and with Ellen's encouragement, stepped into the role of family disciplinarian very early in their marriage. Whether due to his innate child-rearing skills, his commitment to the children, or his wisdom, Randy's firm direction proved to be of great benefit in making peace almost immediately. Kip and Laura were perhaps unusually open to Randy because they had little or no relationship with their own father.

Randy and Ellen's case is important because it illustrates that stepparents need not fear exercising their roles as disciplinarians. To the contrary, avoidance by a stepparent of discipline issues is sometimes interpreted by stepchildren as disinterest. By participating in family rule-making sessions and assuming the role of disciplinarian, as appropriate, you demonstrate to your stepchildren that you care. Even in traditional nuclear families, children that lack discipline show low self-esteem and feel unloved. Participation in family rule-making can also enhance bonding with the stepchild when the stepparent takes the child's side at times when the parent is being too restrictive or arbitrary. The interchange that occurs around issues of family rules and limits can be very healthy for all concerned.

Coming to Agreement with Your Spouse

Most couples spend less than thirty minutes a week talking with each other about family issues. To make peace in your stepfamily, it is imperative that you and your spouse spend the time necessary to come to agreement about family rules, limits, and values. There is no magic to the process. You and your spouse simply need to have a series of very thorough discussions. It is advisable to take notes.

Use the following questions to explore your views:

1. The first issues to consider are family values and expectations.

- What do you want your children to learn about honesty? Telling the truth? Little white lies? Stealing? Cheating?
- What do you want your children to learn about helping others?
- What do you want the children to feel about themselves? Their self-esteem?
- What about sharing with others?
- What are your values about children learning to stick up for themselves?
- What do you want your children to learn about courage and perseverance?
- What do you want your child to learn about respect for others?

• What do you want your children to learn about courtesy?
• What do you want your children to learn about faith?
• What do you want your children to learn about acceptance of other people's beliefs?
• What do you want your children to learn about prejudice?

2. The next issues to consider are family and household rules.

Morning routines
• Who wakes the children? When?
• What is the bathroom etiquette to be? Who cleans up?
• Who makes breakfast? Who cleans up?
• Do children make their own beds?
• Who helps the younger children dress and get ready for school?

Evening routines
• Is a family dinner every evening a priority? If so, how is it scheduled? Who prepares the meal? Who cleans up?
• How clean is the kitchen to be left after use?
• What about bedtimes? When must the younger children be in bed? The older children? Who puts the younger children to bed?
• What about homework?

Chores
• What responsibilities do the children assume to help around the house?
• What about laundry? The lawn? The garbage?
• Must children help with major tasks such as washing windows or spring cleaning? Who washes the car?

Television/entertainment
• How much television? Are there limits on types of shows?
• What are your family rules of television etiquette? Who decides what is acceptable? How loud?
• What about music? When is it acceptable? How loud?

3. The third set of issues to consider are limits. These are the lines of behavior the children cannot cross without consequences.

• How late can the children stay out?
• Can the children go to the park to play at their own discretion?

- Are there any restrictions on books? Magazines? Comics?
- Do you restrict what movies they can see?
- Do you want to know their friends? Their friends' parents?
- What about sleeping over at friends' houses? Or friends sleeping over at yours?
- Can your teenagers attend parties where alcohol might be served?
- What about drugs? How strict is your prohibition?
- What about sex? What are the steps to set limits?
- What about respect for your authority? How much argument will you put up with? What about sassy remarks?
- What about fighting between siblings or stepsiblings? How much will you tolerate?
- What are your methods of enforcing limits?
- What privileges are taken away? When? How?
- Do you have a range of punishments to fit the violation of rules? Do the children understand?

There is nothing unusual in these questions, and this list is hardly exhaustive. Most parents evolve answers as their children grow older. In the remarried family, however, it is more urgent that you come to an agreement. Unless you are specific about the rules, limits, and values to be observed in your home, and unless you develop a consistent strategy to communicate and enforce these rules, discipline will be a continuing problem. I urge you to take the time to work through these questions in detail with your spouse, and write a summary of your conclusions. These agreements will prove invaluable in providing your children and stepchildren with the guidance they need and actually long for.

Set Appropriate Positive and Negative Consequences

You and your spouse must also reach a consensus about rewards, punishments, and your approach to enforcing limits. Again, this task is just as important for the nuclear family as the stepfamily; the only difference is the need for you and your spouse to confront these issues on an accelerated basis.

Appropriate and relevant consequences can be effective not only in getting immediate results but in long-term growth benefits. Humiliation, sarcasm, or physical punishment are damaging to your child's self-worth and motivation. Imposing consequences, such as suspending or restricting a privilege objectively and with a minimum of anger, will allow self-discipline and worth to flourish.

This book is not intended to provide exhaustive advice on how best to discipline children. Many excellent books are available, and these books demonstrate a substantial difference of opinion. At one extreme, certain psychologists favor firm rules and clear consequences that help a child learn quickly the logical consequences of their behavior. At the other extremes are those experts who advocate reasoning with the child as much as possible in the hope that the child will internalize values that promote self-discipline. My personal approach lies somewhere in between. While I prefer to reason with a child who misbehaves in order to teach self-discipline, children are often unreasonable. And so I also advocate appropriate consequences, ranging from a scolding to time out or loss of privileges such as TV or visits to friends.

So much for my personal philosophy of rewards and negative consequences. Far more important is for you and your spouse to discuss your own views and develop a consistent plan to enforce limits. Stepfamilies can be torn apart when the parents fail to enforce family rules without consistent rewards and punishments that the children understand. When you and your spouse undermine each other through inconsistent application of rules, you generate resentment, anger, mistrust, and disrespect among your children and stepchildren, who expect to be treated fairly.

Consistently Enforce the Rules

I encourage you and your spouse to review your list of family rules, limits, and values and to discuss appropriate ways to enforce your guidelines. Here are some questions to prompt your thinking:

- How do you enforce your demand that children stop fighting?
- What if you learn that your child stole money from your dresser? A toy from a store?
- What if you learn that your teenager drank heavily while borrowing the family car?
- How do you handle a child that persists in whining and crying about wanting to visit a friend or go to the movies, after you have said no and explained why not?
- What if you learn that your child is cheating in school?

Once you and your spouse agree about family values, rules, and limits, the next challenge is communicating your expectations to your children and stepchildren. Children resent the imposition of rules that seem arbitrary, and this resentment is even more likely in stepfamilies where there may be a clash of backgrounds and parental expectations, and a whole new set of family rules. I have found that children in a blended family tend to accept new rules if they feel some sense of participation in formulating them. Here is an exercise that will help.

The Family Meeting

Call a family meeting for the purpose of discussing basic family rules. Explain your desire to hear what everyone thinks the family rules are, and whether any changes should be made. To begin the meeting, you should ask each child to describe his or her view of the most important family rules. You can prompt discussion with questions such as:

- What are all the rules about keeping the house clean?
- Is it OK to get angry?
- What are rules about household chores?
- Are there rules about the children fighting?
- What are the rules about staying out late?

During the meeting, appoint a secretary—one of the parents or preferably an older child—to make notes of the rules. To encourage everyone to participate, it is best at the outset simply to brainstorm the rules. Do not be surprised when the children mention complex rules, such as "It's not OK to joke with Mom (Stepmom) in the morning because she is irritable." Don't dispute whether such rules exist. The point is to discover and share what each person *perceives* the rules to be.

Once you have made a list of the rules, you can then go back and have a discussion which might include the following questions:

- Why is the rule important?
- Is the rule fairly enforced?
- Who determines whether the rule is obeyed?
- Can the rule ever be broken without punishment?
- How can rules be changed?
- What rules are made by the parents?

Through this discussion, the whole family will feel part of the rule-making process and you will have a chance for valuable discussion with your children about the reasons behind the rules.

In certain cases, you will have to answer a child's protest about a rule, such as bedtime, with an explanation and assertion of your responsibility as a parent. To end a discussion you can say "I understand your feelings and your arguments, but as your parent I must ultimately make the judgment as to what's best for us all." You might add as a teaching exercise that there are always higher authorities making rules that we might disagree with but must obey. Some bright children may want to argue that all rules should be democratic. Here, the parent team must assert a benevolent authority.

Putting Rules into Practice

Once you have agreed on the new family rules, the most difficult challenge remains—putting the rules into practice. Every parent has difficulty with this task, but as discussed earlier, this difficulty is compounded by the ambiguous role of the stepparent. Only after the stepparent has had success in disciplining the children in cooperation with the biological parent, should the stepparent assert his or her independent autonomy as disciplinarian.

Naturally, there are exceptions. For example, when the biological parent is traveling, the stepparent cannot let the children run wild simply because the remarriage has yet to reach a first anniversary.

Similarly, if the biological parent is working late and a stepchild insists on taking the car or staying out well beyond an agreed-on curfew, the stepparent should not abdicate responsibility or, worse, say "I'm going to tell your mother/father." Even early in the marriage, after you and your spouse have clarified family rules through one or more family meetings, it is important for the biological parent to make it clear that the stepparent has full authority to enforce the rules when the biological parent is absent.

"You're Not My Parent"

By adopting this strategy, you can deal once and for all with the "You're not my parent" syndrome. As every stepparent knows, the "You're not my parent" retort is painful, frustrating, and divisive. A stepchild will exploit your ambiguity by asserting "You're not my mom/dad/parent" whenever it suits his or her need to rebel.

These retorts must be discouraged. Once the parent makes clear that the stepparent has the authority in the parent's absence, then the stepparent can respond as follows:

- "I'm not your father/mother, but I'm the adult in charge now, and I have the responsibility to enforce the rules."
- "I am your stepparent, and I expect you to listen to me as we agreed."
- "That's true, but you also know that I am responsible now, and I've got to enforce the rules."

By taking this firm stand with the backing of the biological parent, the "I'm not your parent" routine will soon disappear.

In some stepfamilies, the parent unconsciously sabotages the stepparent by failing to provide necessary support in the face of unruly or disrespectful children. When this occurs, counseling is often necessary.

Principles of Effective Discipline

While there is considerable disagreement about philosophies of discipline, there is also substantial agreement on certain key principles of how to discipline:

Use discipline to teach a lesson without damaging self-esteem. This is extremely important. Remember that the point of any discipline is to help the child *learn* to internalize self-discipline. In practical terms, this means your discipline strategies should address the child's behavior, not the child's personhood. A scolding is better delivered as "You acted very badly in pushing your baby sister in the mud" rather than "You are a bad boy." Unfortunately, most of us were raised by parents who regularly administered blows to our own self-esteem, and we pass along the damage to our own children. Do your best to avoid attacking the child's basic sense of self-worth.

Avoid derogatory labels. If your child tells a lie, it won't help to call him or her a liar. When you label a child with a derogatory name such as liar, cheat, or loafer, you affirm your low expectations, and reinforce the child's low self-esteem.

Teach the child to feel guilt about misbehavior, not about who he or she is. The capacity to feel guilty is an important part of learning self-discipline. A healthy conscience is an internal necessity for distinguishing right from wrong. To develop the child's conscience, however, you have to take time to explain why the behavior is wrong. You have to teach values—the golden rule, the importance of honesty, respect for others, and the reasons for loving thy neighbor. Comments such as "How could you?" or "You don't care about me" apply guilt in a manipulative and unhealthy manner. The child internalizes guilt about who he or she is, rather than what he or she does.

You want a child to fear the consequences of destructive behavior, not to fear you. The child who cheats or steals needs to learn to fear the consequences of his or her behavior in order to grow up with a basic sense of honesty and abide by the law. Intimidating punishments are appropriate to serious misbehavior, but the child should know the rules in advance and the consequences of their breach.

Do not make rules that you are not willing to implement. When children know the rules and you have made clear to them the consequences of breaking the rules, threats become unnecessary. Rather, you can remind the child of the rules and consequences. If the child misbehaves, you must implement the consequences. Otherwise, the child will not believe you or the limits you have established. Such a child begins to approach life in terms of "What can I get away with?"

Avoid destructive shaming. "You should be ashamed of yourself" is a common but unhelpful admonition used by many parents. Once again, the child who knowingly misbehaves and gets caught may feel ashamed, but you will better serve the child by teaching him or her to feel ashamed of the wrong behavior.

Calibrate your use of force as much as possible. Economy is the best guide in enforcing limits. If you start with a simple reminder, and you are ignored, you can always turn up the volume. In our impatience or frustration with our own lives, we parents sometimes assume the worst and overreact. It is far more satisfying to find that a child may respond to a calm tone.

Express your anger consciously. If you are ignored or the misbehavior is serious, an angry scolding may be appropriate. To be effective, however, your anger must be controlled and targeted. Tell your child specifically *why* you are furious and *what* he or she must do to make amends.

Give the child time to comply. Out of our impatience, parents often expect children to obey immediately. If the children do not, parents immediately turn up the volume. Better to give the child an opportunity to comply on his or her own terms, if possible. If you are concerned about whether you were heard or whether the child intends to obey, ask for an acknowledgment.

Give the child choices, if possible. When putting a child to bed, you might ask "Do you want to get ready now or in fifteen minutes?" so he can feel in control.

Acknowledge your own mistakes. Misunderstandings are common among us all. If you misunderstand when your stepson is due home and confront him about his late arrival, don't feel so invested in being right that you cannot acknowledge an honest mistake. By admitting freely when you are wrong, you gain your stepchildren's respect.

Avoid comparing or lecturing. Comments such as "Why can't you be like your stepbrother?" are very destructive. When parents compare siblings, the parents strike a severe blow at the child's self-esteem. Similarly, lengthy lectures are usually unproductive. It is far better to make family rules and limits clear in family meetings.

Don't get distracted by debates or a change of subject. There is a potential pitfall associated with family discussions about rules and limits. Some children try to debate the merits of a rule or otherwise change the subject through discussion when they get caught breaking the rule. A simple statement such as "Now is not the time to debate whether you can watch TV, because you still have homework to do" is the best response. Even more clever is the child who tries to change the subject by reporting on what happened during a visit at an ex-spouse's home. Don't fall for it.

Avoid manipulative responses. In your frustration, you may be tempted to resort to anything to get a reluctant child to obey: bribery, sarcasm, or emotional withdrawal. These efforts are inevitably self-defeating. You may get compliance, but your child does not learn any values.

Get feedback about your discipline style. It is very difficult for most of us to know whether we inadvertently use any of the destructive discipline techniques such as shaming, intimidation, or prolonged lecturing. You and your spouse should give each other feedback. When providing feedback about the way your spouse disciplines, it is important to choose the right time and place. If your spouse is lecturing your son ad nauseam, don't step in and say "Can't you stop lecturing the child to death."

Instead, create an opportunity for discussion and mutual feedback. Be sure to also ask for feedback about how effectively you discipline. The spirit of this session should be one of mutual learning about how to create more effective communication and positive relationships with your children. Do not offer criticism in a derogatory manner, and try not to take criticism too personally. The goal is to learn together and to become an effective parenting team.

Teaching Values by Your Example

There is one essential to being a good stepparent or parent—you must live by example. A child full of loss needs understanding and acceptance. A child full of hostility needs a calm and peaceful environment. A child whose faith in adults has been shaken to the core needs someone he can count on. A child with low self-esteem benefits from the guidance of a self-confident and supportive adult. A child with poor motivation needs coaching and interest from an enthusiastic person. A child who carries a chip on her shoulder needs a kind, gentle arm wrapped around her. A child with a "negative attitude" needs a positive role model. A supposedly bad stepchild needs a good and loving stepparent.

A stepparent has an extraordinary opportunity to influence his or her stepchild's life by modeling and teaching values. Only by internalizing values does a child develop the psychological foundation for the future. Regrettably, the trauma of divorce often undermines a child's confidence in the values espoused by adults. "My mom and dad are phonies," said one eleven-year-old boy whose parents continued to battle each other three years after their divorce. "They tell me all sorts of things about being good to other people, but look how they treat each other . . . and me!" Anyone who has lived through a hostile divorce can empathize with this boy's parents, as well as the boy. How do you teach the golden rule when your husband fails to make child payments but still expects your son to visit for Christmas? What do you tell your son who wants to see his Dad?

Make teaching values a priority in your family. Almost all children harbor a deep desire to accomplish something great. This natural desire explains in part why young people tend to be idealists. If you want your children to internalize values that can serve them as adults, then the time to teach is as early as possible. There is a very simple question you can encourage your children to ask themselves: *What is the right thing to do?* By making this question important in your family and encouraging discussion of different points of view, you will create a home environment where children naturally internalize a strong set of values.

There is a wide variety of family activities that can help you and your spouse to teach values. Regularly attending a church, synagogue, or mosque is perhaps the best activity, but it is important for you to participate in your child's religious education. Attendance at church school should not be a matter of mere compliance with a parent's demand. If you want your children to internalize the value of a religious education, then you have to make the issues important. Talk to your children about what they are learning, and listen to their views. Don't lecture them, but rather give them the opportunity to explain to you why a story from the Bible, the Torah, or the Koran, is important.

Family participation in charitable organizations is another excellent way to promote family bonding and teach values. Although volunteering as a family is difficult with younger children, it often becomes a memorable family experience for older children.

If you demonstrate interest in and respect for your children's views, then almost any activity becomes an opportunity for teaching values. A movie, a television show, a book, or a newspaper article can become the basis for a discussion about "what is right." Asking everyone in the family what they learned from a movie can deepen what could otherwise be mere entertainment. The key is for you and your spouse to engage your children in thinking about and discussing what they have seen.

On the other hand, lecturing or nagging are prescriptions for failure or rebellion. Giving advice to stepchildren must be handled carefully. Avoid "shoulds" and "oughts," which immediately invite resistance. You are far more likely to be heard if you begin with "May I make a suggestion?" or "I have an idea that might be helpful." Generally speaking, stepparents are better served by avoiding the habit of offering unsolicited advice. You will be far more effective by cultivating your stepchildren's trust and confidence so they come to you for advice when they need it.

Family Rules for Visiting Children

Beverly is a full-time mother to her daughter, Aileen, and son, Niles. She is also a part-time stepmother to her second husband Preston's three children. Recently, she sat in my office with frustration written all over her face. "With the way Preston's kids behave when they're in our house," Beverly complained, "I can see why he divorced Lydia. She

obviously doesn't teach these kids a thing. Everything is a mess, and I'm expected to be the maid."

"What makes me so furious," she went on, "is that I can't get through to him or to them. I don't mind his doting on his kids when they visit, but there have to be limits. . . . Preston is perfectly fine about my rules for Aileen and Niles. He tells me what a great mother I am all the time, but when it comes to his kids, I can't make any rules because I get zero support." In addition to her growing frustration, what prompted Beverly to seek help was the growing tension between her and her own children because of the different sets of rules.

Many a stepfamily has fractured due to the clash of rules and values governing behavior in two different homes. Parents who see their children only on weekends, holidays, and summer vacations are very often reluctant to cloud this precious time with demands that the children obey family rules. "Maybe I'm a Disneyland Dad," one stepfather confided, "but it's not worth it to me to get into a fight with my son about when he brushes his teeth or whether he stays up late when I only see him on vacations." While his father's feelings may be understandable, they can also result in disaster if he indulges his child at the expense of his spouse or stepchildren.

How should your family's rules apply to a visiting child? Among the many stepfamilies whom I have counseled, there have been many answers that have worked. The answer you work out with your spouse will depend on a variety of considerations, such as the frequency of visits, whether you have children living with you full time, and how much space you have to accommodate visitors.

Caught in just such an unhappy position in her own home, Beverly was at a breaking point. She was ready to talk about divorce, but I suggested she ask Preston to join her in at least one counseling session. I was not really surprised when Preston came into my office in despair about what appeared to him as a sudden crisis in his stepfamily. "I knew my kids were hard on Beverly," he acknowledged sheepishly, "but she is such a great mom, I thought she was basically OK with the kids having a great time when they were with us." During the course of this session, Preston admitted he was unaware of the many problems with Aileen and Niles. He hadn't thought about the clash between the families' rules. He soon recognized the need to make changes when his children visited in the future.

Fortunately, Beverly and Preston were not so defensive that each began blaming the other for the crisis in their stepfamily. I explained that each had to take responsibility for where they were. Beverly had let her frustration build without making her feelings known. Preston had been terribly insensitive and had contributed greatly to Beverly's frustration. Each had to be willing to talk at length about what their expectations were for all the children, and what family rules and limits should govern the children during the week and the weekend, visitors included! I encouraged Beverly and Preston to write down their conclusions.

Implementing the new rules also became an issue. I recommended two approaches: either Preston could talk to his children alone, or he could suggest a family meeting to discuss family rules. In either case, it was important that Preston take the initiative and responsibility to explain and enforce the new rules. Otherwise, Beverly would have been targeted mercilessly as the wicked stepmother.

While you and your spouse must work out your own set of family rules for visiting children, there is growing agreement within the psychological community about certain helpful principles to follow. Here are some recommendations for your consideration.

Consider your visiting children as simply living with you intermittently and avoid treating them as guests. Children need the stability which your home can offer. If you treat them as guests, then you create in your mind and theirs a sense of instability. It is better to include visiting children in family meetings and expect them to observe family rules, even when it means confrontation and punishment from time to time.

Acknowledge that things may be done differently in your household than in their other home. One of the advantages of two homes is experiencing differences in values, lifestyles, and ways of living. Explain to the children the principle "When in Rome, do as the Romans." You need not criticize the way your ex-spouse runs his or her home in order to ask visiting children to observe the rules in your home. In fact, any such criticism is counterproductive. Better to explain that the children are fortunate to have different experiences when they are young so they can make informed decisions as adults when they have their own homes.

When explaining family rules, be specific and helpful. If you approach your children with a positive attitude and show them specifically how to please you, their ability to comply is substantially improved.

Try to permit your own children's lives to proceed without interruption when the visitors arrive. If you have made a place in your home for visiting children to keep their toys and clothes, then you avoid the dislocation that can make all the children uncomfortable. When bedrooms are in short supply, you might consider bunkbeds. All of your children's weekend commitments should continue. The challenge is to find creative ways to involve the visitors. Take advantage of those hours when your children are busy for some one-on-one time with the visiting children.

Walk your talk. Noncustodial parents are tempted to use pressure tactics to influence children whom they see for short periods of time at best. You should feel free to enforce house rules such as "no smoking in the house," but you will get nowhere lecturing about the dangers of smoking as long as your spouse allows smoking or even smokes herself. The best way to influence your children is to model the behavior you expect of them. If you maintain your relationship over the years, your influence will be far greater than you expect.

New Family Rites and Traditions

In your efforts to establish rules that work for everyone in the stepfamily, including the visiting children, it is important not to overlook the value of creating new stepfamily rites and traditions. Common memories and shared traditions are part of the emotional fabric that defines family, and sustains emotional bonds. At their outset, stepfamilies lack these common memories and traditions. In fact, the different holiday rituals, religious traditions, and fond memories of the two merging families can just as likely become a source of conflict as an opportunity for bonding.

Parents must pay special attention to creating new stepfamily rituals and traditions that build on the rituals and traditions of their separate family pasts. Here are suggestions that I have provided to clients in the past:

Family wedding. If you are reading this book in anticipation of a marriage, you would be well served to invite your children to participate as much as possible in the wedding preparations as well as the ceremony. If you and your spouse both have children, together take the time to talk with all the children about the significance of the step you are both about to take, and give the children an opportunity to make suggestions about making the ceremony memorable. If an adolescent objects, don't pressure him or her to participate. Also, it is not advisable for the children to participate in the wedding vows, because the focus of the wedding should remain on the commitment being made by the couple.

One caveat to this recommendation is to beware of children becoming torn by divided loyalties. If an ex-spouse is opposed to the marriage, the child may feel like a traitor if he or she participates in your marriage to your new spouse. Be sensitive to your child's fears at this difficult time in his or her life, and do not insist on participation that is not freely offered.

Family anniversary. Most families do not have anniversaries, but stepfamilies do! The day you and your spouse got married was the day your stepfamily was born. Take advantage of this difference and declare a day to celebrate the date that all of you became a family. You might consider an anniversary dinner, and small anniversary gifts or cards to and from each of your children and stepchildren.

Holiday celebrations. Memories of holidays are among the most emotionally charged of all. Whether to put white lights or colored lights on the Christmas tree has been known to become an issue which causes stepsiblings to form battle lines. To head off conflicts about how to celebrate the holidays, discuss your plans with your children and stepchildren in advance. Ask the children whether to use your ornaments, your spouse's ornaments, or a combination of the two well before you bring the tree home.

Even more serious issues may arise if two different religious traditions are involved. If children travel between two homes during the holidays, the children may encounter new religious traditions in both homes. In these circumstances, the children suffer if the adults disparage one another, but the children grow emotionally, intellectually, and spiritually if they learn about celebrations in several religious traditions.

Family newsletter. Before the holiday season each year, you might consider a new tradition of sending a newsletter to friends and family about your stepfamily. A parent or stepparent acts as editor and may write a story. All the children equally submit news stories, cartoons, jokes, sports stories, photos, artwork, and headlines. Each child makes a contribution with his/her name attached—Lenny's Joke, Trudy's Sports Report, Charles's Family Chronicle. It's also a nice touch to add a few photographs of everyone in the stepfamily on vacation, during a celebration, or in the backyard. When the newsletter is complete, solicit names from all family members as to whom the newsletter should be sent.

Stepfamily album. The best way to create a family history is to record it. A stepfamily album can be a perfect way to do so. A stepfamily album is part scrapbook, part photo album, and part sacred family scroll. It should be a special album about events in the stepfamily, big and small. Keep your stepfamily album in a prominent place and share it with visiting friends and your extended family.

New Year's "Family State of the Union." New Year's Day provides a special opportunity for review and renewal. Gather the stepfamily together for a New Year's brunch at which you hold an annual "Family State of the Union" discussion. Kids may start with some laughter or silliness but the embarrassment quickly wears off. Here are some suggested topics:

- Everyone old enough to talk is given time to review the year; talk about changes you might like to make and what you're pleased with.
- Family members identify what significant events they have shared with one another during the year and what those events meant to them.
- You might discuss what you wish to bring into this new year. Use a calendar to plan family vacations and special events. Talk about improvements you might like to see in the family emotional climate. Consider that family members can best support one another in achieving their personal, school, and professional goals.
- New Year's is also a terrific time to remind one another of how far all of you have come:

"A wonderful change I've seen us make this year . . ."
"We've come a remarkably long way this year in . . ."
"An event/goal I admire us for this year was . . ."

Keep this feedback strictly positive. The family will find this recognition an energizing and encouraging way to begin the new year.

Family Awards Ceremony. Once a year a Family Awards Ceremony is an opportunity to recognize the accomplishments and qualities of each person in your stepfamily. Parents create a list of awards so that every child can receive one.

For example:

- Student of the Year
- Pet Caretaker of the Year
- Athlete of the Year
- Big Brother/Sister Award

These awards can be bought by a parent or else be made collectively by the family as a fun art project. The next step is to hold the ceremony. The family can all pitch in to prepare a special "banquet" meal together. The stepparent acts as the Master of Ceremonies. He/she calls each recipient forward.

When the award is received, the recipient gives a brief acceptance speech or thank you. After each award is given, the other family members stand, applaud, and cheer. Everyone should feel like a winner or star at the awards ceremony. This is a great time to present a stepmother who has felt underappreciated with a bouquet of flowers, along with a dinner prepared by everyone else and a special award.

These ideas for creating new family traditions are suggestions only, and I strongly encourage you to modify these ideas to suit your needs and come up with your own ideas. What I want to emphasize is the importance of creating family rites and rituals to support emotional bonding. Even when children recoil at these ideas initially, most of my clients are surprised at how the children finally come around and how much these rituals add to feeling like a family.

Becoming a Parenting Team

The art of discipline in your stepfamily ultimately comes down to one simple concept. You and spouse must become part of one parenting team in which you give your children clear direction and encouragement to respect family roles, rules, and rites. To form your parenting team, you and your spouse must first acknowledge your differences about your expectations of your children, your personal preferences about the atmosphere in your home, and the values you want to observe as a family and to teach your children. There are no shortcuts. Hopefully you will find the exercises in this chapter helpful in this process.

If discipline has become a chronic problem in your stepfamily, take heart in what you and your spouse can accomplish. The time and energy necessary to form a parenting team is worth the effort. Once you and your spouse share a common understanding of family expectations, rules, and rites, you eliminate the source of chronic discipline problems. Your children know what is expected of them, they understand the consequences of exceeding acceptable limits, and they recognize that you and your spouse will stand firm in the face of misbehavior. It may be difficult right now to appreciate what this change will mean in terms of your children's voluntary cooperation within the family, but I assure you that you will be pleasantly surprised and amply rewarded for your efforts.

Chapter 5

STRENGTHENING
YOUR REMARRIAGE

"*D*ivorce?" The question haunted me for months during the height of conflict in my stepfamily. Most couples seriously consider divorce at one time or another in their remarriage. When simmering tensions in a stepfamily come to a boil, the stepfamily's survival depends on the underlying strength of the remarriage. In my own stepfamily, had Sirah not been committed to helping me struggle with my personal conflicts about stepparenting, our marriage might not have survived. I am thankful that Sirah and I had developed the tools to keep our communication open during heightened stepfamily stress.

The statistics on stepfamily survival are not good. *Over 70 percent of remarrieds with children end up in another divorce.* The reasons for this high divorce rate are many, but one is the lack of attention remarrieds generally pay to strengthening their own relationship. The emotional foundation of the stepfamily is the same as it is for any family—the love between the parents. When that foundation is strong, both parents have a large emotional reserve to draw upon in coping with stepfamily conflict. If that foundation develops cracks or becomes brittle, then normal stepfamily conflicts can spell breakdown and divorce.

Most people are accustomed to covering their relationships with emotional Band-Aids. Sex may go flat, resentments may develop as blaming and criticism become predominant, or one or both partners may be holding back so much anger that the relationship resembles a seething volcano, and yet both may unconsciously conspire to ignore or deny the mounting problems. A shopping spree substitutes for expressing hurt feelings, fatigue becomes an excuse for a diminished sex life, work develops into an escape from the problems of living together, and quarreling becomes the mode of maintaining emotional contact without addressing the real issues.

Marriage partners need each other most
when stepfamily conflicts are at their worst.

There is much you can accomplish to strengthen your remarriage, both in how you respond to your mate and how he or she responds to you. Great relationships are created, not simply found! This chapter presents exercises to develop the psychological strength and communication skills to sustain a close, caring love relationship amidst the stresses of stepfamily life.

Making Time to Make Peace

"How can you expect me to find time to talk about my feelings?" complained one of my stepfather clients in response to my suggestion that he and his wife practice a communication exercise at home. "I don't even have a moment to myself."

This complaint is pervasive among remarrieds. Almost every study of stepfamilies places lack of time at the top of major complaints. Five days a week most remarrieds get up, make breakfast, rush the kids to school or day care, fight traffic to work, and then, more than eight hours later, reverse the process: fight traffic to pick up the kids, rush to get home, make dinner, eat, clean up, and collapse. On weekends they shop, clean the house, do the laundry, and run errands accumulated during the week. Often weekends involve either sending children off to another parent or receiving children for a visit. That leaves little time for what is most important to the remarried couple— enjoying each other and their children and friends.

Unrealistic expectations compound the feeling of time pressure for many remarrieds. Another of my stepmother clients only half-jokingly commented, "Daily I'm supposed to spend an hour on exercise, an hour of meditation, quality time with each of my children, stay involved with community affairs, and spend at least one high-quality hour with my husband. While doing all this, I'm expected to keep a lovely home, cook low-fat, high-fiber meals, and volunteer as a room mother, den mother, and earth mother while turning over my compost pile regularly and holding down a high-paying full-time job."

Finding time to strengthen your remarriage is no easy task. Studies show that the average couple spends less than a half hour per week in intimate conversation. Couples prefer to assume that their communication is good until a crisis finally proves otherwise. This assumption is particularly common among remarrieds, who have the experience of a prior remarriage and often believe they have learned enough from a first marriage. In the stepfamily, however, the emotional and physical demands on you and your spouse are so great, and so many critical family issues arise continuously, that you cannot afford to ignore problems in your communication. You make an even bigger mistake if you allow a breakdown in communication to continue on the assumption that things will get better on their own; too often, they don't.

Amidst all the pressure of a new stepfamily, it is easy to find yourself at the mercy of never-ending demands from others—children, an ex-spouse, in-laws, teachers, coworkers—so that you feel at everyone's beck and call. External demands on your time may seem to overwhelm your ability to pursue your own goals. It is precisely in such circumstances that communication with your spouse is likely to break down and your marriage may be at risk.

The first step in strengthening your remarriage is fighting back to take control of your time. Start by getting clear on your priorities.

Strengthening your remarriage will require an investment of time. The result is likely to be better, more satisfying communication with your spouse, a better understanding of your common goals and values, and a more peaceful, efficient household.

Statistics show that unless you pay attention to healing stepfamily conflicts, they are likely to get worse; so too with conflicts between you and your spouse. If conflicts worsen to the point of the marriage breaking down, then you can count on enormous costs—not just in time but in heartache as well—in coping with another divorce.

Consider also the enormous emotional drain, even if you and your spouse manage to muddle through. When one spouse in counseling resists my suggestions of "homework" exercises to improve communication, I sometimes ask the couple to add up the hours spent in arguments during the last week alone. This exercise is usually persuasive. Couples can calculate for themselves the advantages of spending a few hours per week over a period of a few months to end needless conflict once and for all.

"Not Again"

A common problem for remarrieds is the reemergence of an emotional block that plagued a prior relationship. There are few more discouraging realizations in a new marriage than recognizing a conflict from the past beginning to replay itself all over again.

When Jerry, an architect, and Glenda, a real estate agent, first came to my office, they were convinced that their marriage was all but over. They each had one child from a prior marriage, and they wanted their new marriage to work, but something had gone terribly wrong, and they were not sure why.

When Jerry and Glenda met at a charity dinner, the chemistry was obvious. Within a month, they were dating three times per week and having what Jerry calls "the greatest sex of my life." Glenda echoed that she had never fallen in love so completely and with such intensity.

In describing this early stage of their relationship, they both thought their relationship was ideal. Jerry remembered thinking to himself at that time, "Glenda is the exact opposite of my first wife. She was so uptight sexually. We 'did it' twice a month. It's a miracle she conceived my daughter, Zoey. If I walked into the bedroom when my first wife was getting dressed, she would scream and pull away. I couldn't help but feel resentful."

"When Glenda and I first met," he went on, "it was like a dream come true. Not just the way we made love, which was incredible, but how close we felt to each other. I believed she could read my mind—she knew exactly what I wanted and she always said the right thing. I'd never been so in love."

Glenda also described her excitement at finding someone who was not "at all like my first husband." Having been raised by a strict father, Glenda previously found herself attracted to men who were "very dominating and cold." While her first husband had never resorted to physical violence, he had often intimidated her with angry outbursts and belittling comments.

When Glenda met Jerry, she felt relieved that she had finally found a man who was kind and compassionate. "Jerry wasn't pushy or demanding like my first husband," she explained. "He knew how to be warm, affectionate, sincere, and tender. In those early days, we used to stay up all night talking about our hopes and dreams. He had great rapport with my three-year-old son, Cassidy, who seemed to respond to him more than to his own father. It was wonderful, and after six months we had a beautiful wedding at which our two kids laughed and played together. It was a dream come true."

The dream began to fade into a nightmare within six months after Jerry and Glenda set up their household. Quite unexpectedly, Jerry suffered a major crisis at work when he became embroiled in litigation involving alleged design flaws in one of his client's buildings. Jerry, who had been tender and compassionate, now became aloof, anxious, and inaccessible. Glenda tried to be understanding, but her patience began to wear thin as all the household responsibilities became hers while she continued to pursue her career.

"I felt under tremendous pressure," she reported, "I was worried about Jerry, and his problems made my income that much more important to us. At the same time, he just dropped out of responsibility for his kids or the house. I began to feel like a live-in maid to him and his slob of a daughter, Zoey."

"I didn't think she had any idea what I was going through," said Jerry. "I needed support and all I got were complaints."

In this atmosphere of emerging mutual resentment, arguments

regularly escalated into shouting matches. Unknowingly, Jerry and Glenda each began recreating their worst fears in each other. When Jerry became angry and domineering, Glenda began to withdraw. "I couldn't help it," she recalled. "The more he got angry with me, the more I withdrew. His touch felt like an assault. I froze sexually." Jerry read Glenda's withdrawal as a deep personal rejection. His anger only grew worse and the relationship deteriorated until they came in for counseling.

The Repetition Compulsion

Over a period of early therapy sessions, Jerry and Glenda began to understand how their love for each other had become overwhelmed by emotional ghosts from their pasts. We discussed how, on a sub-conscious level, each of us has an inner script of emotional patterns that give shape to our primary love relationships. For each of us, the inner struggle with intimacy is never over. For any remarriage to succeed, it is important to become aware of these emotional inner scripts so that they don't take over in times of crisis.

Jerry and Glenda began to forgive one another as they learned how each had triggered the other's worst fears. Jerry had not known that Glenda's father was so authoritarian as to create in her a reflective fear of authoritarian men. Glenda had not appreciated the extent to which Jerry was hurt by his wife's sexual rejection. Once these scripts became conscious, Jerry and Glenda could each acknowledge how they had been controlled by the past, and they could then choose to avoid the reflexive responses in the future.

One of Sigmund Freud's discoveries that will stand the test of time is the repetition compulsion; that is, whatever is incomplete from the past, we tend to re-create. It is inevitable that unresolved hurts will be retriggered by any intimate partnership. When this occurs, the key is to deal with your troubled feelings without destroying your mar-riage. You don't need to leave a good relationship simply because your partner has restimulated painful memories. If you learn to share and discuss your unresolved hurts from the past, you and your partner can grow much closer.

If your marriage has taken a sudden turn for the worse, and you see in your spouse someone whom you have not seen before, the emotional ghosts from the past may be at work. Instead of allowing the cycle of mutual blame and betrayal to escalate, it would be wise for you to examine what emotional scripts may be controlling you or your spouse.

Some scripts may have their origins in primary childhood memories. For example, if your father was dictatorial, or belittling, you may have married someone who is so much like your father that you feel dominated, or someone who is so much the opposite that you later resent this person for being so meek or compliant. If a parent died or emotionally abandoned you when you were young, you may be subconsciously fearing that your adult love partner might do the same.

Other scripts may have their origins in unrealistic judgments or expectations. If one or both parents catered to your every whim and need, you might be expecting your adult partner to live up to an impossible standard. If you were repeatedly told "Don't settle for anything less," you may become disenchanted with every potential partner to whom you're attracted. For tools to help heal the unfinished business from childhood, please see one of my previous books *Making Peace With Your Parents*.

Emotional scripts may also be of more recent origin. Just as Jerry was deeply hurt by his first wife's sexual rejection, you may have developed a similar sensitivity. Or, if you have previously fallen in love only to be subsequently betrayed by your ex-spouse's affair, you may be reticent to trust, or you may have become overly suspicious. If you previously sacrificed yourself only to be taken for granted by your previous partner, you may now be reticent to make such a commitment again. Here are a few additional examples of emotional scripts from the past:

- I give too much and get too little in return.
- I'm creating the same kind of unhappy marriage my parents had.
- After what I went through with my ex, I'll never be able to trust anyone.
- No one will ever be able to replace my deceased spouse.

When a remarriage falters, there is a tendency to conclude, "I made a mistake." Protective emotional shells thicken. Exploring how old emotional scripts may be playing themselves out in your remarriage can reinforce fears that the remarriage doesn't work. Do not let this fear take over. Remember that your spouse is not the same person as your father or your ex. Your spouse still has all the wonderful qualities that caused you to fall in love, and you are now learning about a few qualities that may be similar to those of a parent or ex-spouse. Sorting out the differences will allow you to sort out your reflexive emotional responses. You and your spouse can then identify the sources of conflict in your remarriage and take steps together to change.

What are the scripts at work in your remarriage?

Overcoming Blocks to Love

When tensions in your remarriage arise, you and your spouse have a choice. You can each take your children and go your own separate ways, or you can recommit to your love, marriage, and stepfamily. That was the choice I posed to Jerry and Glenda. Fortunately, they sought help early enough so they had not lost basic respect for each other. Their love was still alive.

Once Jerry and Glenda understood how their own pasts were contributing to their marriage crisis, the next step was for each to take responsibility for changing the emotional responses that were destroying their love and mutual respect. Each had to stop blaming the other for being cold, domineering, and insensitive. Instead, both had to discern their own specific behaviors that blocked their love.

The following simple sentence-completion exercise can help in this process. I asked Jerry and Glenda to complete the following sentence: I've been blocking my love for you (Glenda/Jerry) by _____.

Here are Jerry's responses:

- taking stepfamily pressures out on you
- getting jealous when you cuddle your son
- working too hard and forgetting your emotional needs
- letting Zoey run all over you
- demanding sex instead of connecting with you

Here are Glenda's responses:

- holding on to my anger rather than letting you know how I feel about being excluded
- turning to Cassidy for affection and ignoring you
- taking out my frustration on Zoey and blaming you for her behavior
- letting myself get turned off even though I find you attractive

This exercise is valuable because it provides specific insight into how behaviors must change to heal the relationship. Instead of turning to me for advice as to what each needed to do, Jerry and Glenda discovered answers for themselves, and those answers are almost always the best ones. You can use this same exercise to find answers of your own.

The great irony about strengthening your remarriage in a period of crisis is that you are likely to find your greatest strength by allowing yourself to become most vulnerable. By acknowledging how you are blocking your love, you uncover ghosts from the past and the behaviors that may have contributed to your first divorce. We all have a tendency to resist such painful self-knowledge. The more we resist being open and vulnerable, however, the more loneliness and frustration are bound to persist. In contrast, by opening up to some difficult memories and emotions from your past, you can learn how you block your love in the present. You are also less likely to seek the impossible from your new spouse. Instead of getting caught in a cycle of mutual blame, you can turn your love crisis into an opportunity for growth and renewal. The result will be a stronger union and a greater love.

The Photo-History Exercise

Once you and your spouse have begun acknowledging your vulnerabilities, there is another exercise that you can use to heal unfinished business from your past, and thereby strengthen your remarriage. Within everyone, no matter how adult, is an inner child who still carries unresolved hurts, needs, and pain. Guided discussion of photographs or home movies of you and your partner as children can be very helpful in uncovering those unresolved feelings. The key is to find a series of photographs from your childhood as well as subsequent eras, then revealing to your mate the deepest feelings associated with the photographs you review. We all have a tendency to try to portray our pasts in the most favorable light, even to ourselves. In this exercise the goal is to access your raw feelings triggered by the photos and to share those feelings without editing. When you review these photos together, use the following questions:

- What were you feeling then?
- What insecurities were troubling you?
- How did you feel about yourself, i.e., your self-confidence and self-worth?
- How were you feeling about your parents? Fearful? Loving? Indifferent?
- What events may have changed your feelings since the photographs were taken?
- Do any of the feelings you had as a little child in the photographs persist today? Toward your parents? Your siblings?

Answer all questions about each photograph. This exercise usually works best if you first talk about one of your photos and then one of your spouse's. Alternate for as long as you feel comfortable, and give yourself permission to laugh, cry, or become angry or silly. Self-disclosure to your lover is liberating.

Coping with Your Partner's Anger

Anger is an inevitable part of any marriage because it is virtually impossible to live so intimately without hurting each other at least occasionally. Sometimes the hurts are small—you forget a birthday, cancel a family weekend at the last minute, or yet again come home late for dinner—and the anger is an irritation. Other times the injuries may be larger—you embarrass your spouse in front of her boss at a company party, invest family savings in a losing venture against your spouse's advice, or have an affair—and the anger erupts into rage. Whatever the cause of anger in your remarriage, one of the most important steps in strengthening your union is to develop skills in accepting each other's hurt and anger without becoming defensive.

Anger is a difficult emotion, whether you are the one dishing out your frustration or the one listening. The emotional intensity of anger often clouds clear and effective communication. Natural tendencies toward self-protection lead most of us to become defensive in the face of an angry outburst. Some couples attempt to cope with anger by suppressing it, only to find their marriages becoming clouded by cold resentments as unresolved emotional injuries accumulate. The better alternative is to learn how to express anger in a way that vents the emotion and openly communicates a wish to avoid a repetition of the hurt in the future.

Three Magic Words: Tell Me More

I recommend that couples use a technique called "Tell Me More" to hear each other's hurt and anger without becoming defensive. The technique requires that the angry spouse ask for an opportunity to express her or his hurt, and that the other spouse agree to listen until the anger is fully expressed. To avoid becoming defensive and to encourage a complete communication, the listener repeats the phrase *tell me more* until the angry spouse has fully vented her or his feelings.

The power of this exercise is best illustrated by example. Lee and Ava sought my help because they were constantly at war about disciplining their children. Lee had two girls and Ava one boy when they married. Ava was enraged because Lee constantly undermined her authority by negating her efforts to enforce discipline. Lee responded with a shrug and a statement that he couldn't understand what Ava wanted from him. I asked Ava to tell him how she felt, and I asked Lee to keep saying "tell me more" until he finally understood what she wanted. Here is an excerpt from their session:

AVA: I am angry that you don't back me up on disciplining the children

LEE: Tell me more.

AVA: We've talked about rules—bedtime, homework, chores—and I thought we agreed on what we expected of the kids.

LEE: Tell me more.

AVA: When I tell the kids to get ready for bed and you then let them stay up, I feel like you have no regard for me. It makes me furious.

LEE: That's not true.

HAROLD: Lee, please stick to "tell me more."

LEE: OK, Ava, tell me more.

AVA: I feel very strongly about discipline—bedtimes are important—that's what we agreed.

LEE: Tell me more.

AVA: When we agree on a rule and then you let the kids ignore it, I feel you don't really care about the kids or me.

LEE: Tell me more.

AVA: Its easier to let the kids get away with it than to discipline. . . . It's not easy to say no . . . but I'm sure it's important . . . very important to what our children become when they grow up.

LEE: Tell me more.

AVA: I don't want to be the one who is a bitch all the time. I love and respect you, Lee, and I want us to bring up our kids to be wonderful people.

LEE: Tell me more.

AVA: I need your help to stand up to the kids. I want us to be a team that the kids can look to for values.

LEE: Tell me more.

AVA: When you let the kids run wild, it feels as if you are rejecting me. It hurts very much.

LEE: Tell me more.

AVA: I love you, Lee, and I want to find a way that we both feel comfortable in enforcing discipline.

LEE: Tell me more.

AVA: There must be ways for us to work these things out so we stop fighting. I'm sure it will be best for us and the kids.

LEE: I'm sure there must be, too.

AVA: I love you, Lee.

LEE: I love you, too. Let's work out a plan.

This result is typical with the "Tell Me More" exercise. What begins as an intense conflict gets resolved in love and agreement. There is no magic, just consistent, complete, and nondefensive communication.

Guidelines for the "Tell Me More" Exercise

Here are the instructions for the "Tell Me More" exercise. Read them carefully, as this exercise can prompt intense emotion that must be handled appropriately to strengthen your remarriage.

1. Find a room in which you both feel safe and relaxed. This room should be pleasant and comfortable, perhaps decorated with flowers and candles or incense. Unplug the phone and put a DO NOT DISTURB sign on the door.

2. Arrange two chairs so that you sit facing each other, close enough to feel in contact but not so close that you violate each other's comfort zone. A conversational distance is best.

3. The invitation to take time out for a "Tell Me More" session should be made by the person who is upset. Once you are fully comfortable, however, the conversation should be initiated by the prospective listener by saying, "I see that you have some feelings that are bothering you, and I would like to hear what you have to say."

4. The listener then restricts his or her statements to the simple phrase *tell me more*. This expression should not be repeated casually or mechanically. There is a natural rhythm to conversation and particularly to self-revelation. If one of you is courageous enough to sit down and express all of his or her feelings, the other must use the phrase *tell me more* as a sincere expression of interest in hearing all the stored feelings your spouse wants to express.

5. When one of you has thoroughly expressed his or her feelings, switch roles. The other now has an opportunity to express all of his or her feelings in response to the phrase *tell me more*. This exercise is not over until both of you feel complete in expression of your feelings.

In addition to these general instructions, I also advise my clients to observe the following recommendations when you are the listener:

• Don't start the exercise if you're excessively tired or preoccupied.

- Don't interrupt.
- Don't be impatient.
- Don't be defiant or arrogant.
- Don't jump to conclusions.
- Give your undivided attention.
- Develop empathy.
- Stay calm.
- Accept your spouse's views and feelings without judgment.

The reason for using the phrase *tell me more* is to elicit enough information from your partner so that you fully understand his or her feelings, what may be behind those feelings, and what your lover may need in order to heal. Use the phrase *tell me more* as often as necessary to be sure you understand your partner's feelings and wants. You may initially be confused by those feelings, but stay committed, and a natural resolution will emerge.

Just as there are dos and don'ts as a listener in the "Tell Me More" exercise, there are precepts to follow as a speaker:

- Don't be afraid to say what you feel.
- Don't try to make your spouse wrong. (There is a fine line between communicating hurt feelings and destructively dumping, berating, and making your lover wrong.)
- Don't rush yourself.
- Focus on one issue.
- Acknowledge your vulnerabilities and weaknesses.
- Show that you care.

Be patient. It may take another "Tell Me More" session or the passage of additional time for forgiveness and reconciliation to evolve naturally.

Eliminating "Yes, But," "So What," and "I Give Up"

Anger is not the only emotion that provokes defensive responses between spouses. Jealousy, frustration, and despair can also become toxic to your marriage if you suppress these feelings by denying their existence or if you deny your spouse's right to his or her own feelings by becoming defensive.

Nicole is a stepmother to Joe's daughters, Jordan and Julia, aged thirteen and eleven. They also have a new baby of their own. After two years of marriage, Nicole became despondent over her inability to bond with the two girls. "I've given my best to love the girls," Nicole remembers telling Joe, "but they won't accept me. They're bitter. And now that I have a baby, I see how much love I have. I feel like I've let you down, and I don't know what to do."

Joe felt that Nicole was setting him up to choose between his daughters and their new baby. "You knew I had the girls when we married, and it was a package deal. I had the baby to make you happy. Now don't make me miserable," Joe insisted.

Joe's response wounded Nicole, and a full-fledged battle erupted. Had Joe instead begun by acknowledging and accepting Nicole's feelings, he could have found an opportunity to unite with her rather than create a division. Instead of taking a defensive stance, he might have said, "I know how difficult it is to love someone else's kids, but I see how hard you are trying to be a good mother. Maybe you shouldn't try to force it. I don't think you should be down on yourself because you feel you don't love Julia and Jordan. Having the baby makes it even more difficult. You're tired, and you naturally love the baby. You know how much I love you and our baby. Let's not worry about whether or not you love Julia and Jordan but instead work on ways for all of us to be a family. Let's let the love take care of itself."

Denying your spouse's feelings is a formula for disaster. In contrast, accepting your spouse's most difficult feelings without becoming defensive almost inevitably strengthens your remarriage. If your spouse complains about the loss of sexual passion since you moved in together, you can become defensive, in which case you and your spouse are likely to become more tense and less attracted to each other. Or you can acknowledge how moving into a hectic household has put pressure on both of you, and you can figure out a way to give yourselves the relaxed time alone that you need. In that way, you will be able to rediscover your passion.

Whenever you find yourself becoming defensive in response to your spouse's feelings, remember that when it comes to feelings, no one is wrong. Feelings are signals to be first accepted and then understood. By learning to check your defensive responses and accept your spouse's feelings, you will acquire one of the most valuable skills for strengthening your remarriage.

"I Love You, And . . ."

There is a subtle form of coercion which spouses sometimes inflict upon each other in the name of love. These verbal traps are important to recognize because they masquerade as acceptance of feelings but are in fact a form of denial. "I love you, but . . ." is one of these traps. When you say to your spouse, "I love you, but . . . ," you actually make a coercive statement which implies "I won't love you unless you agree to do what I say." On the other hand, if you say, "I love you, and I'd prefer if you would . . . ," you communicate your unconditional love, along with your sincere need for your spouse to acknowledge your preferences. If you can learn to use the following four phrases, you may well experience improvements in family relationships.

- *I love you, and . . .*
- I appreciate you, and . . .
- I agree with you, and . . .
- I respect your point of view, and . . .

When you use the above four phrases, you are first of all building care, appreciation, and respect with your spouse, child, or stepchild. You are validating his or her point of view. You are building rapport and acknowledging communication rather than ignoring and denigrating what he or she has to say. Further, you are creating a bond by which you and a family member can look at a difficult situation together and see each other's differing points of view.

"If You Love Me You Would . . ." Exercise

As subtly damaging as "I love you, but . . ." is the expression, "If you love me you would. . . ." This phrase aims at coercion through guilt.

Here are some of the ways I have seen couples use this phrase. If you love me, you would:

- not expect me to discipline your kids.
- not bother me about hassles with your ex.
- not put the kids ahead of me.
- make more money to support "them."

In most cases, "If you love me" statements reflect unrealistic expectations. One partner expects another to create instant harmony or instant love within the stepfamily. We have already seen that these unrealistic expectations are harmful to stepfamily bonding, and part of strengthening your remarriage is to assist your spouse in overcoming such expectations.

Here is a set of questions which I suggest couples use to understand their "If you love me, you would . . ." fantasies:

- How realistic are your expectations?
- What is it that you are looking for from your partner?
- What could you do to create more of what you want and impose fewer expectations on your partner?
- Why are these expectations important to you?
- Why might these expectations not be important to your partner?

Even for those expectations you consider realistic and appropriate, it is helpful to express these as "I would prefer it if you would . . ." (spend more time with my oldest boy, be more affectionate). Remember, it is easier to respond with enthusiasm to a request rather than a demand.

Sharing Heart Talks

While I appreciate the enormous pressures within stepfamilies, both as to time and money, I strongly advocate that all couples, particularly remarrieds with children, make sure to take time every week just to connect emotionally. The problem for most couples is not lack of desire, but making time and following through on the commitment. In a busy household, there will always be demands on your time, and taking time just for the two of you may seem selfish. It's not. Better to think of your time alone as essential to a healthy stepfamily. I recommend weekly Heart Talks.

For Heart Talks to renew your marriage, you and your spouse must be prepared to overcome your own fears of self-disclosure. Relationships often stagnate because spouses are reluctant to share their deepest feelings. There are as many reasons why spouses keep emotional secrets as there are couples.

For Heart Talks to become a source of renewal in your marriage, you will need to discuss what Heart Talks are all about and how to help each other experience a new level of emotional safety and mutual trust. Here are eleven Heart Talk agreements that I advise couples to review periodically:

1. I promise not to interrupt and to listen to you without other distractions.
2. I promise not to withdraw emotionally or to leave physically; I will not reject you for anything you might share.
3. I will make it safe for you to express your most intimate feelings; I will stay open and vulnerable to you.
4. Nothing you say will be used against you or to provoke an argument later.
5. I will be responsible for my emotions, and I will not blame you for how I feel. If I do blame or complain, I will take immediate responsibility for doing so, and stop.
6. I will share the truth from my heart as caringly, honestly, and respectfully as I can.
7. I will love you unconditionally and use any block or conflict

that may arise as a stimulus to more learning and understanding.

8. I will try not to manipulate, defend or control what you communicate.

9. I commit to dealing with and working through any barriers that come up in our Heart Talks until there is resolution and we are once again open and caring with each other.

10. I agree that we can disagree. As we may not see eye-to-eye about all issues, we will each allow the other his/her feelings, understanding and point of view.

11. I agree to finish each Heart Talk with at least one embracing hug and a sincere "Thank you" and "I love you."

"But what are we supposed to talk about?" marrieds sometimes ask. My answer is to peel back the layers that surround that which you want. The human psyche is like an onion. Our personalities are all structured in layers. Usually we share only our outer layers with one another. When we share a few deeper layers, we become overwhelmed with feelings of intimacy and fall in love. To demonstrate what I mean, I give clients the following series of questions. Each level opens to deeper feelings and challenges deeper fears of self-disclosure. Consider using these questions in a series of Heart Talks.

Feeling Safe Is Essential to Love

The Heart Talk diagram below depicts four levels of intimacy and personal privacy. Level E covers emotionally neutral information. In this zone, communication consists primarily of explorations and observations which are mostly emotionally uninvolved (e.g., "What I like most about my work is . . ."; "Things I like to do are . . . "; "Songs I like to sing are . . . "; "My religious beliefs are . . .").

Levels F, A, and S represent zones of increasing intimacy. It is at these levels that you begin to reveal your true self. At level F, you begin to communicate your emotions and desires (e.g. "I feel frustrated . . ."; "I am optimistic . . ."; "I hope . . . "). At Level A, you share more intimate and difficult feelings about yourself and step-family life. The designation *A* is for ambivalence—the feelings that generate uncertainty; it may seem difficult to know exactly what you feel until you begin to explore. Level S is the innermost level of intimacy—secrets. This level represents the territory of hidden feelings and buried fears.

S–Secrets A–Ambivalence F–Feelings E–Explorations

Most people keep the content of Levels A and S a wholly private concern. They share these thoughts, feelings, and wishes with no one, thereby severing a crucial link to potential intimacy. If you are somewhat open and courageous, you can share from these innermost levels of the heart with perhaps one or two special people whom you trust completely. Level S allows for the deepest, most rewarding connection, since by definition you trust no one with these secrets; yet it also requires great skill in sharing yourself. Disclosures at Level S include those dealing with sex, dishonesty, corruption, shame, violence, and rage.

These levels of intimacy form the acronym SAFE, a reminder of the key element for Heart Talks. You and your spouse need to create an emotional environment of trust and safety. Once that is established, you can be completely vulnerable, which leads to personal liberation from fear and therefore a higher quality of love and family care.

Level E: Explorations

1. The personal, family, and work goals I want to accomplish in the next year are . . .
2. A two-week all-expenses-paid adventure I would like to take anywhere in the world is . . .
3. A weekend getaway I'd like to have with you real soon is . . .
4. I think our children should be brought up to . . .
5. If I could have three magic wishes, I would wish for . . .
6. I would like to spend more of our time . . .

Level F: Feelings

1. The two biggest personal challenges I am facing in my life at present are . . .
2. What I am most worried/concerned about this week is . . .
3. An important change I would like to see in you is . . .
4. The five specific things I feel most grateful for are . . .
5. Family life or work habits I would like to change in myself are . . .
6. The best thing that could happen to me is . . .

Level A: Ambivalences

1. A conflict that I have in our family is . . .
2. How I feel when the kids arrive for a "shuttle visit" is . . .
3. How I feel when the kids leave to go to their other parent is . . .
4. The most self-defeating behavior pattern I have is . . .
5. Three things I like least/best about our stepfamily are . . .
6. The way I would feel more loved by you is . . .

Level S: Secrets

1. The last time I cried to myself was when . . .
2. The most dishonest thing I have ever done is . . .
3. I've been secretly resentful about . . .
4. If I were to die within the next twenty-four hours, what I would most want to communicate to you is . . .

5. The most painful aspect of my previous marriage and divorce was . . .
6. Feelings as a parent/stepparent I feel most ashamed of are . . .

Heart Talks are meant for you to discover that we human beings all have the same basic needs, hopes and fears.

Solving Problems as a Couple

While Heart Talks have helped many of my clients to restore feelings of trust and intimate connection, I have also found that couples frequently forget communication skills when stepfamily conflicts become intense.

All of us tend to revert to form under stress. What this means for the typical remarried couple is a tendency to revert to talking past each other rather than talking with each other when a stepfamily crisis arises.

When loving couples run into a communication problem about their children, an inability to appreciate each other's approach to problem-solving is often the cause. More often than not, women approach problems within the stepfamily by trying first to understand what each family member may be feeling. In contrast, men usually go straight to an examination of behaviors and a reward/punishment approach to creating change. As a result, most of the women who see me complain that their husbands "don't listen," while the men complain that their wives "don't understand."

One of the great challenges for remarrieds with children is becoming a parental team. Both members of the remarried couple must learn how to reach a consensus on emotionally charged issues when family stress may be at a maximum. To assist my clients in this regard, I have developed the Couple's Problem-Solving Process. This technique is most effective if you and your spouse have already been using Heart Talks to nurture intimacy. Here are the four steps of the Couple's Problem-Solving Process:

1. *Preparation.* To prepare you must give some thought to the details of the problem to be discussed. Generalities aren't as

useful as specifics. It is important to make notes of your thoughts to facilitate discussion with your spouse.

Thorough preparation also requires that you give some thought to the possible reasons for the conflict. Don't censor your opinions. Gut instincts can be surprisingly perceptive. Again, details are important; make notes.

Finally, you need to consider what each family member may be feeling about the issues. Make note of your feelings as well.

2. *Discussion.* Once you have finished preparation, set aside a couple of hours for your discussion. Review the Heart Talk agreements.

Using your lists, explain to each other your views of the problem, the reasons behind it, and each family member's feelings. Take turns in this process. Be sure to listen to your partner carefully. Remember, the goal is to understand each other's point of view. Therefore, ask questions such as:

- Why do you feel that way?
- Could you explain in more detail?
- What else do you think?

Don't prepare retorts while your partner is speaking. Listen!

Even if your partner's comments feel like criticism of you, try to listen rather than defend yourself. Consider the possibility that your partner's feedback may be useful. Ask for more detail or specific examples if your partner suggests you have been too strict, too lenient, too abrupt, too emotional.

Give yourselves permission to get angry. If unexpected anger flares up, you may need to use the "Tell Me More" exercise to allow the anger to surface without becoming defensive.

Don't hold back your own pain, fears, doubts, hurt or worry. Remember, this discussion is a Heart Talk first and a problem-solving session second. Go ahead and explain how much it hurts when your stepson ignores you or when your child goes back to his mother after a weekend visit. Give yourselves permission to cry, share your despair or your guilt.

When your partner expresses deep feelings, do not feel pressured to respond or fix the situation. What's most important is first to acknowledge his or her feelings. "I can see how you feel," or "That must be hard," or "I didn't know how much it hurt" are enough. Trust develops out of the ability to share deep feelings without judgment, guilt or shame. Let yourselves share your feelings and build trust.

3. *Brainstorming.* Once you have each shared your notes about the problem, the reasons for it, and each family member's feelings, take out a piece of paper to begin brainstorming solutions.

   Don't be intimidated by fears that your partner may not agree with your ideas. Most couples have differences, and this exercise can help you understand and manage them. If you're too tired to brainstorm after your discussions, try again the next day.

4. *Review.* The final stage of the process is to review and analyze your proposed solution to create a problem-solving plan. Evaluate your proposed solutions. Rank them by priority and establish a plan for implementing your solutions. Acknowledge each other for your efforts. Give yourselves credit for both sharing your feelings and developing specific approaches to making peace.

   Problem-solving Heart Talks can be used to resolve a wide variety of conflicts. Listed below are the most common sources of stress in the stepfamily. Check the five that create the most conflict in your home, and devote a Heart Talk to each.

- Communicating with stepchildren
- Family budget, child support
- Chores, responsibilities
- Insufficient romantic or couple time
- Lack of "me" time
- Child custody or visitation struggles
- Ex-spouse hassles
- Midlife crisis, unhappiness
- Child-rearing or discipline issues
- Feeling unappreciated or neglected
- Lack of share responsibility in the family
- Diminished self-esteem
- Spousal resentment quarrels

- Lack of privacy
- Sibling or stepsibling rivalry
- Sexual frustrations
- In-laws, grandparents
- Holidays, vacations
- Religious differences
- Unsatisfactory housing
- Career issues

Supporting Your Spouse During Children's Visits

Parents who see their children only periodically go through an emotional roller coaster in anticipation of their children's arrival, and then another emotional roller coaster when their children depart. So too the stepparent spouses in these homes often become impatient with the emotional upheaval that inevitably accompanies the comings and goings of their stepchildren. The emotional strain visiting children place on a remarriage can be terribly intense, and most remarrieds are totally unprepared for the difficulties unless both have children who visit another parent regularly.

A conspiracy of silence is typical among remarrieds because most parents don't want to acknowledge the intensity of their conflicting emotions when the children visit, and most stepparents don't want to acknowledge their resentments generated by the visit. Instead of pretending that visiting children are a source of joy for both you and your spouse, you would be far better served by a series of Heart Talks in which you discussed all your ambivalent feelings and developed strategies for these emotionally rough transition periods. Here are some issues to consider and suggestions that have helped my clients:

Acknowledge the emotional turmoil that accompanies visiting children. Acknowledge your need for support and be willing to tell him about all your conflicting and painful feelings. A stoic effort to protect your spouse from your distress will create division, not harmony.

Recognize your spouse's need for empathy when children arrive or depart. A hug accompanied by an understanding statement such as "I know this is always difficult for you" is a powerful way to strengthen your remarriage when your spouse's children are about to arrive or depart. Empathy means putting yourself in your spouse's shoes, not pressuring him or her to change.

Discuss your feelings of anxiety, excitement and fear of rejection. With a visit almost always too short, parents are anxious to make the visit a good one. You may worry about planning fun activities, having favorite foods in the house, making the child comfortable in cramped living quarters, creating special opportunities to reconnect, or any number of issues. You may also harbor feelings of rejection by your children. These fears are natural because your children are growing up in your ex-spouse's household. So much change happens without your being there to participate. A visit is a time to reconnect emotionally and you may naturally fear that it won't go well. The best way to lessen these anxieties is to share them with an empathetic spouse.

Acknowledge the parent's need to devote extra time to his or her visiting children. It is tragic how often I hear parents tell me about lying awake at night worrying about how they will manage to spend time with their soon-to-arrive children without creating havoc with their spouses or their stepchildren. This anxiety results from denial. The fact is that parents need a certain leave from their duties to spouses and live-in children to reconnect with and attend to the needs of visiting children, particularly at the beginning and toward the end of the visit. Talk about the issue and make plans.

Make plans for your spouse to spend one-on-one time with his or her stepchildren. This is one of the best ways to avoid having your spouse feel excluded. You and your spouse then actively support each other in planning for the visit, and also nurture the bonding process between your children and your spouse.

Plan family activities together. Don't allow just one of you to assume responsibility for planning family activities when the children are visiting. Ask your spouse for suggestions and engage him or her in the planning process.

Prepare for the heartaches of good-byes. There is no point in pretending that saying good-bye to a child doesn't hurt. In Chapter 2 I discussed ways in which you can ease the heartaches of good-byes.

Acknowledge feelings of hurt and loss. Sometimes visits with children go well; sometimes the visits don't go well. In either case, it is natural to feel the pain of loss when your children leave. Talk about your feelings with your spouse, and about how your spouse felt about the visit. Share your ideas for a better visit next time. Above all, avoid self-recrimination for what went wrong, and do not blame your spouse for the stresses that emerged. It is very hard to be a parent or stepparent to visiting children, and you strengthen your remarriage by each acknowledging that you did the best that you could, and you each look forward to doing better next time.

A New Baby?

One of the most difficult issues faced by many remarrieds is whether or not to have a baby of their own. Even though one or both of you may already have children, it is common soon after the wedding for parents and friends to ask, "When are you planning to start a family of your own?" The answer to this question is a major decision for any couple because a child changes a couple's life irrevocably. In the stepfamily, a new baby has an even more profound effect because the child that may unite its parents, may also be viewed as competition by an ex-spouse, a grandparent, or a stepchild.

Despite the apparent complexities of having a new baby within the stepfamily, there is evidence that new babies generally result in stronger remarriages. Therefore, when my clients ask about the wisdom of another child, I am generally positive and encourage them to explore all the issues that a new child raises.

If you want a child and your spouse doesn't, that conflict can become heated. One of the major causes of divorce in a remarried family is an irreconcilable difference over whether to have another child together. The desire for another child in the stepfamily is often a one-sided matter. A spouse already overwhelmed with parenting responsibilities may not want another child. A childless stepparent, on the other hand, may feel unfulfilled until he or she has a child of his or her own.

The cost of having a new baby can be heavy, economically and emotionally. When baby makes not only three but five, can a remarriage survive the financial pressure and increased stress? Ideally, a couple resolves the issue of conceiving another child before the marriage. Too often there are so many pressing matters in starting a stepfamily that this issue does not come up until later.

Stepchildren sometimes feel very threatened by the birth of a stepsibling. They fear loss of a position in the family when a new child is born. They also fear that a baby with direct blood ties to both parents will be loved more. As in a nuclear family, reassurance and acknowledgment of the children's apprehensions can help to allay such fears.

Parents must also cope with the differences in their own emotional responses to the new child versus the older children. The stepparent who has not previously had children of his own will naturally feel bonded more strongly to the new baby than to his stepchildren. The parent also feels great love for the new baby in part because infants are always the center of attention, but the parent's love is likely to be tempered by concern for the feelings of her older children. One way to minimize the conflict is to include the older children in the childbirth, if possible, and in the expanded circle of love that follows. As in all families, the antidote to sibling rivalry and jealousy is a larger measure of acceptance, love, and understanding.

"I Don't Want to Be Just a Stepmother"

When Dorothy married Kent, she was twenty-four and eager to become a stepmother to his two boys, John and Mark, aged seven and five. "I liked the boys from the first day I met them," Dorothy recalled. "I knew I'd be a great stepmother." Dorothy managed well in her new role, and the boys took to her without the typical resentments and conflicts. After three years, Dorothy wanted to have a child with Kent. Unhappy with his job and feeling a degree of economic pressure, Kent balked. Kent's suggestion was that Dorothy think about going back to work now that the boys were older and doing well in school.

When Kent talked about feeling trapped, Dorothy felt threatened because she so desperately longed to become pregnant. Her maternal dreams made it hard to empathize with Kent. Soon they found themselves involved in below-the-belt personal attacks because neither felt the other was willing to listen. "I've given myself completely to your kids," Dorothy screamed. "All I get is your selfishness."

"You knew I had kids when you married me," Kent retorted. "Don't complain to me now."

These blows and counterblows brought a cloud of fear over their home. The boys became agitated and frightened that they would lose another mother. The yelling matches soon carried threats of divorce.

The first question for a remarried couple faced with a major crisis is the degree of commitment to stay together and "stick it out." Despite the festering hostility, Dorothy and Kent said they still loved each other and wanted to make the relationship work. The fact that they came to see me for professional help was a sign of their commitment. What they needed more than anything else was a specific exercise to listen compassionately and patiently to each other.

Questions to Consider in Deciding to Have a Baby

The following is a list of questions I recommend remarried couples consider in deciding whether or not to add a new baby to a stepfamily:

1. Has one of you ever been a biological parent?
2. Is there an urgency for your decision due to the woman's biological clock?
3. Is the primary child caretaker happy or unhappy about having another child?
4. Will additional living area for a baby be a problem or create competition for space with stepchildren?
5. Will your lifestyle be so compromised by the addition of a new baby that it will cause resentment?
6. Are you prepared to deal with the added financial costs of another child?

7. Is one of you resentful about going through another "bottle and diaper" stage?

8. What will be the impact of a child on the ambitious schedules and finances of a two-career, remarried couple?

9. Is the wife working now? Will she work until childbirth? After the baby arrives?

10. Would mother's physical or emotional health be jeopardized if she became pregnant?

11. Are you under pressure from family or friends to have a child?

12. Do you and your spouse agree upon long-term personal family goals?

13. Are you prepared to be understanding and compassionate about how your stepchildren and children respond to a new baby (with anxiety, jealousy, or confusion)?

14. Are you aware that preteens or adolescents may feel used and resentful if you expect them to be live-in baby-sitters or cooks and bottle washers?

15. What changes do you think will occur in your life, your spouse's life, and your stepfamily life? How do you feel about that?

16. What roles do you expect to play in raising your child?

17. What role do you expect your stepchildren to play in raising your child?

18. How many children would you like to have? When?

19. Are you trying to show someone you are finally a "real" family?

20. How might this decision make or break your marriage?

As unlikely as it might sometimes appear, a stepsister or stepbrother may be one of the most precious gifts parents can give their children after remarriage. Half-siblings can become very close to one another. The younger child often misses the older stepchild when he or she is in the other home. A big brother or big sister is a source of pride and joy as the children learn to share a sport, a hobby, and a history of stepfamily experiences. Of course, a new baby raises issues of sibling rivalry and some jealousy. That is normal and natural. Carefully and lovingly planned, a new baby can become a wonderful bonus for the entire stepfamily.

Having an Affair with Your Spouse

For the couple who feels the pizzazz has gone out of their marriage, I prescribe an exercise I call "Having an AFFAIR with Your Spouse:

- **A.** *Adventure:* The simplest cure for boredom is adventure. When a relationship becomes bogged down by routines, you have to make a special effort to step outside this routine regularly. Take turns with your mate planning a once-a-month adventure just for the two of you.

- **F.** *Fun:* School, music lessons, car payments, individual bills, and all the other obligations of family can easily make a marriage all work and no play. The antidote is to let yourselves go as often as you can. Create a party in your bedroom—nothing elaborate, but a little champagne and chocolate can add something special to an evening at home.

- **F.** *Fantasy:* Give your imagination free reign. Take turns or else create a fantasy together. Indulge in erotica, try switching roles, or write down an erotic fantasy and read it to your mate.

- **A.** *Affection:* There is nothing more welcome when you're feeling down than your lover offering a big hug. In every relationship there will be occasions when one lover needs more from the other. It is important to be sensitive to those times, while responding with considerate, loving gestures.

- **I.** *Intimacy:* Sexual energy is one form of vitality, intimate energy another. Try to think of ways that you and your mate can find true intimacy in everything you do, including even the most everyday activities, such as going for a walk or cooking a meal. Be willing to share your deepest feelings and fears with each other.

- **R.** *Romance:* If you continue to kindle romance, you can continue to experience your partner as a lover. A monogamous relationship is a creative challenge. Buy each other flowers, not for a special occasion but as a surprise. Plan a candlelight dinner or an evening out at a jazz club. Whatever strikes your fancy can help you renew your marriage with the magic of romance.

Having an AFFAIR with your mate is a remarkably effective exercise for a simple reason. Remember when you were dating your spouse. You helped create chemistry in your relationship by focusing your attention on ways to share adventure, fun, fantasy, affection, intimacy, and romance. Is it really a surprise that the chemistry diminished when instead of putting your attention on these aspects of your relationship, you focus exclusively on your work, children's needs, financial pressures, and household chores? By having an AFFAIR with each other, you and your spouse will quite naturally rediscover the passion that brought you together. Give yourselves the quality time you each deserve, and your marriage will not just survive, but thrive.

Chapter 6

HEALING THROUGH COMMUNICATION: FROM STEPFAMILY TRIANGLES TO FAMILY CIRCLES

"You care more about your kid than me."

"Why don't you ever see things my way?"

"You're always siding with your kids."

Such angry refrains can be heard in all families, but they are particularly troublesome in stepfamilies. Whenever a stepfamily comes for counseling, there are usually at least two people who tend to take sides against a third.

A triangle, a three-person emotional unit, is the fundamental building block of any family system. A two-person system, e.g., a single parent and child or marriage partners, may be relatively calm and peaceful, but as soon as a third significant other is introduced, conflict and divided loyalties often develop.

A stepfamily triangle in conflict characteristically has two comfortable sides and one side in tension. Two family members, who are in conflict with each other, each turn to a third family member to seek support. For example, in a stepfather-mother-daughter triangle, the daughter may reject her stepfather. Both the daughter and stepfather then turn to the spouse/mother for support in resolving the conflict. In these cases, the real stepfamily conflict has little to do with the specific complaints of the two individuals overtly battling each other. The real issues are about who has the power, who has the authority, whose side are you on, who is going to be loyal to whom. Making peace in the face of stepfamily triangles requires going beyond the superficial issues to the emotional source of the conflict.

All families have difficulties with triangles, but stepfamilies are particularly vulnerable. What make triangling so destructive are the emotional bonds that predate the stepfamily. Typically, a single mother has lived on her own for one or more years prior to her remarriage. During that period of single parenting, she and her children had one another all to themselves. An emotional bond grew strong, so much so as to become resistant to any man who might intrude to compete for the formerly single mother's love and affection, and who later dares to be a stepfather. The children respond reflexively to the invader. They try to distance the intruder and assure themselves of their mother's loyalty by constantly complaining to her about how badly or unfairly they are being treated. The mother responds by comforting her children, and the dynamics of the triangle are established.

The sheer complexity of stepfamily relationships, coupled with the mixed loyalties among family members, creates a fertile ground for a wide variety of destructive triangles. Fearing a second divorce, a father may side with his new wife "against" his daughter. Unable to control a teenage son, a mother and stepfather may take sides against the troublesome teen who becomes the scapegoat for stepfamily tension.

The Psychological Theory of Relativity

In this chapter, I present a variety of de-triangling strategies. Critical to this process is identifying destructive triangles and understanding each person's point of view in the conflict. You must become familiar with what I call the "Psychological Theory of Relativity." Each person in a stepfamily perceives the stepfamily conflict quite differently because each is likely to have different feelings about preexisting family bonds. Take one example—a daughter living with her remarried mother and stepfather. All three are part of a new stepfamily, but each perceives it very differently at the outset. The daughter may be missing her father and holding onto a reunion fantasy. The mother may be antagonistic toward her ex and anxious to help her daughter bond with her new husband. The stepfather may be feeling uncertain about his new role. Each person perceives a very different stepfamily. By opening yourself to each stepfamily member's unique point of view, you gain new insight into their feelings. Instead of blaming other stepfamily members for continued conflict, you learn to acknowledge and understand their feelings as a first step in making peace.

A stepfamily may have members living part-time in several different households, each with their own set of relatives. Biological, legal, financial, and emotional ties extend across household boundaries to create a wide array of criss-crossing triangles. The experience of "home" and of "immediate family" is different for each member of a stepfamily household. An important task of the stepfamily is to develop communication skills for the consolidation of many different triangles into a new family circle.

Emotional Sources of Destructive Triangles

All families have some dysfunction. Take five families, interview all of their members, and more likely than not you will find at least one member of each family who feels unappreciated, left out, picked on, or abused. The number of adults who harbor these feelings from their own childhood is staggering.

Why? The causes of family dysfunction are many, but one simple factor is that no one person can give equal attention or affection to two people simultaneously. As a result, family life inevitably involves competition for time, attention, and affection. Siblings compete for their parents' love and attention; spouses often find themselves pulled in different directions by the emotional demands of their children, to say nothing of their own parents and in-laws. This competition tends to generate relationship triangles in which two family members become close while distancing a third.

As long as family triangles are constantly forming and dissolving among various family members, no one feels left out for too long, and family competition comes and goes in normal fashion. When triangles become rigid, however, competition can develop into chronic and destructive conflict that at best leaves one family member feeling bitter and at worst destroys a family.

In stepfamilies this normal competition for love and attention frequently generates destructive triangling because other difficult emotions play an unusually strong role. One of these emotions is loyalty. The parent-child bond is built on love and loyalty. A child's worst fear is of being abandoned, and as a result, children become quite upset at the prospect of being disloyal to a parent. When a child asks a parent, "Whose side are you on?" the child is laying claim to the parent's loyalty. A perceived breach is a perceived catastrophe. One of the great difficulties for remarrieds is that certain emotions fueling the conflict are essentially positive. For example, loyalty is an important value which most parents want to instill in their children. Yet within the stepchildren, loyalty all too often leads to destructive triangling. The challenge is finding a balance between respect for loyalty and the opportunity to expand the stepfamily circle of love.

Another major triangle generator is guilt. Most divorced parents harbor guilt about their inability to provide an untroubled home for their children. When one parent gives up custody, the noncustodial parent is likely to deride himself or herself for abandoning the children. It is quite common for children of divorce to feel guilty for driving one of their parents out of the house. To allay guilt, parents and children, particularly when living apart, often attempt to bond in ways that distance other stepfamily members. The result is destructive triangling.

Simple frustration also can lead to triangling. When the realities of stepfamily emotional dynamics shatter the instant love fantasy, frustration follows. To allay the frustration, the stepparent or parent may attempt to bond to the exclusion of a stepchild. Again, this normal response to frustration sets up the potential for chronic conflict as a triangle develops between the stepparent, parent, and child.

Fear is another potent source of destructive triangles. In some cases, fear of another divorce drives a parent to take sides with a stepparent against the children. In other cases, fear of abandonment motivates children to bond with one another against the stepparent, whom the children perceive as potentially taking away their parent. In both of these cases, the emotional triangle ameliorates fear and provides longed-for feelings of stability and safety, but the result is a triangle.

Stepfamily triangles can become particularly destructive because they are largely a psychological avoidance mechanism. The triangling process helps the family members avoid confronting and resolving painful emotions. For example, the child attempts to take sides with his mother against the stepfather to avoid confronting fears of abandonment or possibly to suppress feelings of disloyalty to his own father. A stepfather embraces his children to the exclusion of his stepchildren to avoid confronting his feelings of guilt about his divorce. Because stepfamily triangles are rooted in avoidance, the various participants are often not even aware of how their behavior sustains stepfamily conflict. The pain of destructive triangles may be internalized and be a source of hidden conflict for adult stepchildren. Becoming aware of a stepfamily triangle is the first step to encircling it.

Reaching Out to Resolve Conflict

"It's been over a year since we were married," reported Maria, a thirty-two-year-old stepmother to her husband Keith's nine-year-old daughter, Christine, "and it's not getting any better. In fact, it's getting worse. Christine's got Keith so wrapped around her finger that he is not even aware of how our relationship is suffering."

"I'm embarrassed to admit it," Maria went on, "but the last time I felt this way was when my ex was having an affair. He gradually excluded me from his emotional life. Sure, it's not the same with Christine, but I feel our relationship dying. I try to talk to Keith about it, and he gets upset or withdrawn. Last month, Christine heard me suggest that Keith and I go up to San Francisco for a long weekend. That night she asked her father to a father-daughter Girl Scout trip that same weekend. Keith couldn't let her down, and hoped I'd understand. I was furious because he just assumed I would take a back seat. He didn't even suggest that we go away some other weekend."

When Maria insisted that Keith join her in counseling, he was stunned. "I knew she was having a hard time with Christine," said Keith, "but Maria is a terrific stepmom and I thought we were becoming a family. Christine isn't really negative toward Maria. She just needs a lot of attention from me right now."

Caught in a triangle with his daughter, Keith was unaware of how he was collaborating with Christine's needs to distance Maria. When I pointed out the triangle, Keith balked. "It's not like that at all," he protested. *"We're* not excluding Maria." On closer examination, however, Keith began to recognize a pattern. He always helped Christine with her homework; he used his season tickets for baseball games to take Christine to games; Christine even preferred going shopping with him rather than Maria.

Keith did not perceive this behavior as excluding Maria because he had done all these things with and for Christine ever since his divorce four years earlier. Keith recalled that Christine was very troubled when his former wife Susan left him. Christine had difficulty falling asleep and frequent nightmares. Keith began reading to her every night and, when she was six, taking her to baseball games. They became inseparable on weekends.

When Keith and Maria met, they fell in love quickly. Maria told Keith that she looked forward to having a child with him but that she also welcomed becoming a stepmother to his daughter. He introduced Maria to Christine early in their courtship, and both he and Maria thought stepdaughter and stepmother would get along well. Neither Keith nor Maria really noticed that the first night Maria stayed over, Christine was awakened by a nightmare and required her father to comfort her back to sleep.

After the marriage, Christine grew increasingly possessive of her father. She didn't lash out at Maria with defiance or criticism. Rather, Christine began distancing Maria by pulling as hard as she could on the bond with her father. Baseball, movies, homework, shopping—it was always to her father to whom she turned for help or play.

One of the mistakes sometimes made in such instances is a focused therapeutic effort to weaken the bond between the parent and child in the hope of breaking the triangle. A better approach is to focus on creating a new bond between stepparent and stepchild.

The critical first step is for the parent and stepparent to acknowledge the existence of the triangle.

Once this step is accomplished, the stepparent needs the support of the parent to build an emotional bridge to the stepchild. In this case, Keith was very supportive of Maria spending more quality one-on-one time with Christine. Keith took the initiative to suggest that he and Maria begin alternating taking Christine to baseball games. Maria also invited Christine to several matinees. Although Christine resisted at first, one-on-one fun time led quite naturally to a breakthrough.

In this case, fortunately, Maria stood up for herself early. She did not let the triangle persist to a point where she became bitter or lost respect for Keith. By challenging Keith, Maria broke through the avoidance factor. Keith had become embroiled in a triangle with his daughter because he was unable to confront Christine's insecurities and her fear of genuinely opening up to Maria. Had that avoidance pattern persisted, Maria might have felt she had lost Keith to "another woman," albeit his daughter, and perhaps would have asked for a divorce.

Family Circle

The Family Circle is a high-quality communication experience. It provides a safe, secure, semistructured environment for learning about personal growth and family life. The entire stepfamily sits down together in a circle.

A Family Circle allows each member to gain:

- A sense of belonging and acceptance; "We are all equals here."
- Self-acceptance and understanding through self-observation
- Understanding and acceptance of other family members

- Effective interpersonal communication skills
- Awareness of family and household responsibilities
- Self-confidence
- Problem-solving tools
- Achievement through cooperation with others
- Family growth
- A safe, secure, direct experience of home, love, and family

A Family Circle is more than just a dinner conversation. Regularly scheduled family meetings provide a forum to air complaints, plan family activities, hash out new household rules, acknowledge and share compliments, and have fun. By allowing direct communication among all family members, it prevents the two-person party griping about the third person that often leads to destructive triangling. Here are some suggestions for a Family Circle:

Time. It is best to schedule your meeting for a time agreed upon by all family members. Regularly scheduled meetings are most effective. Although spontaneous discussions may seem more natural, the informality generates short attention spans and undermines the emotional commitment to the meeting. Plan on a one-hour meeting which starts on time and ends on time; only a family crisis meeting should be open-ended. If a routine time each week doesn't work for you, decide at the conclusion of each Family Circle when the family will meet to conduct the next one.

Attendance. Invite everyone who is part of your household, especially visiting stepchildren. A Family Circle is a great way for the weekend stepchildren to adjust and fit in. Invite everyone, but don't force or pressure someone who refuses to attend. At first a child or even an adult may feel resistant. If the family member remains hesitant or fails to show up, you might say, "You are an important part of our family. I/we love and care about you. We need and would much value having you at this meeting. I'd like you to share with me any issues you have about attending. I will make it safe for you to talk about whatever is going on with you, which includes your anger and hurt feelings. I'd love to have you be there for our next Family Circle."

Format. You will add to everyone's focus by taking the phone off the hook so that you won't be disturbed. For some families what works best is a table where each person can pull up a chair; for others, sitting in a circle on the living room floor.

You need a leader to run the meeting and a secretary to record decisions made and future agendas. The chairperson does not dictate what is to be discussed, but instead provides a format for the meeting by soliciting topics for discussion and calling upon each person equally.

For your first few Family Circles, choose a parent, or a stepparent as chairperson. After that, rotate the jobs of secretary and chairperson every meeting or every month. Decide at each Family Circle who will be the chairperson and where, and at what time it will be held. The secretary makes sure each week he has a special notebook for the Stepfamily Journal and a pen to make a permanent record of the discussions held, activities planned, and chores assigned.

Atmosphere. Family members need to be able to share feelings, express their views, and make suggestions in an atmosphere of safety and acceptance, with no fear of begin made wrong, dismissed, or ridiculed. They need to know that their feelings will count regardless of age. Ask each child to express his or her feelings.

Adults must be careful not to dominate a Family Circle. Let the children voice concern, suggest ideas, and offer solutions first—don't jump in too quickly, or the kids will be turned off to the process. On the other hand, some types of decisions must be reserved for the parents. To take an obvious example, adults need to set limits on safety issues. When it comes to major decisions, the children need to hear from both the parent and stepparent. You can let them know that some issues will require further discussion between the parents before a final decision will be made. This will reinforce a stepparent's role as coparent, disciplinarian, and decision maker.

It will take time and many meetings for children to feel comfortable expressing themselves. At first kids may be silly, try to tease one another, interrupt, or be silent and withdrawn. However, once the children know you will give them undivided attention and listen carefully to their feelings and ideas, they will become active members. Be patient, but also firm. Make the process fun and something to look forward to, not a chore.

Facilitator. During the first few months of stepfamily life, or whenever you have a serious or highly charged family issue, your family may benefit from a trusted and valued friend facilitating the meeting, ensuring a safe environment to air feelings, and agreeing upon satisfying solutions. Perhaps you know a successful stepparent who could provide specific guidance or someone with special training in communications skills.

Agenda. A Family Circle is most effective when it has a structure that family members become familiar with. I recommend the following four steps as a broad outline for Family Circles.

Step one: appreciation (10–15 min.). Always start a Family Circle by sharing appreciation and acknowledging successes and thanks, so that each person feels safe, cared for, and positive. One good opener is to have each person share "One specific thing I appreciated about you this week . . . ," with no "buts"; pure acknowledgment. Focus more time on this step in particular during your first few meetings.

Step two: feedback (10–15 min.). You might wish to maintain a Family Feedback box between meetings to facilitate the process of giving feedback. Decorate a shoe box and keep a small notepad and a pencil with it. When a family member sees another doing something positive, that person writes a description of the behavior on a slip of paper, signs it, and places it in the Family Feedback box. It can also be used to record grievances for later discussion.

This is the time for grievances and resentments to be acknowledged, so it is important to encourage everyone to disclose their gripes, large or small. Gripes are not necessarily right or wrong. Resentment and grievances are always one person's way of seeing a situation. So they are always "right" from that person's point of view. The more confident family members become that expressing feelings will not result in ridicule, the more honest, open, and effective the meetings will become.

Sharing a grievance or resentment in an atmosphere of safety, care, and mutual respect in and of itself is healing.

Parents can play an important role by modeling how to gripe effectively and appropriately. Encourage gripes to be expressed as "I" statements rather than "you" statements. In other words, instead of saying "You are selfish," it is better to say "I feel let down."

"I" statements are also helpful because they are much more likely to be received constructively. For example, "I value a clean and orderly house. Last night the bathroom was left a mess—toothpaste on the sink, wet towels and clothes on the floor. Let's discuss how bathroom cleanup rules can be better maintained." Compare this to an accusation such as "Damn it, why do you have to be such a slob?" Take the time with your children to discuss the emotional impact of saying the same things two different ways.

Step three: problem solving (10–15 min.). Once you have reviewed the gripes, create solutions. Knowing how to identify a problem, asking for help, deciding what to do, being accountable, and keeping up morale are essential problem-solving skills. The adults shouldn't instantly dictate solutions but ask for suggestions. Next, consider various solutions until the stepfamily can agree upon the best one. Negotiate. Chose an alternative that each person can accept. Work to achieve consensus rather than a simple majority.

Finally, each person should write down what he/she has agreed to do. Who will do what? When will the matter be discussed again? How can the results be measured? Reevaluate the solutions at the next Family Circle to see how they are working and if they need to be modified. By having an opportunity to express their ideas, choices, and preferences, children are more likely to follow through with agreements and to accomplish their chores and school assignments.

Step four: fun and support (10–15 min.). End the meeting with positive and supportive comments. Each family member should leave the meeting with high self-esteem and a feeling of accomplishment. Everyone needs to feel good about what he or she is contributing to form a satisfying and secure new family unit.

Plan a fun activity after the meeting: a family bike ride, playing a board or card game, or everyone going out for a treat. Use step four to discuss and plan for future activities. When families brainstorm about activities, they often discover unexpected common interests.

Family Esteem Building:
Substituting "Build-Ups" for "Put-Downs"

Whenever you praise someone's positive behavior or attitude ("build-ups"), you strengthen that trait and provide incentive to repeat it. Whenever you humiliate, tease, or diminish ("put-downs"), you create animosity, withdrawal, and low self-esteem. Triangling tends to generate put-downs. An important de-triangling strategy is to neutralize the put-downs with build-ups.

Here is a "Build—Up" exercise to strengthen family bonds:

All the members sit or stand in a Family Circle. A parent or stepparent begins by turning to the person on his or her right saying "Something I value about you is . . ." For example, "Something I value is that you have a smile or hug for me whenever I let you know what's bothering me."

The receiver simply says, "Thank you." Make sure the family member receiving the praise accepts it. Don't allow him or her to deny or diminish the compliment or praise just received. No "Yes, but"; all the person receiving the acknowledgment should say is simply "Thank you."

Then the family member who has just received and acknowledged the appreciation turns to the family member on his or her right and does the same. Keep moving around the circle until everyone has given, received, and acknowledged a positive statement. Finish off with individual hugs and a large family group hug.

Words are powerful, and when ill-spoken, can hurt. When the expressions are "I value your feedback," "I love you no matter what," or "You are special to me," you promote family bonds. But in all families, people occasionally utter painful phrases. At a Family Circle, identify phrases that hurt and therefore generate destructive family communication. Ask the children to clarify phrases that they wish you wouldn't say, such as: "Stupid"; "Shut up"; "No! Because I said so"; "Lazy"; "Just who do you think you are?" Then identify the expressions your kids use that you find unacceptable, such as: "Everyone else gets to go but me"; "I'm telling"; "I hate (you, that food, that chore, etc.)"; "It's not fair." Make a list and vow to eliminate these destructive phrases. Check your progress at the next Family Circle.

When there are triangles, there are always lots of put-downs. Family Circles are a place to break the put-down habit. A good rule is to require two build-ups for each put-down delivered in the home.

Scapegoating

Some triangles blame one person for being the cause of the family's problems. This process is known as scapegoating, and typically involves a parent, stepparent, and troubled teenager. Scapegoating is usually a sign that a family needs professional help. Here is a helpful exercise if scapegoating has occurred.

Look beneath your attitudes. Think of the person whom you blame for family conflict. Identify your judgments (i.e., "always makes trouble"; "never listens"; "lazy"; "a liar") about this person. Write down these judgments on a piece of paper.

Now, reflect upon each of these judgments. Are words such as *always* or *never* really appropriate? Doesn't this person sometimes contribute or tell the truth? Are you limiting your perception of this person by using labels or making global statements that are only partly true?

Now, identify your feelings (e.g., anger, resentment, guilt, frustration, fear) about this person. Write them down. Then ask yourself what is behind these feelings. Are you angry because of what that person has done or how he or she may be constraining your life? Are you frustrated because you do not know how to help?

Now give yourself the opportunity to let go of your judgments and heal your hurt feelings. Try to separate your perceptions of this person's behavior from the reality of this person's being. Give yourself permission to see this person at his or her core as a loving, valuable, and valued person.

As you go through this process, pay attention to what you may be learning. Be patient and breathe deeply. A wide variety of emotions may come up as you recognize the deeper marital and personal stepfamily issues that require your attention.

Turning a Scapegoat into a "Star"

A scapegoat has learned to be a focus of the family's negative attention. That child can benefit from an exercise that can be life changing: "Turning a Scapegoat into a Star."

When a child feels good about him or herself, he or she is capable of being a "star"—a person of higher performance and achievement in all areas of life. A family scapegoat suffers from low self-esteem because he or she has internalized so much negative attention. Here is how to begin turning a scapegoat into a star.

A powerful esteem-building exercise is to turn on a video or audio and interview the new "star" in your family. Go ahead and ham it up so no one tries to be too serious. You might start with a fantasy question such as: "Make believe you have just discovered a magic lantern. If you rub it, a powerful genie will grant one wish for you and one wish for each other member of your family. What are your wishes?"

Choose a few more questions from the list below for this exclusive star interview:

- What qualities do you want to be admired for?
- When do you feel the happiest?
- What words and sentences best describe how you see yourself?
- What kind of work do you want to do when you grow up?
- Where would you like to live?
- If you could change one thing in the world what would it be?
- What accomplishments are you most proud of ?

Play the video or audio for the whole family. Use it for a Family Toast for the new star; note that a "roast," which uses biting sarcasm and teasing, is not appropriate. These tools are fun ways to substitute for negative attention. By treating your child like a star, you may be surprised to find him or her more radiant than expected.

"Stuck in the Middle"

In many stepfamilies, the parent gets stuck in the middle of a battle between the stepparent and children. Both sides may attempt to triangle with the parent against the "wicked stepparent" (i.e., the children's perspective) or the irresponsible and undisciplined child (i.e., the stepparent's views). The parent feels caught in a tug-of-war; torn in two trying to remain loyal to both mate and child. Maintaining a neutral stance can only last so long. Unless this triangling process becomes "encircled" with love and understanding, there is a danger of divorce and/or an alienated child.

Instead of feeling helplessly torn apart you can learn to become a "family peacemaker." This is a person who has developed the skills to facilitate constructive communication among family members; to help build bridges among warring parties. Family peacemaking is *not* a neurotic attempt to take responsibility for everyone else's behavior in an attempt to act as family savior (which eventually leads to failure and playing the martyr).

Facilitating a Peace Talk

The first rule as a facilitator is to remember that your goal is assisting people to solve their own problem, not for you to step in with a solution. You are facilitating, not taking sides or giving advice. The key is to establish a positive emotional atmosphere where everyone feels safety and trust. Stay relaxed; convey respect, neutrality, and warmth. An attitude of seriousness blended with enthusiasm will signal a peace talk is positive, important, and meaningful.

When you model patience and tolerance, each person will learn to be more accepting of the other's point of view. Each party should be acknowledged and supported equally for their contributions. There are many reasons why a facilitator might become more enthused over what one person shares than another. The response may be more on target, be more entertaining, be philosophically more in keeping with one's own point of view, and so on. However, both parties need to be given equal recognition not only for their verbal contributions but also for their listening skills.

Critical to being a peace facilitator is that you create an atmosphere in which the parties can hear criticism and negative feelings without becoming defensive, interrupting, or leaving. Your receptivity, fair-mindedness, and calm presence allow the appropriate and constructive sharing of pent-up feelings in an atmosphere of safety and trust. Be patient, let the feelings unfold. Underneath anger is hurt, and underneath the hurt is caring. The calm and safety you radiate supports a peaceful base for correcting problems in the relationship.

Here are the guidelines for a Peace Talk. Make individual photocopies of these instructions for each person and yourself. Everyone must read and fully discuss these principles beforehand. It is your role to make sure these points are agreed upon at the beginning and adhered to throughout:

Listen receptively: No one was born knowing how to listen effectively to others. It is a skill like many others that gets better as it is practiced. In a Peace Talk, the participants become keenly aware of the necessity to listen, and most people soon respond by expecting it of themselves and one another. Listening is the respectful focusing of attention on the speaker, without interruptions. It includes eye contact and open body posture.

When you conduct a Peace Talk, listen and encourage listening by (a) focusing your attention on the person who is speaking, (b) being receptive to what the speaker is saying (not mentally planning your next remark), and (c) recognizing the speaker when he or she finishes speaking, either verbally ("Thanks, Sam") or nonverbally (a nod and a smile). Reinforce the participants by letting them know you have noticed they were listening to one another and appreciate it.

Equal time to share: It is up to you to make sure both people share the time equally. Everyone is of equal importance. It is not uncommon to have one participant try to dominate. This person is usually unaware that by continuing to talk, he or she is taking time away from a person who is less assertive. If someone goes on and on, firmly intervene, but do so gently and respectfully.

No put-downs: Put-downs are undesirable in a Peace Talk because they destroy the atmosphere of safety and acceptance and disrupt the building of trust. The facilitator should try to prevent put-downs from occurring, and intervene when they do.

Do not interrupt: When faced with a spouse or stepchild's anger or criticism, you may feel tempted to interrupt, to deny or discount that point of view. In a Peace Talk, the correct response is to pause, breathe deeply, and simply say "Tell me more." This exercise cannot be hurried, and you shouldn't rush your spouse or stepchild to express his or her feelings. This exercise demands an open mind and heart.

Stay calm: Most people feel tense under criticism. As soon as you notice your pulse rising or your muscles tightening, breathe deeply a few times and consciously focus on relaxing your body. If you feel particularly upset, politely indicate that you need a break. Take a few minutes to regain your composure. If tears come, that's okay.

Empathize: One goal of this exercise is to encourage empathy; acknowledging and accepting what the other person feels. This does not mean you have to agree. Listening from the heart helps you transcend your personal boundaries to empathize with another person's frame of reference. The more understanding and open you are, the safer he or she will feel about disclosing intimate thoughts.

Acknowledge your "dark side": Simple, humble communications are essential. Own up to your mistakes, pettiness, and weaknesses. Feel free to acknowledge your own demons such as "It's true, I can be selfish and controlling." By acknowledging your own weaknesses, you give everyone permission to avoid having to appear perfect and to acknowledge their weaknesses as well.

As with the Heart Talk, choose a time when everyone is reasonably well rested and create an environment free from interruptions. Learning to facilitate a Peace Talk is one of the most useful and powerful tools for making peace in your stepfamily.

Feeling Excluded

Sometimes stepchildren who shuttle back and forth between two households feel like they belong to neither. Tom was a seventeen-year-old referred to me by his father for "horrible screaming matches" with his stepmother and two stepbrothers. Tom's father feared the conflicts were on the verge of breaking into family violence.

In my first session with Tom, it was clear that underneath his anger he felt deeply rejected and neglected. "I feel left out," he said with bitterness. "When I come on weekends I sleep on the couch or on a mattress in a stepbrother's room. I'm only here because this is the family my father married into. I'm not really wanted."

As part of sorting out many complex emotional and relationship issues, one exercise proved especially meaningful. I asked Tom's entire stepfamily to come to my office. I gave these instructions for the following "Family Break-In" exercise:

> I am going to give you a task to perform as a group to understand better how each of us has a need to belong and be accepted by others. One person will stand outside the family group and try to break in, while the others form a tight circle with their arms locked together to keep that individual out. The person outside the circle must try his or her best to break into the circle, but without physically hurting anyone. You must ensure everyone's safety, but don't be weak or lazy. The family group must try equally hard to keep that person out. Each of you will have a turn to be outside and will have three minutes to push, squeeze, bribe, sneak, climb, or plead your way into the Family Circle. If you do break in, or else when your three minutes are up, you will become part of the circle and another family member will step outside to try to break in. Each of you will have three minutes to be the outsider trying to break in.

The exercise was a mixture of laughter and yelling, pushing and pulling. After the exercise, I posed a number of questions for discussion:

- How did it feel to be excluded, left out, and rejected from the family?

- Why is it so important to feel included?
- If you feel outside the group, what are some positive ways to gain entry and full membership without having to force or break your way in?
- How did it feel to be part of the group keeping someone out?
- What did you learn from this experience about belonging and acceptance in this family?
- What does each person need to do to feel part of this family?
- What can you do to help everyone feel like they have a place in the circle and are a part of the team?

This exercise was a breakthrough. Tom got permission and encouragement to express feelings of being left out. During the discussion, he had an opportunity to share painful feelings common to visiting stepchildren. Tom's Dad tearfully shared that while the divorce was a necessary but painful end to a difficult marriage, he was miserable about being so often separated from his son. Tom felt deep-seated jealousy of his stepbrothers who both got to live with his father, whom he often missed, while he could not. Tom felt he had to compete for his father's attention during the little time he had with him, and so felt like an intruder.

Neither Tom's Dad nor his stepbrothers had been aware of Tom's feelings because he felt embarrassed to express them. The result was a triangle by default with Tom feeling left out, rejected, and excluded.

Tom also needed to vent gripes that bothered him and contributed to the tension of his weekend visits. I suggested a Family Circle. Tom's biggest gripes focused on a lack of his own space in his father's home. Tom complained about not having any privacy, no place to keep his own toothbrush, never knowing whether he would bunk on the couch or with his stepbrothers, and similar issues. Everyone agreed that Tom needed his own space. The family elected to put a lock on the door of his father's home office and buy a new convertible sofa bed. Tom set up an area for his own records and tapes and put up a few pieces of his artwork. A visiting child needs at the very least a bed of his own, a closet for his clothes, and a cabinet for his hobbies and toys.

Several months later, I saw Tom again. He shared, with a smile, that he no longer felt left out. The family had begun holding a Family Circle every Saturday morning so Tom could participate. These discussions proved enormously valuable in encouraging Tom's feelings of participation and acceptance as an equal. He had a forum to deal with all the questions about living together. He felt good about being able to choose the chores he would do. "I hated having to cut the grass that my stepbrothers played catch on with my father when I was gone," Tom explained. "Everyone really understood how I felt. I really feel different now that they listen to me. It's great!"

Stepsibling Rivalry

A degree of rivalry among siblings is normal in every family because they compete for their parent's time, love, and recognition. Stepsibling rivalry can be even more intense and certainly more complicated. When parents remarry, children frequently find themselves inheriting a whole new set of brothers and sisters. The competition is not only for parental attention, but for bedrooms, clothes, toys, and even the places they sit at the dinner table. Stepsibling conflicts can threaten the stability of the remarriage or cause two separate and competing minifamilies. How a parent and stepparent manage stepsibling rivalry in the early stages of the remarriage can make a significant difference in the degree of peace within the stepfamily.

Here are some suggestions for both parent and stepparent to consider in assisting stepsiblings to adapt to a new stepfamily:

- No one likes to be pushed, least of all stepsiblings who find themselves in the same household, not by choice but because their respective parents chose to get married. Therefore, don't expect the kids to love one another and don't insist they do things together. Rather, give them a chance to develop a relationship on their own terms.
- The children will be going through more stress at a time when you and your mate want to rejoice in your union. Don't expect to instantly become one big happy family.
- Some measure of privacy is critical. In many instances, the remarriage means the stepchildren lose privacy, as they move into crowded quarters. Make certain that each child has some area of the house that cannot be violated.

- Make certain to spend one-on-one time with each child, and let your own child know that your love and commitment to him or her is unshakable.
- Remember, in the early stage of stepfamily life, only the natural parent should be the disciplinarian.
- Avoid competing with your mate's ex-spouse. You can never replace a same-sex parent, and should not even try.
- Encourage the children to reconcile their own differences. Adopt regular Family Circles so that the children have a forum to air their gripes and work out their differences.
- Respect each child as unique. Don't get caught up in comparisons or taking sides.
- Be kind and open. Let your children, all of them, know you are always available for a Heart Talk.
- Maintain faith that this too shall pass. Accept, don't resist, the negative feelings. Keep a positive vision that this new family can work it out with patience and care.

A House Divided

Biological bonds frequently create divided loyalties and conflicted stepfamily triangles. In some cases, they can lead to a house inhabited by warring camps.

The Clark stepfamily consisted of two separate camps, frozen in silent hostilities. Peter and Maxine had been married three months earlier. Maxine's thirteen-year-old daughter, Moira, from a previous marriage and Peter's eight-year-old and six-year-old sons, Jay and Ken, were living with them full-time.

The problem, as Peter and Maxine saw it, was that they lived in a house of strangers, and that Moira and Jay did not want to become part of a whole, new family. The children came along for the initial interview but were rather sullen and morose. They resisted my efforts to involve them in the discussion, until I asked each family member to draw a picture of the way he or she experienced the family problem. Peter drew himself in his den with his sons watching television, while his wife and stepdaughter were close together cooking and whispering in the kitchen. Asked why there seemed to be no communication between the den and the kitchen, Peter explained that he and his sons enjoyed watching television together, while his wife and stepdaughter didn't. Peter's pictures immediately showed what neither parent had alluded to during the initial interview, triangles dominated by the parents taking sides with their respective offspring.

Maxine's drawing was equally revealing. She depicted herself and her daughter out shopping, while her husband and his two sons played cards at home. "My daughter is older," Maxine explained. "We enjoy each other's company."

Ironically, the children's drawings revealed a much greater desire to bridge the chasm between the two halves of the family. Moira drew herself walking back and forth between the kitchen and the den. "I'd like it if we could be more of a family," Moira explained. Jay, the older boy, drew himself and his brother, Ken, outside, playing catch with his father, while his stepmother and stepsister were in the car. "My step-mom and stepsister are always so busy," he added, "I hardly see them."

What Shape Is Your Family In?

Psychotherapy depends far too often on one modality alone for exploration and discovery—verbal expression. This is particularly unfortunate when it comes to resolving stepfamily triangles because words alone, through sheer repetition, often conceal the underlying conflict through stereotyped descriptions. The scripts, labels, and familiar accusations become almost predictable to the warring participants.

To discover what "shape" your family is in, drawing is a wonderful medium because it transcends language, introducing the element of the creative and unpredictable. The dominant, verbally well-defended intellect is by-passed for the more intuitive, heartful understanding. Children are often more likely to reveal their unspoken fears and desires thorough family drawings because they are naturally more imaginative and playful. A child can often express his or her feelings in pictures more easily than using words.

The family drawings and subsequent discussions surprised Peter and Maxine. Instead of blaming the division in their household on their respective children's inability to get along, they had to confront how their own attitudes were contributing to the rift. Through further discussions, they began coming to terms with their own disappointments in their remarriage. After a whirlwind romance, the realities of their remarriage were a let-down for them both. Financial pressures, a crowded home, children uncomfortable with one another, arguments at the dinner table, and a growing fear that their marriage would not live up to initial expectation—all these factors contributed to Peter and Maxine separately seeking solace in bonding with their respective children.

The first step in encircling these triangles was for Peter and Maxine to strengthen their remarriage by taking off for a needed weekend alone where they could heal the rift that had developed between them. When they returned, refreshed and with renewed commitment, they were ready to better deal with the children.

Exploring Family Feelings

I recommended that Peter and Maxine experiment with an exercise to help each family member explore feelings of belonging to the new family unit. Here are the instructions for the "Exploring Family Feelings" exercise:

Form a circle sitting on the living room floor. Take a few minutes to be silent to experience how you feel with the members of your stepfamily. Do you find the circle restricting? Do you feel somewhat hemmed in at the sides? Do you feel like you want to fall back or get up? Does the circle make you feel warm and secure or agitated and unhappy?

Look around at each person in the circle, and don't dart your eyes away. Notice the feelings that arise toward each person; don't resist.

Now look at the configuration of this circle. Are all the spaces in the circle equal or are there "holes"? Are all the family members equidistant or are some people closer while others are more distant? Is someone far outside the circle or half in, half out? Who appears to be aligned with whom?

Now, experiment with your circle. Hold hands for two minutes. What feelings does that generate? Change places with another family member. Do you feel uneasy in your new spot? Observe how the family looks different from this new angle, how it may require time to adjust to how the family now looks and feels. How do you feel about the person now occupying your previous space? Notice if you are less secure, more uncomfortable than in the previous position you had in the circle. After a few minutes, ask if someone else would change places with you. If you've had enough time to settle in, you may feel reluctant to switch. Do you still long for your old familiar spot, the seat you occupied in the circle at the beginning? Or are your enjoying changing places with other people? Do you feel confined or comfortable?

Now, experiment with changing the size of your circle. Huddle in close together with your arms around one another's shoulders, forming the smallest possible diameter for your circle. Note how you feel. Now stretch to form the largest possible diameter circle so that you can barely reach one another's fingers or toes. Compare how distance feels versus closeness. Some people in a family need space and get claustrophobic when they feel too crowded. Others may want such closeness and proximity that they would hug, squeeze, and pull to make the circle as small and intimate as possible.

Finally, break up the circle and ask each family member to go to a separate corner of the room up against the wall. From this distance take one another in. Do you have a feeling of relief or loss? Do you feel more happy or alone?

Now, sit down together as a Family Circle and share with the group how you felt during the various phases of the exercise. Each person should have an equal turn to share. You may skip your turn if you wish, but everyone is enthusiastically encouraged to share. And everyone stays in the circle in your own space until the sharing is completed.

There are no "right" responses. Feelings of love, discomfort, closeness, distance, anxiety, embarrassment, relief, and joy are all normal. Each person has a different need and tolerance for intimacy, and that's okay. The key is to accept each person's feelings unconditionally, without judgment. Close with sincere thanks to everyone for being part of the circle and sharing. End by sharing a warm hug.

Sex in the Stepfamily

Sex is a potent energy in a nuclear family but even more so in the stepfamily. Sigmund Freud focused on the Oedipal complex in which a son desires to get rid of the father so he can have the mother's love to himself. The Oedipal triangle has heightened impact in the stepfamily, as a son must deal with guilt about his parents' divorce and an unrelated man sexually bonding with his mother. So does the Phaedra triangle in which a stepdaughter sexually titillates her stepfather. The modern version of the latter myth is the novel *Lolita,* in which a nymphet stepdaughter seduces her stepfather.

The newly remarried couple may be so openly affectionate and sexually attracted to each other as to be arousing to or create jealousy with the children. Teenage stepsiblings, who have not grown up together but suddenly live under one roof, may develop strong sexual feelings for each other, perhaps masked by conflict and quarreling. A stepfather and stepdaughter may be attracted to each other and behave in seductive ways. A new husband may be jealous of the close relationship a mother has with her son, whom she may have relied upon during single parenthood as Mom's "little man." Sexual feelings and jealousies can be particularly problematic because the stepfamily has a weakened incest taboo. Instinctual biological inhibitions must be replaced with knowledge and self-restraint.

Love and tenderness should not be confused with sexual feelings. Stepchildren need to see a loving, caring relationship between their parent and stepparent. It is almost inevitable that the sexual feelings between stepparent and stepchild or between stepsiblings may stir competition and discomfort. When sexuality is suppressed it can lead to hostility, depression, or impulsive acting out.

Sexual feelings in the stepfamily must be understood and managed so they lead neither to guilt about natural feelings nor acting out. Sexual feelings in the stepfamily are widely misunderstood. Parents and stepparents have been reluctant to discuss sexual feelings toward a child or teenager for fear of appearing perverted, crazy, or sick. It is crucial to recognize the difference between fantasy and action. Sexual feelings between stepchildren and stepparents occur frequently. Mature acceptance of these emotions but without any acting out is essential for healthy stepfamily bonding. With open communication and appropriate rules, the sexual storm of adolescence will pass. Love and true tenderness need not be feared; they will prevail.

Sexual feelings toward a stepchild are normal; overt sexual behavior with a stepchild, such as prolonged kissing or even caressing, is tremendously harmful. The fact that sexual activity between stepparent and stepchild may not, technically speaking, be incest, is no excuse. If this type of activity occurs, consultation with a mental health professional should be immediately sought.

The Woody Allen case brought the issue of sexual attraction between stepparents and stepchildren into public focus with a new slant. What if a mother or father has a long-term relationship with another adult who never becomes a stepfather or stepmother in the legal sense? Is sexual acting out appropriate between such a long-term family friend and one of the children who may have reached age eighteen? My answer is an unqualified no.

In the new extended family, where adults may play a quasi-parental role without entering into the legal contract of marriage, the traditional incest taboo requires a broader interpretation and deeper understanding. Contrary to popular belief, the real damage from incest is not primarily genetic abnormalities, but psychological damage to family members and sociological damage to the family unit.

As such, any man who has sexual relations with a mother and her daughter, even if the daughter is over eighteen, is likely to cause emotional damage to the mother, the daughter, and other children in the family, as well as damage to the family as a cohesive unit. This damage is likely to be severe and lasting. As such, the technical legal status of the man as a stepfather or simply a family friend is irrelevant. The incest taboo is appropriate to restrain the normal and powerful sexual attraction that may occur between the mother's lover and the mother's daughter.

What parents, stepparent, and even family friends must understand is that sexual feelings toward teenagers in one's own family are not pathological. These feelings are to be expected. New stepparents are often surprised and sometimes horrified to notice they have sexual feelings toward a stepchild. Feeling guilty is not the answer. Rather, the issue is how to control these feelings, avoid acting out, and yet allow the growth of a warm personal relationship. This process requires self-discipline and open communication. Above all, the stepparent or family friend should avoid any flirtatious behavior or situations that are unduly intimate or provocative, even with teenagers who have reached the age of sexual consent. Also, any tendency toward acting out should be addressed immediately. Unconscious collusion or conspiracy of silence in the stepfamily only makes matters worse.

The parent and stepparent need to support each other's sexual feelings and be open to resolving conflict. The remarried couple must have clear, open communication and maintain their own intimate, sexual bond. Talking about sexual feelings toward a stepchild may be difficult, but a Heart Talk with your mate about such a delicate matter is sometimes essential. If you suspect a problem, better to risk talking about it rather than allowing it to fester.

The discussion below is meant to provide some helpful insight into how to deal with sexual attractions in the stepfamily. Where sexual tension persists and sexual triangles become resistant to encircling, professional help should be sought promptly. The following is a brief look at the emotional dynamics at work in the most common stepfamily sexual triangles:

Father-daughter-stepmother triangle: Dwight and his second wife, Melinda, came for help because his fifteen-year-old daughter, Michaela, had become angry and depressed since his remarriage. "She only cheers up when I take her out alone," Dwight reported. "She refuses to be part of the family."

The elevation of an opposite-sex child to the level of partner is common in single-parent households. After Dwight's wife abandoned him and his daughter, Michaela took on much of the mother and wife role. She did the cooking, helped with shopping, and mothered her younger siblings. She also became her father's friend and confidant.

When Dwight remarried, Michaela responded like a jilted second wife. She was so jealous and resentful of her stepmother, it was almost as if Michaela had been recently divorced. "My new wife and my daughter were each constantly testing me to see who I love more," lamented Dwight. "If I agreed with either one, then I was rejecting the other." They became two women competing to be the center of Dwight's affection.

Encircling this triangle: Michaela needed support in mourning her displaced position in her family. She felt reassured to know that jealous, protective feelings toward her father and "the kids" are understandable and normal. With short-term counseling, she was able to accept her loss and focus on beginning a new exciting chapter of her life. She finally had time to date and got assistance from her dad and her stepmother, who was a physician, to enter an advanced science program for high school students.

Stepson-stepmother-father triangle: Deidre and her stepson Duncan came to see me because they started having screaming matches when he entered adolescence. The arguments had become so violent that his father was threatening to send him to live with his other parent.

Encircling this triangle: Duncan was handsome and well-built; he looked like a movie star. In an individual session, his stepmother Deidre revealed feeling guilty and ashamed about sexual feelings she was having toward Duncan, particularly a couple of times when he would come stark naked out of the shower to ask Deidre for a towel.

"I felt very embarrassed the first time he did it," explained Deidre. "But I was too shocked to say anything. So two weeks later, he did it again. I told him he should be more modest. He tried to blame me about the lack of clean towels."

Often, hostilities between a stepparent and adolescent stepchild of the opposite sex are barely veiled love fights. Bitter quarreling and screaming are a means for both stepparent and stepchild to protect against sexual titilation, rivalries, and frustration.

I advised Deidre to decompose this triangle through a family meeting. She raised the issue of bathroom modesty, and found support from her stepdaughters in suggesting that robes be required as a family rule. In this way, she defused the inappropriate behavior without making Duncan feel guilty. He got the message and soon became careful to put on his robe and be less seductive and provocative with his stepmother. Deidre and Duncan both felt relieved to acknowledge their fantasies and fears. Their arguments markedly diminished in intensity.

Stepsibling triangle: When two previously single parents marry, children find themselves surrounded by a whole new set of housemates. These stepsiblings are more like friends than brothers or sisters. Growing up with a stepsibling of the opposite sex in close proximity can be very sexually stimulating. For example, the eleven-year-old boy with stirrings of sexual feelings may want to play "doctor" frequently with his ten-year-old stepsister.

Encircling this triangle: If a biologically unrelated stepbrother and stepsister have a "crush" on each other, talk with them openly. Explain that flirtatious desires and sexual curiosity are natural feelings, but they are not to be acted upon. Parents need to assert that they are not willing to accept a sexual relationship between stepsiblings, particularly while they are underage and living in your house.

Rearrange the living space so that the stepsiblings are at opposite ends of the hall and if possible, not sharing the same bathroom. While you cannot exercise complete control over the sexual behavior of stepsiblings or any adolescent, you can and must set firm limits about what happens in your home. Sometimes a biologically unrelated stepbrother and stepsister do continue their close relationship after they leave home and later marry each other, but the relationship should be discouraged until the children are well into mature adulthood.

Stepfather-stepdaughter-mother triangle: A stepfather may distance himself from his stepdaughter because he is frightened of his own feelings of sexual attraction. In an effort to deal with guilt over incestuous fantasies and protect his family, many stepdads pull back from their adolescent stepdaughters. In an attempt to shut off his feelings toward her, he may begin to quarrel with this teenager about everything. Not understanding the reason behind the distance and hostility, a stepdaughter may begin to feel unlovable and undesirable. At a crucial time of self-esteem and identity formation, the young adolescent woman may feel unknowingly guilty or rejected. Also, the mother may become competitive with her teenage "beauty" for her husband's attention.

Encircling this triangle: Unexamined fears and fantasies can produce guilt, shame and worry. Sometimes there is a fear of talking about these feelings because people fear they are abnormal. They are not. Strong feelings that are denied can lead a stepfamily to become more disturbed and eventually fail. Intimate feelings that can be shared and defused can bring a family closer. Again, an effective strategy to defuse the triangle is a Heart Talk with the brother, stepfather, and stepdaughter all present. In that safe context, the stepfather can compliment his stepdaughter without being flirtatious or seductive. Just by making these feelings public, they became less threatening. Appropriate loving affection supplants secret fantasy and fear.

Stepfather-stepdaughter-mother triangle (variation 2): Most inappropriate sexual incidents in the stepfamily take place between a stepfather and stepdaughter. While sexual feelings toward stepdaughters are normal, some stepdads fail to deal with their feelings of attraction in a healthy way. Frank, for instance, would give his eighteen-year-old stepdaughter, Maggie, extra long kisses on the lips. Maggie felt uncomfortable, but wasn't sure what to do or say. Then Frank began to "accidentally" brush up against her breasts, and when her mother wasn't around, squeeze her buttocks and make other seductive overtures.

Encircling this triangle: This is sexual abuse. The incidence of a stepfather sexually molesting a stepdaughter is significant. Stepfamilies must confront this potentially volatile and explosive issue early on; an ounce of prevention is worth ten pounds of cure. Therefore, it is advisable to have honest discussions about privacy and propriety early in the formation of a stepfamily. Ground rules need to be established about modesty and restraint. Teenagers should be discouraged from provocative behavior such as parading around in a towel or underwear. Even if a teen disregards these rules, there is no excuse for a stepfather to behave seductively toward his stepdaughter. Again, if that should happen, seek professional help immediately.

Please note that the stepfamily is generally not a sick or disturbed place. With all the sensationalistic publicity given to sexual abuse in the family, fears of incest can inhibit the natural, appropriate physical expression of love and affection. "My stepdaughter and I share a warm hug together every day," said one stepfather, "but I'm feeling self-conscious and inhibited, fearful of what other people might think." At a time when a young person may need a hug the most, a parent or stepparent withdraws affection for fear of being thought of as sexually abusive. Holding a child may be a means to help him or her feel safe and connected. Many stepfamilies are being unnecessarily inhibited from healthy affection and appropriate intimacy by the publicized pathology and emotional disorder within some families.

Family Guardian

You have the capacity to maintain inner peace even in the face of major family problems and personal challenges. For some people, this idea may seem revolutionary because it directly contradicts the long-standing belief that problems must inevitably make you miserable.

You can be the "peaceful warrior" or "family guardian."

Try this experiment with your family today. No matter what problems may come up, smile and say only positive things. Stay receptive and kind, even if you have to work hard at it. Your spouse may yell, your daughter may throw a temper tantrum, your stepson may pout, but you will take up the challenge of sustaining your inner peace. Hang in there. With regular practice at keeping calm, you will increasingly feel as you behave.

Whatever the conflict that arises in your family, seek to be patient, tolerant, and kind. When a stepfamily member frustrates you, stay cool and embrace the lessons of the heart you need to learn. Every family, including your stepfamily, harbors varying degrees of dysfunction. Each person in the stepfamily is taking the necessary steps to become part of a circle of people who love and support one another. Your inner peace can be the center and source for an ever-widening circle of love. Take up the challenge of being the source of peace in your stepfamily.

Nurturing the Spirit of Family

Take the time to meditate, pray, or just "be" as a family. A family meal together at the end of the day is a time to eat in peace and harmony and in the comforting support of the family. A good rule for cultivating peace in your stepfamily is no negatives, complaints, or criticisms during dinner; wait until a Family Circle to handle such grievances. Attendance at the family dinner ought to be expected—a time for positivity and emotional nurturance. Take a few moments when you first all sit down together to join hands in prayer or silent grace.

An antidote to the often conflicting emotions of stepfamily life is regularly finding peace within. The Transcendental Meditation program is a well-researched, reliable means of reducing stress and increasing ease, order, and satisfaction. Meditation allows irritability and frustration to dissolve in inner quiet instead of exploding upon family members. Moreover, inner peace will allow harmony and love to blossom in your stepfamily.

Chapter 7

MONEY MATTERS; LOVE MATTERS MORE

*M*ax is an engineer, and his second wife, Anne, is a publicist. They live in a large four-bedroom, three-bath house with her two children. Max's son and daughter live with his ex-wife, Cynthia, in the home he deeded to her when they divorced. His children visit every other weekend. When Max and Anne sought my help, she bitterly resented how much alimony and child support Max paid to Cynthia, particularly because Cynthia never worked. Max was angry that Anne's former husband paid child support irregularly, at best, while he sacrificed to meet his obligations to his children and to his stepchildren. Anne tried to force her ex-husband to comply with his child support obligations by withholding visitations, but that only seemed to upset her children. Despite their family income of over

$150,000 per year, Max and Anne found their stepfamily in turmoil because every financial decision became an argument.

Most stepfamilies in turmoil cite money as a major cause of conflict. In many stepfamilies, the problems arise out of frustration with a lowered standard of living following divorce and remarriage. A stepfather who pays 50 percent of his income to support his ex-spouse and children may suffer enormous strain in trying to support his new family. Even with his new wife's paycheck, there may not appear to be enough money to go around. A crisis erupts whenever his ex-wife calls about an unexpected bill such as orthodontics for his daughter. He suddenly seems to face an irreconcilable choice between providing for his daughter's needs and providing for the needs of his new family.

The financial tie between ex-spouses also tends to fuel chronic conflict. "I resent the power he still has over us," said one woman of her ex-husband. "He controls our lives through his support check." Of course, the husband's new wife is likely to perceive that same support check not as a draconian exercise of power, but rather as an expression of divided loyalty, particularly if she and her husband have a child of their own. To induce guilt or extract retribution, some ex-spouses send their children to visit dressed in tattered clothes or otherwise coached to remind a parent that they need more financial support.

Even an act of generosity can fuel conflict as some stepfamily members get more than others. When both remarrieds bring children to the new marriage, grandparents sometimes send gifts to their grandchildren and not to their step-grandchildren. When one set of grandparents sends more expensive gifts than the other set, jealousy among stepchildren can boil over into fighting to get even. A parent who only sees his children during weekends or during vacations can spark the same conflict by sending his children home with extravagant gifts or tales of weekends filled with nonstop entertainment that his wife and second husband may not be able to afford.

This chapter examines the emotional dynamics of stepfamily conflicts about money, and presents a series of peacemaking strategies to help resolve them.

"It's Not Fair"

Everyone wants to be treated fairly, particularly when it comes to money. We all want to be paid fairly for our work. During an evaluation, we want a fair review of performance. Even young children soon learn the meaning of fair. Each of us seems to have an inner standard of what we believe is fair, and we strongly object to a violation of this standard.

Achieving a fair property support and custody settlement is the paramount issue in divorce. A lawyer once told me that in divorce there is one big question, "Who gets what?" A divorce becomes a battleground when spouses differ radically on their perception of what constitutes a fair settlement. A husband may feel that an award of 50 to 60 percent of his income to support his ex-wife and children is completely unfair, while his ex-spouse may feel it barely meets her needs.

Financial conflicts between sexes and within stepfamilies highlight a basic psychological problem with the word "fair." On the one hand, most people believe their personal standard of fairness has a certain universal application. The word "fair" takes on an absolute quality, as if the word describes a discernible, absolute measure. On the other hand, each person applies his or her sense of fairness from his or her own perspective, and few people seem to appreciate how their limited perspective shades their application of this standard.

If consensus on a fair settlement is difficult in divorce, maintaining consensus about what's fair in a stepfamily is a herculean, if not impossible, task. The culprit is the inevitability of change. Divorcing couples reach a settlement based on their shared past and certain expectations about the future. On the basis of these expectations, they make plans and assume responsibilities. In most cases, however, the future does not turn out as expected.

When Harris left Betsy, he agreed to provide enough support to keep his two sons in private school. A successful real-estate developer, Harris initially had little trouble meeting his commitment. Two years after his divorce, he met and married June, an estate-planning lawyer. Harris explained his obligations to Betsy and his children, and they thought their financial commitments would not prohibit them from starting a new family. Then, the real-estate depression hit, and Harris's business failed. Betsy was bitter about the divorce and showed little understanding of Harris's situation. Within eighteen months of her marriage, June found herself financing private school for Harris's children and unable to start a family of her own. Harris asked Betsy to try to get by on less so that his sons could stay in private school. Betsy accused him of financial mismanagement. All Harris could say at the end of his story was "It's not fair."

Rickie left Fraser and her two children, a son and a daughter, because she felt compelled to pursue a career as a photographer. Fraser's career progressed steadily as a college professor, but his remarriage and the birth of a son created a significant financial strain. Seven years after her divorce, Rickie's career took off. She married a writer and supported their new family. During the previous seven years, Rickie provided little financial support for her children, although she saw them regularly. Faced with the stress of his new family, Fraser asked Rickie to start supporting her son and daughter. "I've struggled for seven years to make it," Rickie retorted. "I've lived like a pauper. You've got a secure future, tenure, no worries. I want another child of my own, too. It's not fair to come to me now."

In most stepfamilies, just as in those above, there is no easy answer to what is fair from a financial point of view. What you can count on is plenty of people making demands on limited resources for very good reasons. Aside from mortgages, car payments, insurance, and taxes, money must be found for the children's food, clothes, travel, school, dental work, summer camp, and endless special requests. The three words, *it's not fair*, don't seem to be helpful in resolving stepfamily financial conflict. To the contrary, holding on to such a complaint seems to do more harm than good. Making peace with stepfamily financial conflicts requires something more.

The Emotional Cost of Financial Conflict

Forming a new family following the financial conflict (and often devastation) of divorce can be a terrifying step. As long as you or your spouse each worry principally about your own well being and that of your own children, financial conflict is likely to remain a chronic part of your lives. A we/they attitude is inevitable, and both camps in the stepfamily are likely to look at each financial decision in terms of how much do we get versus how much do they get. The alternative to we/they thinking is to embrace the commitment to your stepfamily.

I recommend having a series of financial Heart Talks along the lines described later in this chapter. Then you may want to consult a financial planner so you can make intelligent decisions from an informed perspective. Once you have made an informed commitment to support your whole stepfamily, everyone is likely to feel more safety and trust when money issues arise. When finances become tight, family members are guided by the question "What's best for the family," rather than simply "What's best for me?" As a result, a financial difficulty serves to draw family members together to find solutions, rather than to drive them apart in a competition with one another. Nurturing these values of mutual caring is what becoming a family is all about.

Finding the Wisdom of Solomon

Patrick, thirty-six, is the owner of a service station and father of a daughter, Leslie. His second wife, Dinah, is thirty-four and a mother of two sons, Gary and Danny. They came for help because Patrick had arranged for Leslie to have $4,000 of dental work. Dinah was deeply upset because Patrick had declined to pay for his stepson Gary to have orthodontia.

"Don't you see how much Gary will be hurt when he sees Leslie with braces?" Dinah asked Patrick. "This is going to be terrible for the family."

"Boys don't need straight teeth the way girls do," Patrick replied. "Heck, the boy might lose a tooth playing football. Anyway, we can't afford it, and you know it."

Dinah's proposal was for Patrick to take out a loan on his business. Patrick believed that would be terribly foolish, given recent difficult economic times. They sat in my office, neither willing to compromise. They did agree to keep talking about the problem for a few more sessions before Leslie got her braces.

In our next several sessions, we talked about the many reasons why Solomon's dilemma was simple compared to the dilemmas regularly faced by parents in stepfamilies. Solomon had a simple solution to discover the mother of the disputed child. Rarely is there a simple solution when the issue involves financial equality among children and stepchildren.

In their discussions with me, Patrick and Dinah discovered for themselves the compelling issues involved in the conflict. Most parents and stepparents recognize it is best to treat children within the stepfamily as equally as possible. Patrick recognized that Gary might be hurt seeing Leslie's braces, and he did not want Gary hurt. But the reality is that parents in stepfamilies favor their biological children. "We can only afford braces right now for one child. Leslie is that child," Patrick stated flatly. Dinah understood Patrick's feelings when I asked her who would get the braces if she made the decision alone and only had enough money for one child.

The more we talked, the more Patrick and Dinah began to see that equal opportunity for all the children is a goal rarely achieved in any family, nuclear or step-. I disclosed that I was the only child in my family to go to college. My parents and my older sister sacrificed because I had the ability, and my parents wanted one of their children to get a college degree. Strict financial equality among children is a standard that parents and stepparents too often hold up as a weapon rather than a goal.

I explained to Patrick and Dinah that they needed to expand the realm of resources available to their children. Money was one resource. Parental time, attention and support was another resource. When imbalance occurs among the children from a financial standpoint, parents can restore balance by providing a greater degree of emotional support to the other children.

For this strategy to work, two prerequisites are essential. First, you have to teach your children that their real opportunity lies primarily within themselves, in their own potential, not in what others seek for them. By encouraging this self-reliance, you direct your child on an inward search to discover what he or she is really passionate about doing. Second, you must avoid allowing your children to measure your love by how much money you spend. The real measure of love is time, commitment, and caring.

Some parents find it useful to be meticulous about equality as to the smaller issues so that the children more easily accept the other considerations at work in the big issues. Whether you're a parent or stepparent, the economic challenge of raising your children in a stepfamily requires that you achieve greater wisdom than Solomon. By finding support in your spouse and sharing that love with your children, you can find the wisdom you need.

Safety in Truth

While honesty is important to every relationship, it is essential to the survival of a stepfamily. Only through honesty and the commitment to work through conflicts can all members of a stepfamily develop an abiding trust. Given the many conflicting loyalties and emotional pressures among stepfamily members, a small lie may seem to be a safe and expedient way to make peace. In the long run, such a strategy is doomed to failure because it reflects an underlying fear of confronting and resolving difficult emotional and financial issues. The only safety lies in the truth.

Alan had two sons and Harriet had two daughters when they married. Alan's boys lived with their mother, and Alan paid $2,000 a month in child support. Harriet thought that amount was excessive, particularly because she hoped to have another child with Alan. They had disclosed their finances to each other when they got married, and they were unsure about whether they could support another child. Six months after their marriage, Harriet mistakenly opened a statement from a bank. The statement showed that just prior to their marriage, Alan set up a $40,000 trust fund for each of his sons and had not told Harriet. The loss of trust was great enough to result in their coming in for help.

The tragedy of this lie is that it was unnecessary. No matter how tempted you may be to rely on an expedient fib, I encourage you to reconsider and trust your spouse, your ex, and your children to work with the truth.

For Richer or Poorer

When a couple marries, they usually take vows to support each other in good times and bad. In most marriages, this vow gets tested by the adversities that inevitably arise in most people's lives. If your spouse has children, then this vow may involve a much larger commitment than you anticipate. A stepparent wedding vow also includes a duty to support the stepchildren.

This duty is not so much legal as moral. Custody, property, and support settlements provide that legal obligations of support remain with the biological parents. But life is unpredictable, and biological parents often fail to meet their economic obligations. The stepparent cannot just stand aside if the remarriage is to survive. Morally and emotionally, it is almost impossible to make a lifetime commitment to love and support your new spouse without accepting the obligation to help your spouse support his or her children. To do otherwise is to attempt to compartmentalize your love.

Tempering Power with Heart

In the commercial world, money is often used as an instrument of power. One way to get people to comply with your wishes is to pay them or withhold payment. In the stepfamily, money is also sometimes used as an instrument of power, usually with disastrous results.

"Look what I do for you and your kids," one of my stepfather clients blurted to his wife in my office. "I'm paying for more than my share so I should get to call the shots on the big issues. You've got an allowance for household expenses!"

This stepfather had a very successful heating and air-conditioning business. His first wife had died, and he remarried, creating a stepfamily with his two sons and his new wife's son and daughter. His new wife received little support from her ex-spouse. Even though the stepfamily was comfortable, financial conflict was a constant burden.

Significant differences in earning power are common between spouses in stepfamilies. The spouse with the greater earning power will be tempted by the commercial version of the golden rule, "He who has the gold makes the rules." The result is resentment, guilt, mistrust, and low self-esteem. When I pointed this out to the stepfather, he was embarrassed because he had not noticed how he had been applying the rules of commerce to stepfamily finances.

Although money is an instrument of power, you would be well served to avoid using it as such with your stepfamily. The golden rule to apply in your stepfamily is the good old-fashioned "Do unto others as you would have others do unto you." Before telling your spouse "Look what I do for you," ask yourself how you would feel if your spouse said that to you. I am not suggesting that you give in to every financial whim or that you suppress either your own feelings or good judgment. Rather, I am suggesting that money should be looked upon within the stepfamily as a scarce resource to be well managed for the interests of everyone in the stepfamily. This task is not easy, but you will be far more effective by using approaches that cause the stepfamily to pull together and share sacrifices as well as prosperity.

Becoming True Partners with Your Spouse

What distinguishes a true partnership is a mutual commitment to share financial success or failure, as the fates may dictate. Partners work out in advance how that sharing will take place—who will constitute what to the venture and how the profits or losses will be divided. Partners also make sure they can trust each other; they talk through plans and procedures so no one acts unilaterally, particularly on big issues. Partners also share information freely so that each is as informed and prepared as possible to help the partnership. Keeping one's word is another trait of true partners. They rely on each other without reservation.

Given the complicated financial history that precedes most remarriages, becoming true partners in your remarriage is not likely to be easy. What I have found, however, is that these basic partnership principles provide a very useful goal to assist couples in finding ways to reduce constant conflict about money. Take unilateral decision making as an example. One of my clients came in furious because her husband had agreed to send his two children to Europe with their mother. "He wasn't obligated to do that under the support agreement," she insisted. "He just made the decision to spend *our* money on *his* kids and *their* mother without even asking me. It hurts." Her husband had good reasons for his decision, and they had enough money to send the boys to Europe without impacting their lifestyle. Nevertheless, partners talk to each other about financial decisions, roommates do not. By treating his new wife as a roommate, this husband unintentionally hurt his wife, creating distance and mistrust.

What makes a partnership work is commitment, trust, and communication. Partnership does not mean that each of you has to be 50 percent responsible for family support. Rather, in working out your partnership, you need to assess what each of you contributes to the family. One of you may have more earning power, the other may be more able to devote love and attention to the children. Because one of you may have brought more assets to the marriage, you may want to be clear about retaining those assets if the marriage does not work. The point is that partners trust in and are committed to each other. In that emotional environment, any problem can be solved through close communication and, if necessary, mutual sacrifice. Couples report to me that when they learned to survive the lean times as two partners, the joy of the better times is that much greater.

Make Key Decisions Together; Take Equal Responsibility for the Results

There is a big difference between just listening to your spouse's complaint and genuinely negotiating a resolution of a financial conflict. In the first instance, you may listen while your mind remains made up about how family resources will be spent. In the second case, you attempt to understand your spouse's needs and work out a way to meet those needs while also meeting your own. In a business environment, just listening may be enough if you have the power and authority to make a decision and get your way without compromise. In a stepfamily, unilateral decision making leaves others feeling at best patronized and at worst resentful.

If you want your stepfamily to pull together rather than to be pulled apart in the face of financial conflict, then communicate your desire to encourage negotiation and compromise. Ask your spouse to brainstorm various solutions. Prepare alternative budgeting plans, consider possibilities to reduce expenses. Talk about your mutual needs and clarify how they may conflict. By encouraging participation in the process of solving financial conflict, you maximize the likelihood that everyone will feel fairly treated.

Avoiding Destructive Financial Arguments

Financial decision making in stepfamilies is often stressful, because it always involves the issue of emotional as well as financial support. Unfortunately, the stress compounds the conflict because stress often brings out the worst in people. When under too much stress, you are more likely to say things you don't mean and do things you will later regret. Stress often causes a regression to destructive emotional habits despite best intentions to negotiate rationally and compromise in good faith.

Some of my clients have found it helpful to take a personal inventory of the destructive habits that come into play when they are under stress. By becoming aware of these attitudes, you can catch yourself when discussion of a difficult financial decision starts to break down under stress.

What follows is a discussion of common attitudes that worsen financial arguments.

Blaming and Complaining Don't Work

Blaming is a common defensive habit, particularly among stepparents who find themselves suddenly confronted with overwhelming and unexpected financial pressures. Blaming is a wholly counterproductive communication trap born out of frustration and personal defensiveness. By blaming your spouse, you provide defensive rather than constructive responses, you shift 100 percent of the responsibility for solving problems to your spouse, and you deny your own role.

To make peace in your stepfamily, you must stop blaming.

Overcoming the Need to Be "Right"

The urge to win arises from the need to be one up, which inevitably leaves your partner feeling one down. This competition eventually leads to both of your losing. Even if you win one argument, your lover is likely to feel resistant, defiant, and resentful for losing, and you will pay for your victory through greater hostility in the next round.

Trying to win when you and your spouse disagree is a futile endeavor.

It is ironic how competitive people, who may use team-building skills at work, fail to use those skills at home. Think of your partner as a team member instead of an opponent.

Ruth was in tears because her husband Ozzie had berated her for bungling the family accounting. "She insisted on knowing what we were spending," Ozzie said with irritation, "so I let her keep the checkbook. When it came to tax time, I discovered a mess. No balanced checkbook, no receipts. Damn right I was mad."

On further investigation, it became clear that Ozzie had become a victim of his own self-righteousness. For months, Ozzie had belittled Ruth's desire to become involved in stepfamily financial planning. Once he finally agreed that she could become involved, he turned over the checkbook in a manner to inspire failure. "He told me to go set up an account at the bank," Ruth recalled. "He'd make deposits of $3,000 into the account, I was suppose to take care of family bills, including a $750 monthly check to Lorraine, his first wife. I'm sure she loved getting a check with my signature."

Self-righteousness leads to abrupt decisions and poor planning. It also creates fear of asking questions. No one is willing to ask questions if he or she fears looking stupid or feeling humiliated.

We human beings are incredibly self-righteous. In an argument we know how "right" we are and how obviously "wrong" the other person is.

The best way to cure yourself of the self-righteousness habit is to acknowledge that everyone has a right to ask questions, everyone has a legitimate point of view, and every questions deserves a considered and considerate response.

Beyond Either/Or Thinking

In the best relationships between remarrieds, stepfamily financial pressures become an opportunity for creative thinking and cooperative planning. An obstacle to this process is a tendency which we all have to see solutions in terms of either/or choices, rather than to expand our thinking to find a third alterative.

Wes and Nadine came to see me because they were struggling with how to be fair to all their children. Wes's daughter lived with her mother, Nadine's son and daughter lived with her, and Nadine and Wes had an infant. Wes came from a relatively prosperous family; his parents were paying for his daughter's education and were talking about a trust fund for the baby.

Nadine resented that Wes's parents ignored her children. Wes wanted his stepchildren to feel part of the family, but he also felt the sacrifices would be too great to try to provide the same financial support to his stepchildren as to his own children. Nadine had framed the issues as "either we treat all the kids the same, or we accept that we're not really a family."

I suggested that other couples in similar circumstances had found a third alternative. Both Wes and Nadine could contribute to a family account designated to help balance perceived inequities among the children. For example, the account could be used to make sure that all the kids had equal opportunities for vacations and no one felt left out when it was time for new clothes. Once Wes and Nadine let go of their either/or thinking, a dilemma that drove them apart became an opportunity for a creative solution that brought them together.

Avoid Financial Threats and Personal Attacks

When frustration levels run high, as is inevitable when the stepfamily is under financial pressure, it is easy to fall back on threats and coercions to get your way. Here are some examples of what my clients have said to one another:

- "Unless I start getting the check on time, you can forget your weekends with the kids."

- "You won't listen . . . so I'm leaving."

- "Unless you stop sending (your ex) money every time she asks, this marriage is over."

The problem with these coercive statements is not that they lack justification. In each of these cases, one stepparent had tried for months, and in some cases for years, to resolve an ongoing financial conflict. The problem with threats is simply that they at best succeed in generating compliance coupled with resentment.

If you feel so driven by frustration to begin making threats, you probably need a mediator. You might try one of the Heart Talk techniques described in this book, but if you don't get anywhere, then get counseling.

Some couples allow their arguments to degenerate into personality attacks because they have simply developed the bad habit of criticizing each other rather than facing the reality of their problem. As I have said, when it comes to feelings, no one is wrong. When it comes to how you express your feelings, however, you have an important choice to make. Do you want simply to vent your rage? Or do you want your feelings to be understood so you can find a solution to your conflict?

I advise my clients to refrain from personal attacks even if it means leaving the room to let off steam and then resuming the discussion when you are in control. To resolve disputes in your stepfamily and particularly disputes involving money, it is essential that you create and maintain an atmosphere of mutual respect where negotiation and compromise can flourish.

Becoming Overprotective

Sometimes a well-intentioned effort to take care of your spouse can precipitate unnecessary financial conflict. Rick married Ellen after a five-month whirlwind romance. He had no children, and she had a son and a daughter. Having been a single mother for eight years, Ellen was relieved to marry Rick, who was a very successful entertainment executive, and who accepted her children as his own.

Problems began to develop in their relationship soon after she lost her job. They had set up their household with separate accounts, but after losing her job, Ellen found herself and her children totally dependent on Rick's income. Rick's response was "Don't worry, I like taking care of you." He expected Ellen to enjoy what he perceived as her new financial freedom.

Ellen came in troubled by her feelings of resentment toward Rick. "I've never been dependent on a man," she explained. "I know he doesn't intend to be demeaning, but whenever I have a question about money, his answer is "Don't worry, I'll take care of it." Ellen felt guilty about her growing resentment. "I should be appreciating all he is doing for all of us. What do I have to complain about?"

The more Ellen and I talked, the more clear it became that she would not be happy as a wife who shopped and took care of the home. Her children were eleven and fourteen and had become quite independent. What Ellen needed from Rick was not overprotective reassurance but rather help in redirecting her career.

I suggested that Ellen have a Heart Talk with Rick. She later reported that he was surprised about her real feelings. After a six-month job search, Ellen found a new job in magazine editing.

Costly Denial

Another emotional trap that sometimes complicates stepfamily finances is denial. Here are cases which illustrate the variety of ways in which denial compounds an already existing problem.

Samantha and John had a retail store that sold ethnic furniture, rugs, clothing, and jewelry. They both had a retail background and started this venture shortly after their marriage. Samantha brought one child to the marriage. John supported one child living with his ex-spouse. The store prospered from the start, and believing they were now living the charmed life, Samantha and John significantly increased their standard of living. They bought a new house and soon had a child of their own. After four years of prosperity, sales at the store began to flatten and then decline. Refusing to acknowledge the downtrend in the economy, Samantha and John continued their lifestyle. Eventually, sales at the store could not cover expenses. They went into debt to keep the store open, only to find the situation getting worse. When their home went into foreclosure they finally woke up. With both marriage and personal finances in a crisis, they came in each blaming the other for extravagances when in fact, they had both gotten caught in the folly of their own fulfillment and denial.

Denial compounds stepfamily conflicts and particularly financial ones by allowing the problem to grow before it gets addressed. In most cases, parents and stepparents persist in denial because they fear the truth and are unaware that denial is at work. Here are the symptoms of denial:

- Refusing to discuss a problem
- Failing to consider the worst possible outcome as well as the best
- Telling yourself or each other everything will be all right without any foundation or specific planning
- Avoiding concerns expressed by your spouse or friends
- Convincing yourself or your spouse that "it's not my/our problem"
- Trusting that your ex will change with no concrete evidence.

If these behaviors sound familiar, then you and your spouse need to have a realistic Heart Talk about the problem at hand. You may find that a counselor can be helpful in enabling you to overcome the denial and start working together to solve your problem before it grows worse.

Heart Talks About Money Matters

Many marrieds wind up in conflict about money because they never discussed critical issues at the outset of their relationship. For many couples, there is a mutual conspiracy of silence about money. During the early stages of a relationship, financial discussions can seem terribly unromantic. When so much seems to be going right with a relationship, it is easy to assume that financial issues will take care of themselves or at worst can be worked out after the marriage. The problem is that many couples continue to postpone candid financial discussion until a crisis develops.

Money is too important in any marriage to be relegated to the netherworld of unexamined assumptions and unspoken agreements. In the stepfamily, to postpone thorough communication about your financial status, your philosophy about money, and your financial priorities is to dramatically increase the odds that your remarriage will fail. Because money is so important to stepfamilies but so often ignored, Heart Talks about financial issues can be enormously useful to remarrieds.

Financial Heart Talks require preparation to be effective. You need to do homework on the issues of concern. You may want to learn more about the community property laws in your state, and how community property gets divided in divorce. You may also talk with a financial planner. A little research may lead you to think more thoroughly about basic issues of family accounting, whether to pool your earnings, whether to maintain separate checking accounts, how to allocate financial responsibility for your spouse's children, how to maintain ownership of your home, and how to maintain ownership of IRA accounts and other investments.

The concerns couples have about disclosing feelings about money issues are in some respects justified. Money raises questions of boundaries. Who gets what? Love is primarily about sharing. How do we merge? By setting aside a specific occasion, time, and location for a financial discussion that you acknowledge as a Heart Talk, you and your spouse assist each other in empathetic communications about difficult and divisive issues. You create an atmosphere of safety and trust where you both can be honest with yourselves and each other. Remember that if you resist your fears about merging your finances or deny your concerns about supporting your stepchildren, those fears and concerns will slowly generate conflict, even though the emotional process may be unconscious. If you can acknowledge your fears and your concerns, you and your spouse can create financial arrangements without conflict.

Yours, Mine, and Ours

Sometimes remarrieds blindly go on maintaining separate accounts with the thought that he will support his kids and pay half the rent, while she will support hers and also pay half the common expenses. This approach often fails because the stepfamily winds up divided into separate groups. A more common (and successful) approach is to supplement the separate accounts with a joint account for household and family expenses. Some couples find that the commitment to the joint account grows as each becomes more confident in the marriage. Still other remarrieds put all their money into a common pot to use for the stepfamily as needed. There are numerous variations on these approaches to household accounting, and different approaches are appropriate for different stepfamilies depending upon the relative wealth, earning power, and support obligations of the parents and the relative needs of their children or stepchildren. The key to minimizing conflict about money issues remains the clear understanding between you and your spouse.

There are other financial issues you need to discuss thoroughly with your spouse. Support obligations are among the most important. It is not enough to know that you or your spouse has an obligation to pay a specific sum, say $1,200 per month, to support children who live outside your home, or to know that your spouse must also pay $1,500 per month in alimony to his ex. Discussing court-ordered support obligations is the starting point, but you also need to know what the understanding is regarding unexpected medical or dental bills and plans for education costs.

How would you as a stepparent feel about contributing to these costs from your income? Remarrieds often fail to discuss these issues early in their remarriage because it is easier to assume there will be enough money than to define the limits of what you are prepared to do for your stepchildren. If you wait for a financial crisis to prompt examination of these issues, you wind up discussing them during a period of emotional turmoil and you limit your ability to plan for contingencies. Have a Heart Talk with your spouse about support obligations as early as possible in your remarriage.

Guilt can complicate support obligations to an enormous degree. Divorced fathers often feel guilty for abandoning their former wives and children, particularly if the father chose to end the marriage. To compensate, some fathers regularly pay more than legally required amounts in child support and alimony. When these fathers remarry, they wind up caught between their desire to support a new family and guilt about abandoning their old family. Finding the right balance is the key to resolving this conflict. Two steps are necessary. The father must confront his guilt and lessen its destructive emotional impact. Exercises to be described in Chapter 8 will help. Effective Heart Talks with the new spouse then may be possible as well.

Here are the other financial issues that merit Heart Talks:

- *Work.* Do you both want to work? Is work optional for either of you?

- *Another child.* Can you afford to have another child? When will your current children be on their own? Will one of you stop working? How do you feel about taking care of your spouse's children while giving up having a child of your own?

- *Differences in family wealth.* Are there substantial differences in family wealth that will benefit your children as opposed to your stepchildren? Are your spouse's parents more able to give to their grandchildren than your parents to theirs?

- *Budgets.* Have you and your spouse worked out a detailed budget? Do you review it regularly? Does it include a savings plan?

- *Money demands from an ex.* Does your ex or your spouse's ex frequently request more money? Do you accommodate these requests? Are you motivated to do so by guilt?

Financial Heart Talks can have enormously liberating outcomes. One of my clients became anxious about a layoff notice, because she would no longer be able to support her children as she and her new spouse had agreed. She was afraid to tell him, and was hoping to postpone any discussions about her job until she found a new one. I told her that she would only make matters worse through delay, particularly if she was not successful in her job search. I suggested a financial Heart Talk. A while later she reported, with great relief and renewed confidence in her spouse, that he was very understanding. Instead, he suggested they work together as a family to cut back on expenses until she found a new job. By trusting her ability to have a Heart Talk, she avoided a family crisis.

Teaching Children the Value of Money

Hank and Sara came into my office with Hank complaining that he felt like a plastic credit card. They both worked, and they both had custody of their children from previous marriages. "Sara's girls expect to get whatever they ask for," Hank complained. "Now my son is getting into the act. I would like to have a child with Sara, and we won't be able to if this keeps up."

"Their father has always spoiled the girls," Sara admitted. "But since the divorce, he has been so cheap. . . . The support agreement doesn't provide us anywhere the lifestyle the girls were accustomed to." Sara went on to suggest that her ex-husband was hoping that his daughters would come to live with him because Hank and Sara could not provide the same lavish lifestyle. "Every time the girls go to visit, they come back reminded of what he can do for them and what we can't," Sara lamented.

Sara escalated the stress in her remarriage by pushing Hank to compete with her ex-husband in an area where Hank was certain to lose. I suggested that Sara, Hank, and their children would benefit if they shifted the competition to their own playing field and focus on the values their children were learning. Sara's ex was teaching his daughters to measure love with money. Whatever the girls might learn about in the commercial world, I suggested they would be better served by learning a different set of values in their stepfamily.

Trying to teach your children about money is a difficult task, particularly in stepfamilies where children moving between two homes may encounter different values. Here are some guidelines that have proven helpful.

Assure children about your commitment to their support. A child's greatest fear in divorce is being abandoned. Your child's basic sense of safety and security depends on confidence in his or her parents' commitment to provide support. By communicating your sense of personal commitment to support your child, you encourage a sense of responsibility in your children.

Expect children to help with family finances through prudent spending and possibly part-time work. Stepfamilies are often under so much financial pressure that everyone must pitch in to make it work. Money should be a topic at regular Family Circles. You and your spouse should also set house rules that encourage thrift.

It can also be very helpful to encourage children at an appropriate age to begin earning some of their own pocket money. Baby-sitting, mowing lawns, and paper routes are a few ideas for part-time work. Earning money helps children develop a sense of responsibility, achievement, and independence.

Don't Confuse Net Worth with Self-Worth

Children of divorce are often exposed to the worst frailties of the human psyche—jealousy, bickering, betrayal, and vicious arguments. What's worse, they encounter these qualities in their parents and family members. As a result, children of divorce are particularly susceptible to the message in our materialistic culture that the only reliable measure of a person is net worth.

Children need to be taught that the true measure of self-worth is personal integrity. Are you true to yourself? Do you have a basic sense of self-esteem? Can you build close personal relationships? Do you feel your life has meaning?

These are the qualities essential to personal happiness. I have seen countless numbers of clients who are wealthy but miserable because one or more of these qualities is lacking in their lives. Given the trauma of divorce, most divorced parents have great difficulty modeling these qualities for their children. Rather than let your children develop a materialistic cynicism (i.e., what really counts is how much money you've got), short-term counseling is advisable to help your children understand their own needs and to find the path to their own personal integrity.

Encourage your children to discover their own passionate interests. Ask children of divorce what they want to do in life, and many will respond, "make money." These children are motivated by their own fear of personal vulnerability. What they fail to appreciate, however, is the correlation between success and a passionate interest in a particular type of work. Successful people generally do not identify making money as a primary goal, even if they have made millions. Time and again successful people report that building houses, making movies, developing a new computer program, or otherwise realizing a personal dream was and is their goal. Money is the by-product.

Children who are motivated by fear are constantly concerned about how much money they have. Children who are motivated by passionate interests are constantly concerned about how to achieve their next goal and what they need to do to compete. Give your children the reassurance that money will follow achievement, and that the real challenge in life is to discover what you want passionately to do.

Do not denigrate your ex for giving gifts, and don't make a child feel guilty accepting. Sara fell into a trap set by her ex-spouse. By flaunting his lifestyle to his daughters, he prompted Sara to criticize him as a "bad father" and to attack the girls for accepting his "bribes." As a result, Sara wound up trying to compete with her ex and heightening the emotional distress felt by her daughters.

Once again, it is helpful to remember that what you resist persists, and what you accept lightens. By resisting her ex's display of wealth, Sara exacerbated the conflicts surrounding it. Had she simply encouraged his daughters to accept their fathers gifts graciously, the whole wealth issue would lose importance. Sara could then focus on the real issue—what the girls wanted to do with their lives, what their interests were, and how Sara and Hank could support them. There is no reason to make your children feel guilty about money that follows from success, or about their parents' success.

Demonstrate to your children that the time you spend with them is more important than the money you spend on them. Children thrive when they get attention, respect, recognition, and encouragement. But giving these gifts takes time, a commodity in very short supply in most hectic stepfamily households.

In Chapter 3 I emphasized the critical importance of one-on-one time to encourage bonding between stepparent and stepchildren. Younger children are generally more open to spending time with parents than older children, who may balk at losing time with their friends. It often seems easier for everyone to finance a teen's next wish rather than take the time to discover his or her real needs.

I have a busy practice, two teenage stepsons and a daughter. I am not suggesting in the least that any of this is easy. I am certain, however, that I do much more for each child by taking time to listen to what's on their minds, than by giving them money to buy the latest video game.

Make it clear that you will not be ruled by fads and advertising. With the jealousies and divided loyalties in most stepfamilies, you ignite endless conflict if you surrender to the impulse to buy what the kids want because "everybody else has one." If you make this mistake once, you invite constant pressure from the children and stepchildren to buy the next fad. You also fuel complaints that "It's not fair" if you buy Nintendo for your stepson but don't buy the latest new clothes for your stepdaughter.

With children immersed in our advertising culture and faced with constant peer pressures, it is difficult to say no. One effective strategy to deal with this pressure is to give your child financial choices. For example, you might ask them to choose between new sneakers and a new video game. By providing choices, you help the children to confront limits and to evaluate their true needs, essential tools to prepare them for the realities of adult life. Another strategy is to offer "matching funds." You pay a percentage of a big ticket item; if the children want it badly enough, they will earn the balance needed. This strategy eliminates the handout philosophy which is counterproductive.

Create an atmosphere where the children can ask about and understand family finances. When your children and stepchildren are old enough, you can ease the pressure of their demands and help them learn about money by letting them know about the limits of family finances. If family finances become very tight, it can be very helpful to discuss the problem at a Family Circle. You can solicit suggestions about cutting back on expenses. When children and step-children are invited to participate in figuring out how to cut back, they tend to transform the problem into an opportunity for family bonding. In contrast, children who are simply told to cut back often wind up resenting these orders. Lacking insight into the problem, they assume that family resources are being diverted to other family members—a stepparent or stepsibling—and that "It's not fair."

When Values Clash

"I can't understand Warren," Delores complained of her ex, who had married Marie, a twenty-three-year-old. "He's trying to drive Meredith (their fifteen-year-old daughter) crazy. Meredith has been asking War-ren for a new ski outfit for months, and he had promised her one. The first thing Marie does when Meredith arrives is show off her *three* new ski outfits *and* her new skis. Then Marie announced that they're having a baby."

Meredith was devastated by her father's insensitivity and jealous of her stepmother, particularly given the relatively small age difference. "Meredith feels that Marie is getting everything Marie dreams of, while Warren ignores me and his two daughters," Delores exclaimed. Her solution to this clash in values was to go out and buy Meredith the new ski outfit, and send Warren the bill.

In cases such as this, merely trying to balance the financial scales is not enough. Meredith was bound to continue visiting her father and encountering the same clash of values. Although Delores worked, she did not earn enough to compete with Warren. Moreover, I advised that Meredith would suffer terribly if she got caught in a competition where Delores tried to make up to Meredith for a perceived rejection by her father.

Resolution of this financial conflict required a meeting of the minds between Warren and Delores. To some degree, a clash of values between homes is healthy for the children of divorce as long as the children learn to appreciate why their parents have chosen a different lifestyle. Where a lifestyle choice involves an apparent rejection of a child, however, the clash of values is too extreme. The child cannot be expected to interpret such disparity in attitudes. The divorced couple has a responsibility to improve their coparenting through mediation or therapy if they cannot resolve this clash of values on their own.

In this case, Meredith was traumatized because her father seemed to be abandoning her for her youthful stepmother. Visiting stepchildren often resent their stepmothers because their father seems to be devoting himself to her needs at the expense of his prior family. In some cases, this is true; but just as often, fathers support their prior family at the expense of their new family. In Meredith's case, however, there were other signs of rejection. Her father did not have any pictures of his two daughters in his new home, and he did not arrange for them to have any space they could call their own. Meredith and her sister always felt like visitors, and even though Marie tried to be friendly, Marie's flaunting of Warren's affection and their lifestyle wounded Meredith in an unreasonable, albeit perhaps unintentional, manner.

Delinquent Child Support Payments

One of the most pervasive financial conflicts in stepfamilies is the failure by ex-spouses, usually fathers, to honor child-support agreements. In most cases, child-support payments are chronically late, and in many cases, the payments stop altogether.

Continuing child support depends on maintaining a reasonable relationship between the ex-spouses. Whatever agreement may be reached and approved by the court, the agreement is only as good as the goodwill between the ex-spouses, unless you are prepared for a costly enforcement effort, and even then, an angry spouse may flee rather than pay. Child support becomes a source of intense financial conflict when coparenting by ex-spouses begins to break down. To avoid this conflict, it is best to treat late child-support payments as a symptom rather than a cause.

When discord grows between ex-spouses, address the problems early. A father is unlikely to keep sending regular support checks if he feels he is being abused. Rather than become indignant, it is better to acknowledge the other's feelings. Neither cajoling a noncompliant father to make prompt payment nor becoming indignant is effective. It is critical to arrange a meeting, preferably with a therapist or mediator, to help work out the ill feeling. If the father feels fairly treated, he is more likely to resume regular payments.

Finally, delay in addressing the problem only compounds it. So, too, do unilateral enforcement efforts such as denying visitations. Berating the father in front of the child or putting a child on the phone to ask for money is damaging to the children and to the relationship between the spouses. All of these unilateral enforcement efforts should be avoided.

If a mediation effort fails to resolve the problem promptly, i.e., within a matter of months, then you should proceed expeditiously to legal action. Attorneys are expensive, and the process of going to court is emotionally as well as financially draining. Nevertheless, you are far more likely to be effective if you promptly obtain a court order rather than allowing the problem to drag on with growing bitterness and resentment, perhaps causing the father to feel he has nothing to lose by moving out of state. Generally speaking, courts retain the power to intervene in child support matters until children reach age eighteen, and it is becoming increasingly common for courts to allow wage assignments so that the noncustodial spouse's employer pays a certain percentage of the noncustodial spouse's wages directly to the spouse who has physical custody of the children. In some states, arrears in child support payments can result in suspension of professional licenses. Federal legislation is also likely to assist in this area.

Prenuptial Agreements

A prenuptial agreement is a written contract, signed by a prospective husband and wife after full disclosure of their finances, that specifies how property is divided in the event of one spouse's death or their divorce. In simplest terms, the more affluent spouse agrees to provide a specific sum to the less affluent spouse in case of death or divorce, while the less affluent spouse agrees to waive any claims on the estate in case of death or under state law in case of divorce, other than as specified in the prenuptial agreement. The net effect of a prenuptial agreement is that the less affluent spouse agrees in advance to take less in the event of death or divorce than he or she might be entitled to, while the more affluent spouse retains the ability to control what happens to his or her property and, particularly, to assure that a remarriage will not impair his or her children's claim on the estate.

In a premarital agreement, the less affluent spouse gives up certain protections provided by state laws. Therefore, these agreements are often the subject of litigation. The less affluent spouse may attempt to avoid the enforceability of the agreement by claiming there was misrepresentation or lack of understanding. Most matrimonial lawyers are aware of these pitfalls, and the more affluent spouse's lawyer will probably suggest that the less affluent spouse be represented by a lawyer. With lawyers on both sides, the agreement is more likely to stand up in court. It is also less likely to get signed in the first place. With enough open discussion, mutual love and respect, an understanding about a prenuptial agreement may be reached.

Adoption

Jerome and Gwen sought help because Jerome wanted to adopt his eleven-year-old stepdaughter and her nine-year-old brother. "I am tired of Gwen chasing after David for the child support," explained Jerome. "David rarely sees his kids, he doesn't support them, and I love them very much. I've been their father for the past six years. They call me Dad now."

"I would be very happy for Jerome to adopt Ronnie and Andrew," Gwen added. "It would solve so many small problems, like the kids having a different last name than ours. But how do we approach them? They both get very excited when their father does come to visit."

In appropriate circumstances, adoption is a wonderful step in cementing the commitment of a stepparent to his or her stepchild. "Stepfamily adoptions occur most commonly in cases such as that of Jerome and Gwen, where a stepfather adopts children who have substantially lost contact with their biological father, or where their biological father is no longer willing or able to provide support. As long as the biological parent remains alive, however, his or her legal consent is necessary for the adoption of a minor child to occur. Consent can be waived in cases where the biological parent may be alive, but has completely disappeared.

Adoption resolves a wide array of issues that can cause major or minor conflict in stepfamilies. Both the stepparent and the child become more secure in the relationship. The stepparents' legal obligations to the child are clarified, as are the child's right to support from the stepparent, including participation in the stepparent's estate. Institutions such as schools, which might not recognize the role of the stepparent, acknowledge and include the former stepparent as a parent. The stepparent can also sign medical releases, and other consents as may be necessary for minor children from time to time.

With all the benefits of adoption, there are also cautions to be considered. Adoption legally severs a biological tie. When children are asked if they would like to be adopted, the children can face an emotional dilemma. They may wish very deeply to retain a bond with the absent parent, but given the parent's absence, they may feel compelled to acquiesce in the adoption out of their insecurity and fear of abandonment. It is important not to allow a well-intentioned desire to adopt your stepchild to become a test of your stepchild's loyalty or a manifestation of competition with the same-sex natural parent. Adoption creates rights and responsibilities, but it does not create relationships. If you are thinking of adoption in your stepfamily, you would be wise to discuss it with a counselor familiar with the complexities.

Love Matters More

For the stepfamily to function as an effective unit, each member must make contributions that go far beyond bringing in a paycheck. To overcome financial adversity you need to be able to bank on a strong family team. Parent and stepparent, as co-captains, need to instruct, support, and encourage the children to pitch in with meal preparation, kitchen cleanup, laundry, home maintenance, and grocery shopping. Every stepfamily member can and must be taught to be a good team player. This approach allows children to contribute and feel their value. They learn that while money matters, love matters more.

Chapter 8

PERSONAL GROWTH THROUGH STEPFAMILY CONFLICT

*O*ne of the greatest challenges in healing conflict within your stepfamily is taking full responsibility for your own emotional responses that may be sustaining that conflict. I know how difficult this can be, from my own experience. Before Sirah's sons came to live with us full-time, I had thought of myself as a tolerant and easygoing parent to my daughter. When the boys arrived and challenged my comfortable routine, a darker side of my personality emerged, and I found myself becoming the family dictator. In retrospect I see how my authoritarian attitudes brought out the worst in the boys. Regular screaming matches became inevitable. Only after I finally began to recognize my role in the conflict did the possibility for healing appear.

Few of us are eager to recognize our own weaknesses. On the

contrary, it is only human to assume that chronic conflict in your stepfamily is primarily someone else's fault—a recalcitrant stepchild, malicious ex-spouse, an intrusive in-law, insensitive spouse, or an overbearing stepparent. One of my greatest challenges in assisting couples to resolve stepfamily conflicts is enabling the adults involved to recognize how they are contributing to the conflict. As long as each member of a stepfamily fails to recognize his or her role, making peace is virtually impossible.

My purpose in this chapter is to assist you in examining your role in creating or sustaining stepfamily conflict. The goal is not to prompt self-criticism but rather self-understanding. Once you recognize how your own reflexive emotional responses may be adding to stepfamily conflict, you can then take steps to change. This process of insight followed by behavioral change is the essence of the personal growth process. Instead of being at the mercy of your emotions, you knowledgeably embrace your feelings and choose to respond in ways that promote harmony rather than conflict.

Coming to Grips with Guilt

When guilt becomes excessive, this normal barometer of a healthy conscience can grow into dysfunctional self-punishment. Divorced parents and some stepparents are frequently subjected to excessive guilt which leads to behaviors that create unintentional conflict in their stepfamilies. In most cases, excessive guilt arises out of the divorced parents' unrelenting self-recrimination for putting their children through the trauma of divorce, and their subsequent inability to provide daily guidance, love, and support to children living in another household. Divorced fathers are particularly prone to this type of guilt because their children usually live with their former spouses, while the divorced fathers become stepfathers to their second wife's children.

"Phillip and Brian came crying to me, asking why Ned doesn't like them," complained Rosalyn in an accusatory tone while sitting across from her second husband, Ned, in my office. "He hasn't opened up to his stepsons at all, and what makes it worse is how he dotes on Tina and Christian (Ned's own daughter and son) when they visit on weekends."

"It's not that I'm trying to exclude Rosalyn's boys," Ned explained defensively, "but when Tina and Christian visit, that is all the time I have with them. It is my responsibility to make up for my not being there for them. I feel terrible about the divorce and the problems they are having with their mother. Tina still asks me why I had to move out and leave her and her brother. Whenever she asks that, I die a little bit inside. Rosalyn doesn't understand, but I won't make it worse by making Tine and Christian feel they can never have 100 percent of my attention.

"I'm not asking him to make it worse," Rosalyn interrupted. "I can see that Tina and Christian are hurting, but it's not going to get better if we go on like this. All I want is for Ned to open up a little more."

Rosalyn's request was well-founded, although her accusatory tone was at best unhelpful and probably destructive. Ned was paralyzed by his own guilt. Not only had he allowed his guilt to block his ability to bond with his stepsons, he had also created an emotional climate of regret and remorse for his own children. They all remained emotionally transfixed by the past and unable to discover the joys of creating a new stepfamily and anticipating a positive future.

When a parent acts out of guilt, even well-intentioned actions often end up generating conflict in a stepfamily. Beth has become obsessed with guilt for having given up custody of her two boys following her divorce. After several years living alone, she married Grant, a man much more successful than her first husband, Dean. Beth also became a stepmother to Grant's three children. Beth and Grant came for help because they had begun fighting about how much Beth was spending on her own children.

"I told Grant when we got married that I felt terrible for abandoning my two boys," Beth explained, her voice cracking with emotion. "All I've been doing is trying to make up to them for my not being there when they were younger. That can't hurt, can it?"

When parents act out of guilt, they rarely appreciate the consequences of their actions on others within the stepfamily. Beth was unable to see that her constant demands upon Grant for money were creating antagonism by forcing him to choose between his own sons and her children. She also failed to recognize that Grant had been attracted to her precisely because she did not seem to place much emphasis on possessions, and he had thought she would help create the close family that he always desired. Instead, her own efforts to "make up" to her children for the divorce led her to create conflict that neither she nor Grant expected.

"She wants too much," complained Grant. "As much as I want to be a good stepfather, I can't make up to Beth's kids for what she and Dean didn't provide, and I am not about to sacrifice what I want for my kids. Somehow this has all gone wrong. I wanted to have a family, not just be a plastic credit card all over again. That was a big part of the problem in my first marriage."

"You have no idea how it feels," Beth asserted. "Not having your own children with you is something you can't understand until you live it. Don't you think I want to be a good stepmother to your sons? Haven't I tried? But the more I give to your children, the worse I feel about what I can't give to my own."

In this case Beth's guilt not only alienated her second husband, but her efforts to use money to "make up" for her absence from her own children's lives also exacerbated animosity with her first husband. "Dean isn't any more happy about the situation than I am," Grant explained. "The focus of what the kids need is getting lost. We need to get back to some basics."

When a parent acts out of guilt, the motivation becomes assuaging the parent's emotional distress, not meeting other stepfamily members' needs. Beth had become obsessed with showering her children with new toys and clothes at every opportunity to make up for her own failures. Her obsession made her insensitive to Grant's desire to create a close family and to her first husband's belief that the children needed her time, not more toys. As the conflicts escalated, her children soon became uncomfortable with visiting her. Beth blamed Grant and Dean for turning her children against her. Fortunately, Beth and Grant finally came for help, and Beth began to examine the real motivation behind her behavior.

In some cases, a father may wind up alienating his new wife because guilt renders him incapable of saying no to his ex-wife. Excessive guilt impairs a parent's or stepparent's ability to take everyone's needs into account and make well-reasoned decisions. In many cases the parent or stepparent obsessed with guilt is not fully aware of the problem. Surprisingly, guilt can result in maladaptive preoccupation even among parents who are fully aware that they are feeling guilty and as a result creating stepfamily conflict.

Guilt is a natural, perhaps inevitable part of going through divorce if you are a parent, but at some point it is essential to recognize that there are limits. Just as it's okay to feel anger, but it's not okay to hurt someone physically, it's okay to feel guilt, but not to the point of emotional self-injury or incapacity. When guilt motivates you to make amends, it can be healthy. But guilt becomes maladaptive when it becomes a daily diet. Unrelenting guilt is a self-destructive self-punishment that you don't deserve and which does not serve you, your children, or your new family. Excessive guilt keeps you stuck in the past and impedes fully accepting and making the most of the here and now.

It is important to distinguish between effective care and concern versus excessive guilt and worry. Love and concern for your child are uppermost to good parenting. The difference between guilt and concern is that concern leads to positive action; guilt immobilizes you in self-punishment. If you then let guilt and worry play an inordinate role in your emotional life, the result is depression. Guilt, worry, and depression impair your ability to be a concerned, effective, and loving parent.

Parenting driven by guilt breeds tension and conflict in the stepfamily. One mother felt so guilty about possibly favoring her own children over her stepchildren that she set up a terrible competition between them. Each began to scrutinize what the other child got at every turn. As a result, all of the children grew up feeling bitter about being treated unfairly.

When you feel chronically guilty you may be inadvertently teaching your children to stay miserable, blame you for their troubles, and not take responsibility for their own happiness and well-being. The result is a vicious cycle that can be perpetuated into your children's adult years. The more unsuccessful or unhappy your child, the more guilt and worry you feel. The more guilt you feel, the more your guilt reinforces a child's mistaken belief that you are responsible for his or her happiness and self-esteem. *The more you have guilt, the more miserable it makes your child feel!*

Forgiving Yourself

Whether you have custody of your children now or whether you see them only on weekends, it is essential that you forgive yourself for causing your children pain through your divorce. You cannot make amends by remaining emotionally crippled by the past, and chronic feelings of guilt are as crippling as a broken leg that has never healed. Forgiving yourself is a healing process essential to your ability to be an effective parent or stepparent.

Again you can't heal what you cannot feel. The first step in forgiving yourself is to acknowledge your feelings. Focus on your feelings about your divorce and your children by completing the following sentences:

- I still feel guilty that . . .
- I regret that . . .
- If only . . .
- I wish I had . . .

Now go back and ask yourself how you feel about your responses. Don't censor yourself. Do you want to hide? Do you feel ashamed? Do you feel anxiety sensations in your body—pain in your chest, heaviness in your shoulders? Do you want to cry? Let your feelings flow as they will. Remember, when it comes to feelings, no one is wrong! Divorce is painful, and your feelings are natural.

Lighten Up

Now that you are more in touch with your feelings, you can help them heal by letting go and allowing yourself to discover a source of inner peace. Light is the source of all life and warmth on earth; the source of all healing and growing. Visualizing a healing light is now used as an adjunct to standard medical treatment, including healing wounds and cancer recovery. A healing visualization can also help lighten your emotional burdens. Follow the instructions below:

Unplug the phones, put a Do Not Disturb sign on the door, find a comfortable chair, and give yourself a chance to relax and let go. Close your eyes and take five very slow, deep breaths, exhaling through your mouth. Begin to notice the soothing effects of settling down. Direct your attention to your toes and feel them relax. Let your attention slowly glide up your body—feet, ankles, calves, knees, thighs, hips, abdomen, back, check, neck, arms, face—and stop at each part to feel relaxation taking place.

Now imagine that you are floating in space or lying in a warm meadow. Create any mental image that you find peaceful, relaxing, and enjoyable. Let the world slip away, and drift naturally in your reveries. From this safe and relaxed place within you can perceive yourself without self-criticism. You can feel the release of letting down your defenses. As you progress in your relaxation, you can feel the love and inner peace that are deep inside you.

When you are feeling relaxed and comfortable, picture the person(s) you have injured, as realistically as possible. Observe your feelings and thoughts as they arise. You may experience some tension in your chest, shoulders, or neck. Your breathing may become shallow or feel constricted. Without resisting the feelings and sensation as they arise, continue to focus your attention on the peaceful images you created in the relaxation exercise. Remember to breathe slowly and comfortably, letting go of any tension. Continue to relax, unwind, and feel comfortable.

Imagine a white light surrounding your body. Let it fill you with healing and grace. Imagine the white light focusing on the area of your body in which you experience guilt or remorse: your stomach, perhaps your heart, maybe your head. See your emotional pain surrounded by this goodness and light. Now imagine the light penetrating and dissolving the guilt. The more the light saturates the guilt and hurt, the lighter you become. Imagine the guilt entirely diffused in the light. Like the darkness in a room is dispersed when you turn on the light, the self-punishment is no more. Be at peace in the goodness and light.

Use this visualization process daily for a time to help lighten and dissolve your emotional burdens. Each time you do the exercise, take a few deep breaths and imagine a healing light sweeping over you. The light can be seen as emanating from any source comfortable to you—God, spirit, or love. This inner light can assist in healing the pain and bitterness in your heart. Each time relax for five or ten minutes in this inner light. After the exercise, if you experience a lingering pressure in your head or some irritability, be sure to take additional time to rest. Lie down, take a few deep breaths, and let yourself unwind. You may practice this technique as needed. Repeat the exercise until your "heavy" feelings lose their intensity and become "lighter."

Stopping Self-Punishment

To stop punishing yourself, it is essential to identify and work through the hidden or unconscious resistances that block letting go of guilt and experiencing more love and kindness. This exercise is a quick way to find out what thoughts and attitudes are working against your intention to make a deeper peace with your past and yourself.

Take a sheet of paper and draw a vertical line down the center of the page to make two columns. In the left-hand column write "I forgive myself." Then close your eyes and notice your immediate thoughts. Do you hear yourself saying something that contradicts the statement "I forgive myself"? Look for anything sarcastic, doubting, or bitter that is a barrier to self-forgiveness. Whatever response comes to mind after "I forgive myself" should be written in the right-hand column.

In the same fashion, continue to write "I forgive myself" on the left, as well as your gut response on the right, until you start to feel a release from the resistances that are holding you back. These are what block forgiving yourself and regaining your peace of mind. When you have written "I forgive myself" three times in a row with ease and acceptance, then you have completed the exercise.

Some people uncover all their resistances in one page of "I forgive myself" treatments. Many find it takes a number of such self-treatment sessions. This exercise is about learning to *treat* yourself with love, kindness, and dignity rather than continuing to punish yourself with self-recrimination. This treatment is what you deserve, and your kids deserve to have a peaceful, happy parent.

The following is an example from one parent's list of "I forgive myself" treatments and the responses that arose:

I forgive myself	Who am I to forgive myself?
I forgive myself	But look at what I did to my kids!
I forgive myself	It's all my fault
I forgive myself	I am a home wrecker
I forgive myself	How can I?
I forgive myself	Things happen
I forgive myself	Maybe . . .
I forgive myself	Okay
I forgive myself	Peace

"Forgiving yourself" treatments are most effective if they are specific. Create a list of statements that address your specific guilt feelings. For example, you might use:

I forgive myself for the divorce.

I forgive myself for giving up custody of (names of children).

I forgive myself for being unable to celebrate (name of child)'s birthday.

I forgive myself for my child's learning disorder/delinquency.

Using "I accept that . . ." and "I have faith in . . .", similar treatments help you accept what you cannot change and trust in the future. Here are some examples:

I accept that I can't be there for (name of child).

I accept that I want to help (name of child) with his/her homework.

I have faith in (name of child)'s ability to make the most of his/her life.

I have faith in my ability to help (name of child) in the future.

I have faith in my remarriage and stepfamily.

As an additional completion, you may want to sit down, close your eyes, and visualize your child(ren) accepting your forgiveness as you say, "I'm deeply sorry that I haven't always loved you the way you needed to be loved. I'm sorry about the divorce. I'm sorry your heart was split in two. I'm sorry for your pain. It's hard for me to admit but sometimes I was so selfishly involved in my own life and my own problems that I neglected your needs or failed to recognize you were hurting. You are a special, beautiful blessing in my life. I love you deeply and know how much you love me."

Once you lighten your emotional burdens and forgive yourself, a basic shift in your personal growth can ensue. Many people report that they felt blocked in their capacity to love and be loved prior to working through their guilt. Afterward, you feel more whole and centered, and ready to be a more loving parent and/or stepparent.

Letting Go of Grievances

Just as important as reducing excessive guilt about the past is letting go of grievances. The complex emotional dynamics in stepfamilies almost ensure that you and your spouse will have hurt each other early in your remarriage. You are also likely to have hurt your children, or your stepchildren will have hurt you. I frequently see remarrieds who harbor grievances from the early days of their remarriage. Making peace requires letting go, even where the grievance may be justified.

Colin and his second wife, Deanna, sat in my office talking about an event that had happened ten years ago. Colin's daughter, Hannah, lived with her natural mother at the time, visiting Colin and Deanna during summers and holidays. Hannah needed surgery, and Colin offered Hannah the opportunity to have the surgery during the summer when she would have two months to recuperate while visiting. When Colin proposed this idea to Deanna, she flatly refused. Colin had promised a vacation with Deanna in Europe, and Deanna was unwilling to spend the entire summer nursing Colin's daughter.

Now sitting in my office, the issue emerged once again. "Deanna was so selfish about Hannah," Colin complained with pain in his voice.

"Sylvia (Colin's first wife) wanted to take care of Hannah," Deanna countered. "Colin wants to believe Sylvia would have agreed to our keeping her, but it just wouldn't have happened."

Colin and Deanna were once again engaged in rehashing a grievance from the past. Each had a position, neither was about to change. The result of holding on to the grievance is a constant irritation and diminished affection between Colin and Deanna, even though Hannah long ago had the surgery and recovered fully.

To make peace in their stepfamily, Colin and Deanna had to let go of their grievances. Deanna harbored a grievance of her own, namely that Colin had postponed having more children, and now Deanna was having difficulty conceiving. Colin, who had two children, was not particularly eager to have more.

I advised Colin and Deanna to let go of their grievances with the following technique. Each agreed to write down his or her grievances, then each read the grievance for the last time to the other. In doing so, each:

- Acknowledged that he or she played a role in the incident, whether by provocation, neglect, or simply keeping silent
- Acknowledged that the incident was not malicious
- Recalled a series of positives about the relationship
- Agree these grievances would be put to rest for good

Each then burned the paper in a symbolic act of "letting go."

This simple exercise of clearing by fire and acknowledgment can be very effective in putting the past behind you. As a follow-up to this exercise, you must control any urges to recall the incident at a later date. When you commit to letting go of grievances in this manner, you allow mutual respect and consideration.

This strategy does not preclude discussing painful issues that have not been settled or taking steps to see that past hurts are not repeated. Forgiveness does not mean whitewashing or being a patsy. You can bring up the past in a way that resolves your own bad feelings, but without hostility. For example, you may not be ready to let go of a grievance involving an affair. In that case, you should refrain from using the grievance as a weapon. When the grievance comes up, you might simply say, "Sometimes I feel really bad about the affair you had two years ago, though I'm trying hard to heal and forget it." Working together to prevent a repetition of the hurt is far more valuable than holding on to past grievance.

The goal of the exercise is to communicate your hurt effectively once and for all, then choose to let go and heal. Instead of remaining caught in the past, you embrace the here and now.

Coping with Rejection

Few stepparents are prepared for how much it hurts to be repeatedly rejected by their stepchildren. In some cases, stepparents cope with the pain by trying even harder to be good stepparents. In other cases, a stepparent may tell himself, "I'm an adult, and this child's hostility shouldn't get to me." In still other instances, a stepmother may deny the rejection altogether, until a silent inner fury boils over into a screaming match with the ungrateful child.

Denial transforms rejection into resentment and rage, very dangerous emotions to the long-term well-being of a stepfamily. One of the most often cited reasons for stepparents walking out of remarriages is the pain of rejection. Unfortunately, once the damage is done, walking out often doesn't resolve the emotional issue. I have had divorced stepparents seek counseling to cope with damaged self-esteem long after they had left their remarriages.

The normal psychological forces of attraction and repulsion guarantee a dose of rejection for almost every stepfamily member. Stepparents bear the brunt of rejection from stepchildren, but stepparents may also incur rejection from their spouse's ex. Stepchildren may be rejected at times by their stepparent or stepsiblings, and parents often wind up caught in the middle, a target of anger both from their own children and a new spouse. When grandparents and step-grandparents enter the picture, the opportunities for rejection multiply.

Throughout this book I discuss a wide variety of cases in which rejection occurs. In each case I examine the causes of the breach in the relationship and suggest ways to bridge the communication gap. An essential component of the process, however, is learning to acknowledge the pain of rejection and restore your own self-esteem. Otherwise, the communication strategies may fall flat because you may be holding back or harboring resentment.

Rejection hurts. It's like a slap in the face. There are a variety of techniques you can use to lessen the pain and repair your self-esteem.

Many of my clients have found the following five techniques particularly helpful.

Dissolving Emotional Pain

The first step is to acknowledge how much you hurt. Denial is a short-run and ineffective coping mechanism. Personal growth comes from accepting your feelings and your pain, whereby you heal and broaden your insights.

One way to break through denial is to write down how you are feeling. Use the following sentences as a prompt:

- I feel rejected because . . .

- I feel left out when . . .

- I feel unappreciated . . .

- It hurts me that . . .

The pain of rejection often creates physical symptoms. It is important to acknowledge these feelings as well. You might write down where you hurt, such as "my neck is tense, knot in my stomach, headache." Or draw an outline of your body and identify where the rejection seems to show up as a physical symptom. Feelings are not rational. They just are. Give yourself a chance to accept them.

By opening up to your feelings, you may find yourself hurting more than you thought. Give yourself permission to let go; surrender to the tears if you start to cry. If your spouse tries to comfort you, let him or her be by your side, but do not try to turn off your tears in order to please your spouse. Tears are your own healing process. You can explain later, and there are other techniques below in which your spouse can play an active role.

Teachers of yoga have long recognized the power of breath to release pain and restore peace of mind. A simple breathing exercise can be very effective in restoring inner tranquility, particularly after you may have had a good cry.

Sitting comfortably, take a slow, deep breath, gently expanding your abdomen. As you gently inhale, close your eyes and picture the energy of life streaming into your body. Pause, then exhale slowly, this time envisioning the expulsion of any inner feeling of self-deprecation or self-hate. Pause, then repeat the slow inhalation process this time, noticing a wave of compassion filling your body. Pause, then exhale, picturing the tension and resentment flowing out of your body.

Repeat this process for five to ten minutes. Combine the visualization of loving qualities entering your body on each inhalation and self-hate leaving your body on each exhalation. This process restores your awareness of who you really are.

The Healing Heart

Rejection is a blow to the heart. Your spouse can help you heal from this blow by providing a loving and tender touch.

Sitting comfortably on your bed, ask your spouse to put one of his or her hands on your chest over your heart and the other hand on your back over your heart. Close your eyes together and feel the healing energy streaming between your spouse's two hands, embracing the wounded heart in your chest and creating a healing wave flowing within you. With each beat of your heart, you can let go of the pain and resentment while you rediscover inner feelings of love and hope. Some couples find this exercise so comforting that they share it with each other for perhaps ten minutes every evening.

Comforting Your Inner Child

Each of us has within our psyches a core sense of self from childhood. This animated set of memories from the past is often called the "inner child." Rejection as an adult and particularly as a stepparent is likely to trigger painful memories from the past. These old memories amplify the pain of current rejection.

If you resist old memories of rejection, they will continue to erode your self-esteem. Better to treat this crisis in your stepfamily as an intense personal growth seminar. Allow your old memories to emerge and give yourself the comfort you need. Take each memory of a prior rejection and reframe it to coincide with all your strengths as an adult. For example, if you were rejected by a group of children at school, acknowledge all the strengths of your inner child which your childhood tormentors failed to see. Embrace your inner child with compassion that allows you to appreciate your strengths and recognize the shortsightedness of your playmates. Go through this reframing exercise with each painful childhood memory of rejection.

Through this reframing process, you provide your inner child with affection and praise that you may have missed. Comforting your inner child through active reframing can heal old wounds to your self-esteem and restore feelings of inner strength. By comforting your inner child, you also reduce the emotional impact of rejection in your stepfamily. As pain from the past diminishes, the significance of current emotional conflict takes on more reasonable proportions.

Silencing Your Inner Critic

Each of us engages in an inner dialogue which psychologists call self-talk. Sit quietly for a moment, and you are likely to notice this ongoing dialogue as thoughts emerge spontaneously. Depending on your mood, schedule, work, and personal or financial pressures, your self-talk may range from positive and optimistic to negative and self-critical. Stepfamily conflict often brings out the harsh inner critic.

In most instances, the harsh inner critic is unreasonable and unnecessarily harmful to basic self-esteem. Self-punishment neither helps you cope with rejection nor serves the interest of your stepfamily. One way to silence your inner critic is to engage in directed self-talk:

Take a piece of paper, and draw a line down the middle. At the top of the left-hand column write "Inner Critic." At the top of the right-hand column, write "True Self." Now, write down your worst self-criticisms under the left-hand column, but answer back in the right-hand column with your best qualities. For example:

Inner Critic	*True Self*
I'm not a good stepparent.	I'm a very good and loving stepparent.
Nobody loves me.	My husband loves me dearly.
It's your fault that the girls hate you.	I have been a kind and loving stepparent.
You're just feeling sorry for yourself.	I have every right to feel hurt and take time to heal.
Anybody would be a better stepparent than you.	Stepparenting is difficult and I am doing a good job.
You don't have the strength to stick it out.	I have the courage to grow and a loving husband to help me through this difficult period.
You don't deserve to be happy.	I deserve a wonderful family and I'm going to have it.

By silencing your inner critic, you gain perspective on your family situation. Rejection is an inevitable process in stepfamilies, and the rejection has nothing to do with you. What you need is the personal strength to heal the wounds of rejection and develop your own self-esteem so that you can respond to stepfamily conflict with compassion and love. This may seem like a tall order, but that is why living in a stepfamily is a great incubation of personal growth.

Making Anger Work for You

Getting angry is an inevitable part of living in a stepfamily. The blending of two families almost assures that people living closely will hurt one another, at least occasionally, and the result will be angry feelings. Anger is the normal, natural emotional response to being hurt by someone you love. Whether those angry feelings lead to a prompt resolution of conflict or a prolonged escalation of conflict depends upon how the anger is expressed. Learning to express anger constructively is an important skill for every person in your stepfamily to acquire, so that daily conflict can be quickly resolved without prolonged recrimination.

Whether anger is constructive or destructive depends on how you develop your intention when you first start to feel angry. Intention is subtle, and it can be easily overlooked amidst the surging adrenalin that accompanies anger. How you formulate your intention at the earliest moments of feeling angry is absolutely critical.

If your intention is merely to strike back, then your anger is almost inevitably destructive. You wind up trying to put down, punish, or manipulate, while the positive goals of communicating needs and changing the relationship go unmet. Your anger spurs hostility and bitterness and freezes the relationship in an event of the past. You explode in rage to punish your stepchild. Whether you scream at the top of your lungs or sulk in cold silence, the goal remains the same—vengeance and retaliation.

In contrast, if your intention is to communicate your pain and your need to change the relationship in positive and specific ways, your anger will be constructive. This intention makes anger supportive and imbues your expressions of anger with a commitment to a positive outcome. You assertively communicate your hurt feelings and explain what specific changes you need. Consider for a moment the following characteristics of destructive anger versus constructive anger:

Destructive anger is often a self-fulfilling prophecy in which anger begets anger. Destructive anger usually involves the following elements:

1. Manipulative comments to coerce your lover ("If you loved me, you would . . ." "If you don't like it, leave.")
2. A lengthy monologue to control and dominate ("Let me finish; I've got more to get off my chest." "I don't want to hear your excuses.")
3. Global, all-encompassing accusations that use words such as *never, always, should,* and *ought* ("You never listen." "You always do this to me.")
4. An attempt to make your loved one wrong and guilty ("You know how much I count on you." "This shows you don't really care.")

5. An uncontrolled outburst of anger, impatience, and yelling to intimidate your loved one ("Look at what you've done now.")
6. The use of old resentments as ammunition ("This is just like the time you . . ." "You're just like your mother.")
7. The use of emotional blackmail; playing the martyr ("Telling you this hurts me more than it hurts you." "I'm wasting my breath talking to you." Sighs and moans that signal "poor me.")

Constructive anger is committed to positive outcomes and is shaped by the following characteristics:

1. Gets immediate attention through an assertive but warm statement ("We've got to talk now, I'm angry . . ." "I'm upset and need to explain why . . ." "I'm hurting, please give me your attention.")
2. Communicates your hurt using "I" statements to express your feelings ("I feel let down, disappointed, and hurt." "I have trouble when you . . .")
3. Communicates specific requests for change ("I am hurt when you don't call me if you are going to be late. I am busy, too . . .")
4. Leaves you open to your family members', relatives', loved ones' feelings and points of view ("I can see how you feel." "Now I understand the miscommunication, so what can we do to avoid this problem in the future?")
5. Empowers both of you to change a destructive pattern through mutual cooperation ("Since we both want . . . we'll need to watch out for . . ." "What could we have done differently?")
6. Expresses patience while expecting determined effort to change ("I want you to stop hurting me, but I know it's going to take time." "It's normal to have ups and downs, but we have to change . . .")
7. Prepares emotional ground for forgiveness once the relationship begins to shift to a new footing ("I still think you're terrific, and I love you. What we need to work on is . . ." "I value you greatly, and . . .")

The more skilled you become in expressing anger constructively, the more you will find that even intense arguments can be resolved quickly and effectively.

Defending Your Stepfamily

Sometimes it is necessary to stand up to disapproval of the remarriage by one spouse's parents and/or the stepchildren. Your parents' dreams for you, like your own, may not have been to marry someone who already has children. Parents may be unsupportive and mistrustful. They may wonder if your spouse sees you as nothing but a meal ticket.

After a whirlwind courtship, Chad married and moved in with Stephanie and her two children. According to Chad, "When I brought Stephanie and her two children to meet my family, it was a total disaster. Mom was determined not to like Stephanie and made little effort to hide her judgments."

His parents expressed worry to Chad about all the responsibility he was taking on, and they made sarcastic comments about Stephanie and the permissive way she raised her children. They said to Chad privately, "Why do you want to spend your time and money raising someone else's kids?"

Chad later shared, "I wanted to tell them all just where to go, but I decided to keep my mouth shut and pray the visit would soon be over."

When Chad's mother called to invite him to spend Christmas with the family, she failed to mention Stephanie or the children. Chad asked his mother, "What about Stephanie?" His mother snapped, "What about Stephanie? Can't you come without her?"

As soon as Chad related the conversation to Stephanie, she became furious. "It hurts that your mother doesn't like me. If you have to go, then you may as well go without me and the kids."

Chad felt caught in a bind. He didn't want to say no to his parents, yet he wanted to spend Christmas with Stephanie and the children. Asking Stephanie to give his family another chance and join him on the trip, Chad was surprised to hear Stephanie tell him, "As long as you let your mother get away with her tirades, I'd rather not see her. I'm also losing respect for you and mistrusting your love for me because you're a mama's boy." Feeling conflicted and depressed, Chad came to see me.

In his first session, Chad expressed hurt at being caught "in the middle" between his parents and new family. His anger and frustration over the current dilemma left him feeling paralyzed. For Chad, holding his hurt and anger inside was no longer a viable choice. He said that his stomach felt like it was tied in knots and that he had become increasingly short-tempered with Stephanie and the children. The time had come for him to learn how to stand up for his new stepfamily.

I pointed out to Chad, "Your desire to not hurt anyone may be good, but the effect of your submissiveness is to keep you a boy instead of a man. It's the common conflict of wanting to please Mom and Dad versus the desire to become an independent adult with your own wife and family."

As part of therapy, I encouraged Chad to express his anger to me in a role-playing exercise, as though I were his mother. At first he held back, saying "I don't want to raise my voice to my mother." Recognizing that he didn't need to act out his rage toward her in person, he then let himself get involved in the role-playing exercise. Shaking his fists, swearing and shouting, he hurled a tirade of feelings at me as I played his mother:

- "I hate it when you reject and criticize Stephanie and the children."
- "I have a right to my own life."
- "Don't lay your fears and insecurities on me."
- "I want you to love and accept my wife Stephanie."
- "I need your support in becoming a parent."
- "I want you to open your hearts and be real grandparents."

Once Chad let off steam and had a good cry, I suggested we continue with the role play.

CHAD: "Please tell me why you've been so cold and critical to Stephanie and her children."

MOTHER: (played by me): "Do you really want to know? I'll tell you. I don't like the fact that she's already been married. Why doesn't the children's father pay for their share instead of depending on you? Then there's the way she dresses—like a seductress. That must be how she caught you."

CHAD: "Are you jealous I married Stephanie?"

MOTHER: "That's not why I don't like her. I never expected that you would come home with a divorced woman with two children and say 'We just got married.' Then you tell me that she's an artist but unable to make a living at it. You don't have that much money to waste, do you? I feel like she is taking advantage of you and us."

CHAD: "Why do you care?"

MOTHER: "Because I love you and want what's best for you."

CHAD: "You do?"

MOTHER: "Of course I do. Otherwise, I wouldn't care who you were with. But I need to hear from you that you are happy with Stephanie and your stepchildren, and then we need some time to adjust and accept your choice."

At this point we stopped the role-playing exercise because Chad had discovered that underneath the disapproval and negative judgments were his mother's concern for his happiness. As I explained to Chad, it's natural to be hurt when your excitement is not shared by your parents. Give them time to adjust; a stepfamily is not what they dreamed of or expected.

Two months before Christmas, Chad flew to Philadelphia for a convention and arranged to meet his mother so they could spend some time together. He told her "I love you, Mom, and I've always enjoyed spending our Christmas with you and Dad. But my family now includes Stephanie and our two children. While I know you might not approve of my marriage to Stephanie, I want you to know that it hurts me to see her and the kids rejected by you. Stephanie, the kids, and I love one another. I'm going to stay home this year to celebrate Christmas with my wife and kids. I would very much like you and Dad to fly out over Easter to get to know Stephanie and the children. Let's start anew."

Having expressed his feelings without blame or criticism, Chad listened without interrupting while his mother described her anger at him for not being invited to meet Stephanie before he made plans for the wedding. He made a conscious effort to remain relaxed, attentive, and receptive. Watching his mother closely, he was able to see the concern and love underneath her angry remarks and criticisms.

Before leaving, Chad gave his mother a hug and said, "Mom, you're special to me. You're entitled to your feelings and opinions, as I am to mine. Stephanie wants you to like her and be grandparents to the kids, and I hope someday you will. You've done your job as a parent by sharing your concerns with me and now you can relax. I am responsible for and feel good about my wedding and new family. Even though I don't always do things the way you and Dad would like, I want you to know I love you."

When he discussed the visit with Stephanie, she began to see that Chad valued his relationship with her and the children enough to stand up to his mother's disapproval. Feeling that their commitment to each other was solid, they became less affected by what Chad's mother thought about their marriage and stepfamily. This trial by fire, while painful, actually served to strengthen Chad as well as his remarriage.

Role Reversal:
Seeing Yourself as Others See You

If you are having trouble communicating with your stepchild, you might want to take a moment to figure out how your stepchild is perceiving you. A "Role Reversal" exercise can be especially powerful and enlightening when you are stuck in repetitive arguing with your stepchild.

A seven-year-old stepdaughter was once again dawdling and procrastinating about getting dressed and ready for school. When her stepmother found herself becoming more and more frustrated and once again ready to yell, she stopped and instead suggested a game. "Let's reverse roles," she suggested. "You be the mother and I'll be Julia; maybe we can learn something together."

"Brush your teeth and get dressed now, Julia," said Julia.

"No!" the mother yelled. "No, no, no. Stop rushing me."

"We have to leaving in five minutes or you'll be late for school again," said Julia.

"You're always hurrying me and being bossy," said her stepmother.

Julia took her stepmother's hand, put her arm around her shoulder, and lovingly said, "Sweetheart, I'll be more cheerful and less grumpy in the morning. We'll have fun getting ourselves ready in the morning. I'll have a smile on my face when I wake you up."

This stepmother found this exercise to be a stunning revelation. The stepmother had felt dragged out of bed to get Julia ready and was communicating this attitude to Julia. The role play took only a few minutes, but created a shift in attitude that brought them much closer together and ended the conflict.

This "Role Reversal" exercise can sometimes be a humorous way to learn how your stepchildren perceive you. If you can summon the courage to engage in a little role-playing exercise with your stepchildren, remember that the purpose of the exercise is to learn how you are perceived. The children must be assured that they can be frank and even exaggerate the role playing. The point is not that you are "Mrs. Clean," "Mr. Dictator," or "Mr. Cold," but rather that your stepchildren may perceive you that way. Once you get the feedback, you can change the relationship to create harmony and communication.

Watching the Family Movies of Your Mind

There is another exercise I recommend to obtain feedback about how you are perceived. This exercise is particularly useful with older children. Psychotherapy puts a premium on words. But there is another way of knowing, a more intuitive, holistic awareness that exists alongside, though often dominated by, the intellect and rationality. This intuitive portion of the mind provides awareness through movies-of-the-mind. By first contacting and then directing these inner images on a deeper level than you may have previously explored, it becomes possible to feel less conflicted about family issues and to allow certain suppressed feelings to surface.

Close your eyes for a few minutes and let yourself relax. Breathe deeply from your abdomen and feel the relaxation that flows through your body. Now, in your mind's eye, see a beautiful meadow with wildflowers and grass. Perhaps you even visualize butterflies and hear the sound of the breeze blowing through the leaves.

Then see your entire stepfamily—spouse, stepchildren, children—running through this field of flowers. Look at yourself and each family member closely. See each person's facial expression and how their bodies move.

Regardless of how far from real life the notion of you and your family running through a field may be, let yourself go with the fantasy and watch this inner movie unfold. As you watch, ask yourself these questions. Is everybody running or does one refuse to run? Who is running faster? Who is running at a slower pace or dragging? What do their bodies look like as they run—stiff, relaxed, loose, tight? Take your time and watch your movie unreel, noting everything that's happening.

This visualization lets you look at your family members in a new light, to see yourself and them in a way that may reveal what you believe about them. You will probably find that your images of the way you and they run across a field are a parallel to the way the family has moved through life. This exercise is particularly useful if you and other family members do the exercise and discuss it together.

After you've done the exercise, here are some guidelines to help you interpret it: Is the father or stepfather running faster than the mother or stepmother? Who is out in front? Who is being left behind? Who is looking out for whom? When legs move freely and they're relatively relaxed as they run, it is a sign of a relatively relaxed home environment. Rigid legs or strain usually indicate conflict. If one person is left behind, further discussion will generally reveal a family member who feels left out or excluded. When the parent or stepparents tends to self-pity and martyrdom, he or she usually has stiff limbs or is dragging in the visualizations.

Step Inside Your Shadow

In psychology the shadow refers to the dark side of human personality: the rage, fear, jealousy, and violent feelings that lie unconscious beneath the surface, masked by the more pleasant, proper, and appropriately socialized outer presentation.

If your shadow side remains unexplored and untamed, it is all too easy to project your disowned lying, selfish, and vindictive tendencies onto a stepchild. *To make peace in your stepfamily, you must see and reown your own shadow, and come to grips with the inner enemy you have been so ashamed of and reviled.* When you see a stepchild as inferior, immoral, disgusting, or psychopathic, turn the mirror around to see what you can learn about your personal shadow.

To identify your shadow, reflect on who in your stepfamily pushes your buttons. Whom do you revile, resent, or hate? What traits in a stepchild are you particularly repelled by? Why do you find these qualities so repugnant? Are fights with your stepchild over cleanliness, household chores, schoolwork, or "showing respect" somehow reminiscent of your own childhood experiences? Did either of your parents or a sibling make degrading comments that left you feeling inferior? What specific remarks did they make that you've never forgiven them for? What other instances as a child made you feel rejected, put down, humiliated, or scorned? Write down specific comments.

One stepfather found he was using the same yelling and intimidation he hated his father for using to belittle or shame him as a child:

- "How could you be so stupid?"
- "I told you not to do that!"
- "If you ever raise your voice to me, I'll smack your head off!"
- "I don't have to explain anything to you. You'll do what I say."

A stepmother was able to recognize her use of guilt-inspiring comments that she despised her mother using on her as a child:

- "After all I've done for you, you don't even appreciate me."
- "You don't care about anyone but yourself. You're incredibly selfish."
- "Look what I have given up for you!"

The need to make peace suggests that a war has been raging, and perhaps that war has been raging within you, long before you became a stepparent. Parenting is never easy. In the process of wanting to influence, guide, and protect children, you—like your parents before you—may resort to emotional weapons that have harmful psychological consequences. By becoming more conscious of your disowned shadow and your own hurt inner child, you will be able to choose more constructive responses; to stop old patterns of guilt and intimidation.

Drawing Out Your Shadow into the Light

As an additional helpful exercise, try "drawing out" your shadow. Draw images that symbolize the disowned and uncomfortable parts of yourself you generally choose not to see. Focus on emotional expression rather than the normal concerns of art, with no critical editing of your inner visions. The simple act of drawing is healing because it takes shadow feelings that have felt out-of-control and gives them a conscious image. If painful or frightening images come up, keep drawing. You may also try drawing a healing light surrounding these images.

Draw pictures of your stepchild to learn more about the shadow you have been projecting. First close your eyes to fully experience the negative feelings which you harbor. When the negativity has reached a peak of intensity start to draw your rage, hatred, or disgust onto paper while your eyes are still closed. When it feels right, open your eyes and continue to draw using different colors and images to vent your cruel, murderous, or arrogant feelings. Take some time to vent your anger safely—pound a mattress, scream into a pillow, or have a good cry. Feelings and memories may come up that you have been repressing for a lifetime.

A Child May Express What You Suppress

In an effort to avoid the label of "wicked stepmother" or "cruel stepfather," some stepparents fall into the trap of suppressing their feelings to the point of causing personal and family dysfunction. Families are emotional systems, and your suppression of your feelings may find expression in a stepchild's maladaptive behavior.

Marie and Gary sought treatment for Gary's thirteen-year-old daughter, Donna, who had been arrested for drug abuse and shoplifting. Gary and Marie had been married for two years. Marie had tried desperately to "love Donna as my own and make us a happy family." Unfortunately, no matter how hard Marie tried, Donna would continue to unleash her rage upon her. Having lost the security of her first family, Donna has a deep resentment and mistrust.

Only when Marie was able to learn not to take these attacks personally was she able to be more effective. Marie made the mistake of trying to replace Donna's biological mother. Instead of being a successful "rescuer," Marie seemed to make the situation worse.

Whenever Marie began to feel anger with Donna's unruly, disobedient behavior, she would suppress her frustrations. The more Marie would repress her anger, the more irritable and angry Donna would become. The more Marie tried to be a pleaser, the more Donna would explode.

Underneath it all, Marie was outraged by the treatment she was receiving. All the while, her husband Gary stood on the sidelines. I explained to Marie that it was a mistake to hide her hurt and anger.

I made two recommendations to Gary and Marie. First, Gary had to take charge of enforcing discipline. Second, Marie had to stop suppressing her anger and allow herself to develop an authentic relationship with Donna. I encouraged Marie to tell Donna that she was angry and that she would not put up with Donna's disruptive and uncooperative behavior. We discussed the importance of anger as a natural emotional response to being hurt. Unless you express the anger, you invite further hurt.

In this discussion, I reminded Marie of five essentials to express anger effectively:

1. Identify the hurt that caused the anger.
2. Demand that the hurtful actions not be repeated. Be specific.
3. Express your emotion with warmth or even heart to communicate you care. Avoid the "silent treatment."
4. Express your feelings vehemently but consciously. Do not let yourself get out of control or fly off into a rage.
5. The purpose of effective anger is to communicate, not to punish.

While anger is perhaps the most common and troublesome suppressed emotion in stepfamilies, beware of others as well. If you have not spent enough time with your spouse clarifying values, roles, rules, and limits and values, then your own role as stepparent may generate anxiety. In that case, other family members may feel ill at ease or on edge as well. The solution is a family meeting to address these issues.

Depression is another common emotion that needs attention but often gets ignored. Depression is often a sign of unresolved loss. It can become troubling for stepparents who believe they are not living up to their own expectations. If you were a victim of the "instant love" fantasy, or if you otherwise thought your good intentions and commitment as a stepparent would assure the love and respect of your stepchildren, then some depression is natural. You need to give yourself permission to mourn your loss of expectations and reapply your commitment with the expanded knowledge of stepfamily dynamics that you are gaining.

Negative Expectations May Become Self-Fulfilling Prophecies

Parental expectations can have an enormous impact on children. Some studies show that expectations alone will cause children to improve their performance and behavior, while malignant expectations can create misbehavior. Stepfamilies provide particularly fertile ground for such malignant expectations because conflict and animosity from a prior marriage often spills over into the stepfamily to color perceptions.

Malignant expectations show up in subtle ways with subtle but nevertheless damaging consequences. For example, if a stepchild fails to empty the garbage as asked, does it mean that he hates you or is trying to show disrespect? Or might he simply have forgotten? If you choose the former interpretation, you set the stage for an argument before you even know the facts. If you choose the latter, you open the possibility for inquiry and correction of the problem.

By choosing the strategy of positive interpretation, you won't feel cheated, the children won't feel guilty, and both of you can focus your energies on creating a new and pleasing routine. If you give the benefit of the doubt (he didn't hear me, she was upset about school) and make benign assumptions about a stepchild's actions (or lack of), you will feel better and your relationship will be smoother. This does not mean that chronic misbehavior should be explained away, but if you are going to make a more "malignant" assumption, first check its accuracy with your child and with your partner.

Sarcasm is one of the most common and destructive ways that

parents project negative expectations. Parents sometimes add a sarcastic qualifier to an acknowledgment that would otherwise serve to build self-esteem, such as:

- "Thanks for washing the car. I thought I'd never live to see it."
- "That was the first nice thing you've ever said to me."
- "That was a good report card. I'm amazed you don't have D's."

Sarcastic qualifiers may be explainable as an expression of frustration with a child who has been very difficult. Nevertheless, both you and your child will be better served if you acknowledge positive behavior with sincere appreciation instead.

Dealing with Family Frustration

Almost every stepparent feels at one time or another, "I've had enough. I'm ready to quit." No matter how much you may love your spouse, it is natural at times to feel overwhelmed and trapped. The first step in dealing with these feelings is to recognize that almost every stepparent has negative feelings about her stepfamily (such as "If it weren't for those stepchildren, I could have my own baby," or "The stepchildren are taking over my life").

Quite often stepparents are reluctant to acknowledge the existence of these feelings, or are guilty or ashamed about them.

My advice in dealing with these negative feelings is: accept them, but don't dwell on your frustration. Paradoxically, by accepting these feelings, they will tend to diminish. If you resist them, they tend to persist. Guilt and shame are counterproductive. If you recognize these feelings for the normal products of frustration that they are, you can let them pass without becoming engrossed in them. You are then free to turn your attention to what you can do to lessen conflict and create more satisfying relationships in your stepfamily.

When to Seek Professional Help

If conflict persists or escalates in your stepfamily, despite all your efforts to make peace, then you would probably benefit from seeking professional help. The results of therapeutic intervention in stepfamily conflicts are generally good. In fact, given the high divorce rate among remarrieds with children and the complexity of stepfamily relationships, I would recommend that stepfamily members seek professional help whenever conflict seems to be excessively prolonged. A few sessions with a therapist familiar with stepfamily issues can make an enormous difference.

If one or more of the following signs and symptoms apply to your stepfamily, I urge you to seek professional help promptly:

- You and your marriage partner are repeatedly caught in bitter conflict and hostility.
- You feel chronically overwhelmed by problems and feel you cannot cope.
- You or your mate seeks solace in binge eating, illicit drugs, or alcohol abuse.
- Family arguments lead to physical combat or threats of violence.
- The boundaries of intimacy are violated, and someone in the stepfamily is sexually harassed or abused.
- You and your spouse have sexual problems that you haven't been able to resolve on your own, even after making a sustained effort.
- A child in the family is "that troublemaker," the source of many unresolved disputes between the two of you.
- Stepsiblings continually use physical or psychological abuse to deal with jealousy and rivalry.
- You're in a severe emotional crisis, and the support of family and friends isn't enough.
- Someone in the family may be suffering from a serious mental illness.
- Any family member is significantly depressed or having suicidal thoughts.

- You and your mate remain emotionally withdrawn from each other (when you frequently think the remarriage was a mistake).
- A child's school performance, peer relationships, or behavior remain deteriorated months after the previous marital breakup or after the new family has been formed.

Couples in crisis routinely prolong their emotional distress through denial. We all have a tendency to hope conflict will lessen by ignoring it. If any of the above symptoms apply to your stepfamily, what you need is the courage to acknowledge the crisis and get help. Many forms of help are available, including premarital counseling, stepfamily workshops, stepparent groups, stepfamily classes, family therapy, and adolescent or child therapy. Following is a brief summary of what you can expect from these various sources of help.

Premarital counseling. An ounce of prevention is worth ten pounds of cure. Before walking down the aisle, remarrieds ought to talk with a therapist and/or attend a stepfamily workshop. Premarital counseling can provide an opportunity to avoid major confrontations and divided loyalties at the beginning of stepfamily life. Premarital counseling can also help you to prepare the children for the overwhelming changes that take place when forming a new family. Especially if either partner has had a painful first marriage, it is better for unresolved issues to be played out in therapy, rather than in the remarriage.

Often just a couple of sessions with a counselor versed in the special problems and stages of development of the stepfamily allows prospective marriage partners to explore and clarify their needs, fears, and expectations, as well as those of their children. If these discussions reveal the couple's expectations to be at opposite ends of the spectrum and irreconcilable, it's far better to discover it before the marriage ceremony than to put yourselves and your children through another family breakup and divorce. Such a possibility prior to taking the nuptial vows is often too frightening for some people to handle, but most often partners who are smart enough to go for premarital counseling wind up with a much stronger union and a better functioning stepfamily. While starry-eyed lovers are the stuff of romance novels, realistic love partners stand the best chance of living happily ever after.

Stepfamily workshops and classes. Most people don't need individual counseling. They need a good education as to what is normal and what expectations may be unrealistic. A stepfamily workshop before or soon after the marriage allows participants to learn a good deal about the universal elements of stepfamily conflict. A skillful seminar leader encourages attendees to open up about feelings, an experience that would be inappropriate in any other gathering. In one of my recent workshops, a father expressed relief that he could share his guilt at the breakup of his previous marriage. Another participant was relieved to learn that "I'm not the only stepmother who resents being the cook and maid when the stepkids come to visit." Stepfamily workshops are burgeoning, and the Stepfamily Association of America has chapters that are active in over forty states.

Stepfamily classes are for stepparents and parents alike. Remarried couples have a forum in which to learn communication skills, discuss finances, examine rules and discipline in their blended families, and explore ways to welcome the visiting stepchild. Most of all, a support group for remarrieds with children allows you to meet others with feelings and experiences similar to your own. These groups also create special events (picnics, camping, play days) for fun.

Stepparent groups. Another valuable source of help is a stepparent group, in which members generally meet once or twice a week to provide support. For too long, stepparents have felt secretly bitter and ashamed for not possessing the instant love and know-how expected of them. They struggle with the issues behind the scene, afraid to "air dirty laundry in public." A stepparent group is often co-led by a man and a woman who are mental health professionals who have been stepparents themselves. Therapists who have experienced firsthand the emotional isolation and conflicts of stepfamily living often make good facilitators. The bond of "we're all in this together" is very healing. Often it is a relief to realize that someone in the group is struggling with a situation that is much worse than your own! Stepparents gain insight and solutions to difficult problems. Mutual support inspires confidence and provides a safe place to vent feelings about what is happening at home.

Marriage, family, and child therapy. If there is chronic fighting or hostility in a stepfamily, then a workshop, class, or support group alone may not be sufficient. Many stepfamily problems involve a number of people in destructive relationships. Marriage or family therapy allows you to look at what is going on in the system with a trained, objective person. We can never see ourselves the way an outsider can. The professional's office provides a safe setting for explosive issues to be aired.

A child often suffers serious psychological wounds in a situation in which both father and mother have remarried new partners and yet continue the hostilities that originally led to their divorce. A child caught in the middle between warring parents frequently engages in acting out or delinquent behavior, or else becomes emotionally withdrawn. The child's symptoms are manifestations of divided loyalties and internalizing the parental conflict. A therapist can be very helpful to a troubled teenager or child, in individual consultation or meeting with the entire family.

How to Choose a Therapist

Most people spend more time buying a car than searching for the right psychotherapist! There is nothing mysterious about psychotherapy, and no therapist can perform magic. Any psychotherapist can only assist you in discovering how you can solve your marriage and stepfamily problems; not solve them for you.

The empathic ability of a therapist, rather than his or her theoretical persuasion, is critical in determining whether you can benefit from counseling. Therapeutic strategies and techniques can be very helpful and genuine. Other characteristics to consider are authentic, nonpossessive warmth and sense of humor.

The importance of carefully choosing a psychotherapist cannot be overemphasized. Seek referrals from your local Stepfamily Association of America chapter (see Appendix C), mental health agencies, family doctor, and other stepfamilies. Visit two or three counselors, therapists, or ministers with the intention of determining who would be most suitable. It is helpful to include your marriage partner in this evaluation.

When making your final decision, consider the following questions:

1. Is he or she a licensed psychotherapist who is respected by the professional community and general public?
2. Does the therapist have a pleasant disposition, a sense of humor, and appear to be functioning well in his or her life?
3. If you specifically need family therapy, marital counseling, a support group, or a child evaluation, does this professional have specialized experience and expertise in this area?
4. Do you feel safe, comfortable, and at ease with the therapist?
5. Is the therapist honest, nondefensive, and empathetic?
6. Is the therapist willing to explain his or her approach to your problem, including strategies, goals, and length of treatment?
7. Is the therapist very rigid in his approach or flexible and open to your input?
8. Does he or she listen silently like a blank screen, or do you feel you are getting some sensible and generally helpful input?
9. Does the therapist answer your questions and concerns directly rather than always asking what you think?
10. Do the therapist's strategies and techniques show care and concern for you as well as others?
11. After the session, do you feel more hopeful and empowered with higher self-esteem?

The therapist should be willing to explain his or her assessment of your marriage and stepfamily, along with strategies and treatment goals. It is also reasonable to ask for an estimate of how long treatment will take. Significant benefit can often be obtained in a short number of sessions. The Chinese symbol for "crisis" also means challenge and opportunity. Psychotherapy can be opportunity to face the crises of stepfamily life and convert them to opportunities for personal growth and family renewal.

Up from Depression

Are you or your spouse depressed? If you and your spouse have lost the passion in your marriage or if you are troubled by chronic conflict, one cause may be that one of you is significantly depressed and in need of treatment. Depression is an inherent part of the human condition that everyone suffers to some degree at one time or another. For some people, however, depression may be so severe that psychotherapy alone may yield few positive results. In these cases, a psychiatrist can prescribe antidepressant medications which make severe depression a highly treatable illness.

Most people are unaware that low energy, lack of sexual passion, and an impaired ability to love and be loved can be the biological result of severe depression. Almost as painful as being severely depressed is being the mate of someone suffering from this disorder. No matter how hard you try to be intimate and stimulate passion, nothing seems to work. Both people tend to blame themselves and each other. It is easy to blame being in a stepfamily or scapegoat a child as a cause of suffering.

People who suffer from depression may fail to seek help and appropriate medical treatment because they fear the stigma of "mental illness." This is an unfortunate irony because biological depression is a highly prevalent and well-recognized medical disorder, one as treatable as diabetes or hypertension.

The primary symptoms of depression are anhedonia (reduced enjoyment and pleasure), boredom, loss of concentration, difficulty in decision making, neglect of personal appearance, early morning awakening, low self-esteem, outbursts of rage, exhaustion, insomnia, reduced sexual activity, feelings of guilt, worthlessness, or stupidity, suicidal thoughts, and a diminished capacity for love and affection.

Severe biological depression may result from or lead to a biochemical imbalance in the brain. Antidepressants, taken as prescribed by a psychiatrist, are nonaddictive and highly effective. Some people resist taking antidepressants because they are "drugs" and therefore perceived as "unnatural." This is unfortunate because antidepressants restore a natural biochemical balance. Proper medication used in conjunction with psychotherapy can bring immediate relief and in most cases an effective end to severe depression. If you or your spouse suffer from the symptoms of depression, consult your family physician or a psychiatrist for help.

Conflict will not disappear from your marriage as a result of classes, workshops, support groups, therapy, or antidepressants. Nor should it. Conflict can be the basis for positive change and progress.

With compassion and knowledge, conflicting forces in your step-family can be used to strengthen your stepfamily and enhance your personal growth.

Conflict Is a Challenge to Growth

Making peace in your stepfamily is likely to be one of the most significant personal growth experiences of your life. The process is dynamic, both among members of your stepfamily and within you. Resolving conflict is an essential and inevitable part of becoming a stepfamily and an ongoing part of blending two different family histories. As such, stepfamily peacemaking requires that you become adept at integrating seemingly opposite values, and at teaching others this skill.

Every member of the stepfamily faces the ongoing challenge of integrating apparently opposing feelings. For example, stepparents must integrate their desire to love their stepchildren with a desire to have children of their own or to love their own children. Parents must integrate loyalty to their own children with loyalty to a new spouse. Stepchildren must integrate love for parents who have separated with the need to be part of a new family. These are just a few of the conflicts that have ramifications throughout stepfamily relationships and deci-sion making. When children move between households, both families must recognize that the joy of every reunion has a sadness of depar-ture built in. Tension between ex-spouses can be reduced, but rarely disappears entirely. Children who have suffered the trauma of divorce can regain self-confidence and security, but memories of the trauma remain and get played out from time to time.

What you gain from this constant challenge to integrate opposites is a steady expansion and deepening of your sense of self. For exam-ple, you begin to recognize that you are big enough to incorporate love of your children and your stepchildren, despite all the conflict you may have endured with your stepchildren. You learn that your capacity to give is bigger than you thought, and you open yourself to a wider array of feelings than ever before. You are also likely to find depths to your own personal strength that you have never anticipated. This expansion of the self is the essence of what personal growth is all about. What you will also gain from the growth process is a greater sense of humor. Life in a stepfamily teaches the futility of taking ourselves so seriously and becoming too embroiled in petty concerns. The more you appreciate the emotional dynamics of your stepfamily, the more you may be surprised at how often you end arguments in laughter. When it comes to resolving stepfamily conflicts, humor is often the best medicine.

Chapter 9

FROM EX TO EXTENDED FAMILY: FORMING A PARENTING COALITION

*T*he single most important factor in the positive emotional adjustment of children following a divorce is a stable, loving relationship with both natural parents. In most stepfamilies, however, chronic friction between ex-spouses is the norm, and not only the children but the whole stepfamily suffers as a result. Children are torn by divided loyalties, and stepparents become frustrated, witnessing their stepchildren's emotional turmoil exacerbated by petty battles between their parents.

Our understanding of how children cope most effectively with divorce has progressed over the past twenty years. When divorce rates began to rise in the early 1970s, some psychologists thought that getting children out of a bad marriage environment would more than compensate for the trauma of divorce. We soon learned that the emotional needs of children following divorce were not so easily met, and the research results began to suggest the importance of a continuing connection with both natural parents. The courts responded with the concept of joint custody, which evolved into the norm for child custody arrangements.

In many cases, joint custody has not lived up to expectations. This apparent legal solution to assuring children of contact with both natural parents is not an effective emotional solution. As long as parents remain embroiled by their own emotional antagonism, exercise of their rights under joint custody agreements becomes a source of chronic conflict that throws the children into emotional turmoil rather than providing the children an emotionally stable bond with both parents as originally intended. Remarriage by one or both of the natural parents further exacerbates the problem when one of the natural parents perceives the new stepparent as an interloper or competitor.

The new direction in stepfamily counseling goes beyond attempting to facilitate a better coparenting relationship between ex-spouses. The newest research on stepfamilies indicates that children of divorce can thrive if they can feel part of two stable and related households. This goal requires formation of a parenting coalition involving both natural parents as well as one or both stepparents.

A parenting coalition diffuses the tension between ex-spouses and allows the evolution of two independent but related households with their own set of values, rules, roles, and relationships. These households have permeable boundaries which allow the children to move back and forth, feeling part of each and comfortable with both, despite often significant differences between the household in discipline, expectations, or finances.

This chapter is about making peace in your stepfamily by forming a parenting coalition. It may sound like an unattainable ideal if your stepfamily is currently plagued by chronic friction between ex-spouses. If your ex-spouse is abusive to you or your children, many of the goals of this chapter may not be appropriate. With this exception, any progress you make forming a parenting coalition is worth the effort, if not for you then for your children.

War Games Divorced Parents Play

There is simple wisdom in the old saying, "Two heads are better than one." The first step in forming a parenting coalition is recognizing that three or four parents can be better than two. The principal obstacle to forming an effective parenting coalition is neither the stepparents nor the children. The obstacle is almost always the divorced parents who remain locked in postdivorce emotional wars. All too often, parents enlist their children as pawns in the ongoing battle.

Here are some of the war games divorced parents play with one another, often unwittingly at the expense of their children:

Spy: When children return from a visit to an ex-spouse, some parents quiz the children for information. "Who is your father dating now? What did your father give (his new spouse) for her birthday? Where is your stepfather planning to take your mother for vacation?" In this war game, parents use their children to acquire information that might be useful in financial disagreements or visitation dispute. While the parents arm themselves with information, the children are torn by feelings of insecurity and disloyalty.

Provocateur: In sending children to visit an ex-spouse, some parents create emotional distress that makes the children very difficult to handle. Parents who bad-mouth each other to their children prior to visits may succeed in torpedoing the visit, but only at the expense of the child's self-esteem and trust.

Messenger: Some parents use their children to underline their lack of respect for each other. Parents demonstrate this mutual disrespect by refusing to address each other directly and using the children as messenger. ("Tell your father that he better send the support check on time or you're not visiting next weekend.") By using a child as a messenger, parents may succeed in showing their contempt for each other, but only at the expense of putting the child in the middle. The child perceives his parents as not caring enough about the child to talk to each other directly.

Propagandist: Some ex-spouses use their children to deceive each other. Trying to manipulate her ex into increasing his support, one mother instructed her son, "Tell your father the roof is leaking and we need to get it fixed." The roof wasn't leaking, but the mother knew her ex would never check. Trying to keep his ex from learning about a big promotion (and pay increase), one father instructed his son, "Don't tell your mother about the new car. If she finds out, she'll try to get more money, and I won't have enough to really have fun when you visit." These propaganda tactics may serve in the battle of one-upmanship between ex-spouses, but only by breeding dishonesty in the children.

Saboteur: Some parents prepare their children to sabotage an ex-spouse's remarriage. For example, one mother told her daughter that new school clothes were out of the question because her father was spending his money on his new wife. When the stepmother tried to be friendly, this girl was antagonistic. This strategy succeed in creating enough conflict between the father and his new wife to cause them to seek counseling. The mother achieved her psychic victory at the expense of creating jealousy, and mistrust in her child.

Children are the true casualties of these war games between ex-spouses. What makes these cases even more tragic is lost opportunity to provide better parenting for the children. When parents and stepparents move toward forming a parenting coalition, they do not just call a truce in their war games, but begin to cooperate in sharing their parenting responsibilities. In doing so, the two households coordinate efforts to alleviate the burdens of parenting while most effectively meeting the needs of the children. Competition between spouses and the stepparents diminish, while communication about the children increases. Adults in parenting coalitions feel comfortable discussing their views about the children, and may meet periodically to make certain that communication remains open and unclouded by emotional static from the past.

Cooperation Benefits You

I would not even begin to suggest that forming a parenting coalition is easy, but here are some of the advantages that suggest the effort would be worthwhile:

- You have more information about the child's needs and behaviors.
- You have three or four people working together to solve problems, rather than two parents working at cross purposes.
- Each of you, parents and stepparents, are less likely to be manipulated by the child.
- You can more easily combine resources for the child's benefit—medical needs, a school opportunity, or even a vacation.
- You lessen tensions surrounding major events, such as holidays, graduations, or weddings.
- If your child develops a discipline problem, you can respond with a coordinated effort in both households.
- You create safety and trust with the child who feels he or she can move between households without feeling guilty or disloyal.
- When a child has a continuing discipline problem, you know that the problem is not a result of sabotage from the other household.
- Should professional help for a child appear to be indicated, you know that you have input and cooperation from all the responsible adults in the child's life.
- By demonstrating cooperation among the households, you model for the children positive qualities such as trust, cooperation, self-confidence and optimism about the future.

In reviewing the advantages to a parenting coalition, it is obvious that the children are not the problem. The real obstacles are unresolved emotions among the adults, particularly ex-spouses. Here are some exercises to get past the emotional blocks to a parenting coalition.

Discharging Rage Appropriately

To discharge rage, you have to get in touch with your feelings and allow a physical and emotional release. Rage often remains repressed because the intensity of the anger may be frightening. Rage is anger so intense that its object is to destroy. Most of us are unwilling to recognize such intense anger within ourselves. Instead, a conversation with an ex provokes an intense headache, or a clenched jaw.

To get in touch with rage toward your ex, you need to create a safe environment and give yourself permission. Go into your bedroom, close the door, and find several pillows on the bed and imagine that they are your ex. Now recall the last incident that made you furious at your ex. Rather than control your fury, surrender to it by pounding the pillow and telling your ex exactly how you feel. Do not be afraid to use expletives or phrases such as "I am going to bash your head in" or "You can't push me around anymore." Let yourself go. No one will be hurt by your release of your fury. The more you let go, the more intense your rage may become. This release of violent feelings in the safety of your bedroom will result in an emotional clearing to allow a new quality of communication to develop between you and your ex.

One trial of this exercise may provide the emotional release you need. Or, if your symptoms of repressed rage persist, you may want to repeat this exercise. It is important to lie down for a minimum of ten minutes after the exercise to allow your feelings to settle down and to regain your sense of composure.

Writing the Wrong

While rage may be a deep, destructive emotion that fuels irrationality between you and your ex, accumulated resentments can be equally problematic.

In an exercise I call "Writing the Wrong," make a list of specific resentments toward your ex. For example

- "I resent you are a Disneyland Dad while I do all the dirty work."

- "I resent when you yell at me over the telephone."
- "I resent when you make the unilateral decisions about holidays and summer visitation schedules."
- "I resent that you make such a big deal about picking up the kids in your new Mercedes."

It isn't necessary to list every last resentment. At a certain point, when you have filled up a page or more, you will have reached a critical point. Rest a few moments and see if other strong feelings emerge. After you have added any additional resentments, stop to inhale and exhale deeply. Let any feelings come up, and don't be afraid to cry.

Under no circumstances should you use your "Writing the Wrong" exercise to hurt and attack your ex-spouse. This list of resentments is not to be mailed, and under no circumstances is this ever to be shared with your children. You are healing old wounds, not seeking to make new ones.

The Power of Forgiving

Another useful technique to complete an emotional clearing is a visualization exercise that I call "The Power of Forgiving." When I suggest this exercise, some clients reject the idea of forgiving an ex-spouse. The reason to forgive is not for your ex, but for you and the emotional well-being of your children. Forgiving frees you from emotional bondage to your past.

Unplug the phone and put a DO NOT DISTURB sign on the door. Close your eyes, relax, and visualize you and your ex in an appropriate setting, perhaps your current home or the home you shared. If you find it difficult to visualize your ex, express your feelings while looking at an old photograph of him or her.

With an ex-spouse in mind, say in your own words, "Out of a desire to make peace and for the sake of the children, there are some things I need to clear up with you." Now proceed to let your ex know the resentments you still harbor as if you had his/her undivided attention. Each painful memory or hurt could be described as specifically as possible. Review your list of resentments, if necessary. Remember the incident, feeling, or conflict that upset you, and describe your stuck feelings to the visualized image of your ex-spouse. However unrealistic it may be, picture your ex accepting your hurt and anger, and understanding fully your point of view.

It is not important to cover every hurt of your entire relationship. You may want to spend an entire session or two on a major traumatic event. Imagine you have complete permission from your ex to finally "let it out." As you describe your resentments and anger, give yourself permission to release any hurt, fear, or sadness. Playact, exaggerate your feelings, scream—do anything safely to let go of your feelings. If you are afraid of making too much noise, shout into a pillow. You are not to wallow in your hurts, but to release them safely and appropriately. If you become distracted or feel emotionally blocked, don't strain but gently bring yourself back to the process. Remember that your intention is not to harm your actual ex-spouse. Hostile thoughts are okay, violent action is not. Rather, you are using this imagery to acknowledge and heal old resentments and move on. After doing this exercise for approximately twenty minutes, you may feel complete for this session or else emotionally fatigued.

At the end of this exercise, a few moments of guided relaxation are advisable. Get comfortable, close your eyes, and imagine your body and emotions filled with lights (for example, red lights for anger and blue lights for peace and relaxation). Visualize the lights changing from red to blue and from blue to red, and notice your physical sensations. Gradually change all of the lights in your body to blue and experience feeling lighter. Notice the tension easing in your body. Allow the light to fill your body as you relax and let go.

Overcoming Fear and Mistrust

One of the most troublesome emotional legacies of divorce is lingering fear and mistrust between ex-spouses. The reasons for divorce may be many, but almost always at least one of the marriage partners feels deceived and betrayed. In some cases, the betrayal takes concrete form through an affair. In other cases, the betrayal is ambiguous, arising out of a gradual disaffection.

Lingering feelings of betrayal tend to fuel post-divorce fear and mistrust, particularly as to issues involving children. Ex-spouses are quick to interpret each other's actions as an attempt to win the children's loyalty or otherwise maneuver the child-rearing responsibility to an unfair advantage.

I have witnessed the problem in my own stepfamily when Sirah's boys periodically showed up for a summer visit without jeans or some other essential piece of clothing. Sirah immediately perceived her ex as manipulating her into spending more on the boys. When the boys returned home with new jeans, Sirah's ex immediately perceived Sirah as attempting to compete for the boys' affection by flaunting wealth. What followed sometimes were acrimonious arguments and accusations by telephone. Having watched this pattern over two summers, I made my own inquiry and discovered benign behavior where Sirah and her ex had perceived intentional one-upmanship. The boys as young teenagers insisted on packing for themselves with the not-to-be-unexpected result of forgetting important items. Once the boys arrived in need of clothes, Sirah took them shopping because she enjoyed it. The nefarious intentions which Sirah and her ex ascribed to these simple events were mostly in their own minds, and grew out of their mutual lingering feelings of betrayal and mistrust. This type of misunderstanding is not unusual. My clinical experience indicates that my stepfamily is the rule, not the exception.

Alleviating fear and mistrust between ex-spouses is a task that takes time. These negative feelings only diminish when the ex-spouses rebuild a responsible coparenting relationship where each person keeps his or her word and respects one another's needs, autonomy, and privacy. The problem in many cases, however, is that the coparenting relationship cannot get started because each of the ex-spouses is so inclined toward mistrust of the other. Someone has to be willing to take the first step by attempting to lessen the fear and mistrust from the past so that those feelings do not cloud discussion of current child-care issues.

A Vision of Possibilities

One way to lessen anxiety and mistrust from the past is to replace those feelings with love and self-confidence in the present. This can be so simple. By creating the direct experiences of love and self-confidence, you inhibit fear associated with mistrust. A technique called creative visualization can assist in this process. You might experiment with the following exercises. In each case, you need a quiet room, a comfortable chair, and twenty minutes to be alone.

1. Close your eyes and visualize yourself with your spouse. Now recall an incident when you believe your ex lied or betrayed you. Notice the anxiety and anger, particularly the physical symptoms on your body—head pounding, shoulders tensing, stomach churning. Don't resist these feelings. Then imagine yourself transported from this tense encounter to a safe and beautiful retreat, such as the beach, a lake, a mountaintop. Experience the anxiety and tension dissolving and serene self-confidence flowing throughout your body. Imagine yourself ready to travel back to a meeting with your ex, while you remain supremely self-confident and able to talk to your ex without feelings emotionally impaired by fear of betrayal from the past.

2. Close your eyes. Recall a recent incident when you got into a yelling match with your ex about the children. Be aware of the anger filling your mind and body. Pause. Now go underneath your anger and anxiety to visualize your love-filled heart—powerful, radiant, healing, alive. Imagine your heart is able to withstand all challenges, sending renewed love to every part of your body and beaming light all around you. Your anger and mistrust are merely a creative challenge, an opportunity to love and be loved even more deeply and courageously. Close your eyes and return to the safety of your eternal ear whenever you need to feel peace, renewal, and balance.

3. Close your eyes. Take a few deep breaths, and imagine a healing light sweeping over you. The light can be seen emanating from any source comfortable to you—God or universal spirit or love. Allow the warmth and light to assist the healing of your pain and bitterness of your spouse's betrayal. You have released the venom from your emotional abscess; this is the time to heal. Bathe your wound in this healing light, and allow your strength of heart to emerge into your awareness. Be as

peaceful as possible for about ten minutes in this spiritual "treatment."

These visualization exercises are intended to help you generate emotional well-being that can serve as an antidote to crippling fear and mistrust lingering from past betrayal. These exercises are not intended to create feelings of warmth or bonding toward your ex or to lull you into experiencing trust when you should be worrying. The goal is to recover a sense of emotional balance that will serve you in creating a businesslike coparenting relationship with your ex. It is impossible to build such a relationship if your old feelings always cause you to assume the worse. (However, avoid using these exercises to create a mood where you always assume the best.)

Reframing

Another very useful exercise for reducing the emotional volatility of coparenting relationships is called "Reframing," which replaces suspicion and anger with trust and empathy. Reframing is trying to understand a situation from another point of view so that you can discuss it rationally rather than reactively. In coparenting relationships, the simplest way to reframe is to imagine yourself viewing or interpreting the same facts from your ex-spouse's point of view.

Reframing is an active process that you can use to avoid jumping to premature conclusions and creating unnecessary conflicts. In order to master this technique, you might try reframing several recent conflicts with your ex. For instance, while you may initially interpret your ex's offer to pay for private school as an attempt to show off his wealth, reframing may help you see that he or she really just wants the best educational opportunities for your children.

Reframing is a critical skill to be mastered by all members of a parenting coalition. In a emotionally charged situation, most people are quick to interpret events as threatening and thereby to create conditions for conflict.

Setting Boundaries

In some cases, a parenting coalition is difficult to form because one or both of the ex-spouses have not yet come to terms with the finality of the divorce. One stepmother caught in such circumstances expressed her frustration. "I feel totally excluded when it comes to my two stepdaughters," she said. "Suzanne, Ty's ex-wife, is on the phone to him all weekend when his girls visit us, and he puts up with the calls because he doesn't want to hurt her."

In cases where both ex-spouses remain attached to their former relationship, the excluded stepparent needs to intervene with his or her spouse and request a Heart Talk about the need to let go so that the new stepfamilies can evolve. In cases where one spouse remains attached, the other spouse needs to address the issue directly, whether through a personal meeting or by letter to set emotional boundaries and establish limits on communication. In both circumstances, one or both of the divorced spouses have work to do in coping with loss. The discussion in Chapter 2 should be helpful. Where the attachment persists long after the divorce, therapy is advisable for the spouse unable to let go.

From Bitterness to Businesslike Meetings

When significant bitterness remains between exes, one parent may need to approach the other with a proposal to clean up their relationship. Despite bitter feelings, you are both genuinely concerned about your children's development. Share your concerns about how your conflict might be hurting the children, and request a meeting to discuss some of the problems and consider some possible solutions.

Be prepared to discuss three essential components of a new businesslike parenting relationship—attitudes, communication styles, and negotiating principles.

Here are some proposed changes in attitude ex-partners need to agree to:

- Stop criticizing each other as parents, particularly in front of the children

- Control anger so that issues can be rationally discussed
- Let go of resentments from the past as much as possible
- Acknowledge that you both have needs for respect and support
- Stop using the children to carry messages
- Stop leaning on the children for emotional support
- Stop trying to make the children feel disloyal for developing closer relationships with their stepparents
- Stop trying to use the children to punish each other by encouraging them to be more loyal to one parent than another
- Focus on what's best for the children in any situation or dispute
- Respect each other's privacy
- Respect each other's parenting styles and differences as to discipline
- Stop looking to each other for praise or appreciation and instead recognize that good parenting is a mutual responsibility
- Encourage the children to feel comfortable in each of their homes
- Encourage the children to develop friendships with their stepparents
- Encourage the children to express their feelings and to feel safe in doing so

Here are some proposed suggestions as to how to make your decision-making process more businesslike:

- Acknowledge that the children will benefit if you can reduce conflict and create a safer emotional environment
- Stop making assumptions about one another's views or intentions and try to reach more detailed agreements
- Start putting your agreements in writing, even if it's a brief note or letter
- Try to understand each other's point of view on every issue
- Stop jumping to conclusions and begin asking more questions
- Keep appointments, except in emergencies
- Build more trust by honoring agreements
- Avoid unilateral decisions about the children
- Recognize that the stepparents play an important role in the children's lives and start including the stepparents in the decision making

- Acknowledge that each of you will check with your new spouse before making an arrangement involving the children
- Focus on finding solutions that work for the children rather than trying to prove each other wrong
- Clarify boundaries between the households by limiting phone calls, minimizing requests for favors, putting visitation schedules on paper, scheduling meetings in person or by phone, and respecting each other's autonomy when the children are visiting the other parent

Finally, here are some suggestions for improving your ability to negotiate resolution of conflicts rather than winding up in shouting matches:

- Identify the issues that were cause for chronic conflict
- Prepare a list of issues, and compare notes
- Prioritize the list of issues from easiest to most difficult
- Schedule a series of meetings, preferably including the stepparent, to discuss one or two of the issues at the meeting
- Avoid pressuring each other into agreement
- Address no more than two major issues at any meeting
- Seek help from family mediation as to issues about which they could not reach agreement
- Come to each negotiation meeting as prepared as possible to discuss the issue
- Remain open to new ideas and alternate solutions throughout the negotiation sessions

Review these suggestions and draft your own proposals for changes in attitudes, communication styles, and negotiating principles to make peace in your stepfamily by building a parenting coalition.

Making Peace with Your Ex-Spouse

We human beings all share a destructive psychological trait which often strikes with a vengeance in the evolving relations between stepparents and a spouse's ex. This trait—often known as the tendency toward "enemy making"—involves an unconscious process whereby we repress our own hostile feelings and project those feelings on the person whom we may not really know but we instinctively fear.

A parent instinctively fears a same-sex stepparent, because a parent believes the stepparent may attempt to replace the parent in the child's heart. So, too, a stepparent often fears a same-sex parent. Stepparents often believe that the same-sex parent may try to break up the remarriage.

The irony of the enemy-making process is that it thrives on lack of contact between the two people who regard each other as enemies and usually withers when genuine contact is made.

A session or two with a psychotherapy professional can often allay the mistrust of two people who have never met, particularly when they discover common ground in a mutual concern for the children's well-being. This common ground exists as a potential basis for a constructive relationship between most stepparents and same-sex natural parents. Nevertheless, the key to finding this common ground is establishing direct communication between the two people who considered each other enemies. A peacemaking and parenting coalition begins to evolve out of the communication process.

When the New Wife and Ex-Wife Compete

Often, there can be great competitiveness between the new wife and the ex-wife. However, each must be prepared to accept the other as he or she may be. You cannot expect to form a parenting coalition on the condition that the wife or ex-wife change. Furthermore, any effort to bad-mouth the other person or influence her behavior through the children will only make matters worse.

Once you have accepted that the other person will be a significant part of your life, you can acknowledge the importance of establishing a cordial relationship, and begin to work toward a parenting coalition with the ex or new wife.

From Competition to a Coalition

The process of making peace between the same-sex parent and step-parent—a mother and stepmother, a father and stepfather—can be emotionally complex. Here are principles that you should try to apply as appropriate:

- Create opportunities for direct communication
- Avoid criticism of one another
- Discuss feelings of competition
- Acknowledge that the parent will always be the parent
- Acknowledge that the stepparent may love and wish to provide the best for the children without attempting to replace the parent
- Give children the permission to love the parent and the step-parent as different people in different roles
- Involve the absent parent, particularly the noncustodial father or mother, in decision making
- Create opportunities for the noncustodial parent to participate with the child in school, church, and afterschool functions
- Accept each other without a demand for change
- Not try to force a close relationship if the parent or stepparent would prefer a cordial and businesslike relationship
- Avoid self-righteousness; acknowledge your weaknesses
- Accept that each may have different values and encourage the children to learn from the differences
- Look to your current spouse for support and appreciation of your parenting efforts; not look to your children or stepchildren
- Work cooperatively to create a parenting coalition

As difficult as it may seem to form a parenting coalition, it would also be a mistake to underestimate your ability to succeed. Ideal parenting coalitions do exist where the children feel supported by two sets of parents and comfortable moving between two separate but related households. Nat, Joanne, Connie, and Dan are one such group of parents.

Nat divorced Connie when their sons were ages seven and five. He retained custody while Connie pursued a career in dance. Within a year, Nat fell in love with Joanne and they married. From the outset,

Joanne encouraged Connie to play a role in the family. By welcoming Connie, Joanne disarmed both Connie and her own fears. They cooked Thanksgiving dinner together the first year of Joanne's marriage. Nat felt somewhat awkward, but the cooperation between the two women was infectious. With such a good start to the relationship, Connie remained part of Nat and Joanne's extended family. When Connie married Dan four years later, a pattern of mutual support and acceptance had already been established. Dan brought one son to his marriage, who was happy to meet his stepbrothers living with Nat and Joanne. Both couples had children of their own, raising the total number of children among the four parents to five, three boys and two girls. Holidays for these two families are one part chaos mixed with two parts love for a remarkable celebration. These two couples are a lighthouse of love and a great hope for the future of the family in America even as the traditional nuclear family gives way to the complex and dynamic extended stepfamily.

Changes in Visitation or Custody

Coping with change in custody is one of the greatest challenges to a parenting coalition. Emotional bonds to children grow very strong. It may be that only another stepparent can appreciate how much a stepparent may love a stepchild. The prospect of giving up custody raises all the old issues of loss and sacrifice that may have been long ago resolved. However, if it becomes clear that a change in custody would benefit the child (for instance, enabling attendance in a special school), this should take place. Once the parent and stepparent losing custody have had an opportunity to express all their feelings, including anger and resentment, in a supportive atmosphere, they too will begin to weigh the pros and cons of the proposed change. Ultimately, any change for the children's good should receive their support.

What Is Best for the Children?

The impact of various custody and visitation arrangements on the emotional well-being of the children is the subject of increasing professional attention. Psychologists are far from having well-defined answers to questions such as: How often should young children visit their noncustodial parent? What is the emotional impact of a change in custody? What happens when siblings split up, one living with the biological father and the other with the biological mother? What emotional effects follow from frequent changes in visitation schedules?

The growing number of stepfamilies virtually assures that the mental health community will provide more detailed and better answers to these questions over the next decade. Nevertheless, here are some available guidelines to consider:

- Regular contact with both parents is preferred to support the emotional development of the children following divorce.
- Young children generally require a higher degree of emotional continuity than older children. For example, children under three do best with a primary caretaker. Alternating custody between mother and father is probably not wise.
- After the age of three, children are generally able to spend more time visiting the noncustodial parents, but the child needs to be told when the visits will occur and what activities may be planned. Going to the store or doing errands may be enough.
- Changing visitation plans at the last minute is traumatic. Children develop expectations and anticipations of seeing "Mommy" and "Daddy." Changing schedules leads to disappointment and undermines a basic sense of trust.
- Older children require and deserve more information and consultation about visitation. They have friends and plans of their own. Older children do better if they have input as to the visitation schedule and planned activities. They are also more able to accommodate changes if they are given appropriate notice when rescheduling occurs.
- When older children, particularly teens, express a desire to live with another parent, be supportive in examining the idea. It took great courage for your teen to make the suggestion. He or

she is struggling with the pros and cons—school, friends, feeling more comfortable with one parent or stepparent than the other. You can assist your child's emotional development by encouraging your child to identify and weigh the factors that he or she thinks would best meet his or her needs and serve his or her growth as a responsible, self-motivated person.

Once a decision is made to change custody arrangements, it is important for all members of the parenting coalition to support the process. Children are perceptive. The parent or stepparent who begrudgingly accepts a change in custody risks burdening his or her child with guilt and shame about "being disloyal." No one is served by sending a child off to live with another set of parents and burdening the child with a huge dose of guilt in the process.

The way to avoid creating guilt is for both sets of parents to discuss the impending move with the child. For example, when my stepson Michael proposed leaving Toronto and moving to California, I encouraged him to write down his hopes, concerns, fears, and goals for the move. I also suggested Michael identify what he expected to lose (his Toronto friends, watching his baby half-brother and sister grow up, etc.). Once Michael made these notes, I suggested he have a Heart Talk with his dad and stepmom in Toronto and later with us in California. In this way, all of us were able to empathize with the emotional struggle Michael faced in choosing to make a radical change in his life.

School-Year Parents Versus Summertime Parents

A parenting coalition is especially important to children who move between families separated by long distances. With the children in these cases usually spending the school years with one set of parents and the summer with another, the opportunities for mistrust and miscommunication are large. At the same time, conflict can be minimized if the parents respect two basic principles.

First, differences in climate, geography, weather, and culture increase the likelihood that the basic rules and routines of the two households will differ markedly. In our own case, the differences in lifestyle between Southern California and Toronto are great. In addition, when Sirah's boys visited during summer, a vacation attitude prevailed. It can be tempting for one set of parents to criticize the routines or values in another household, but such criticism only breeds resentment among the parents and divided loyalties among the children.

Long-distance parents and their children are best served by the parents' showing respect for one another's differences and encouraging the children to follow the rules and routines of each household while they are there. When Michael visited during the summer, I did not allow him to protest our no-smoking rule just because he was allowed to smoke in Toronto. Similarly, I did not expect Michael to resist any household rules in Toronto with an appeal to our routine in Southern California. Parenting coalitions who respect one another's differences can expect their children both to respect the rules of each household and to appreciate the opportunity to learn from the different rules, routines, and values of two different households. Mutual respect within the parenting coalition also saves the children from the emotional pressure of divided loyalty and the temptation to achieve their ends through manipulation and deceit.

The second principle in maintaining a long-distance parenting coalition is for the parents to communicate regularly and to encourage the children to remain in touch with their parents in the other household. A monthly conference call is the minimum communication required among long-distance parents so that absent fathers or mothers who see their children only during the summer feel involved in their children's upbringing. If you are a summertime parent, you should also arrange to make contact with and receive regular communications from teachers and coaches. Even if you can only provide your children with advice or encouragement by phone, the fact that you take the time to keep up on their progress will show that you care.

Suggestions for Long-Distance Parenting

Whether you are a school-year parent or a summertime parent, you need to stay in communication with your child during the time your child is away. Here are some suggestions:

- Write letters often. A short note every week is better than a long one every two months.
- Enclose a stamped, self-addressed envelope so that your child can write back to you with ease and need not depend on anyone else to stay in touch with you.
- Call regularly—once a week if possible—and let your child know when to expect the call. When you make a phone date, keep it. You need not run up large bills—short calls at the low-rate periods are fine, and don't feel embarrassed about telling your child you need to be economic on the phone.
- Buy your child an inexpensive cassette recorder and show him or her how to use it. Exchange tapes. Again, enclose a self-addressed, stamped envelope to make it easy for your child to make a tape and mail it to you.
- Agree to share experiences long distance—i.e., follow the same team, watch the same TV show, or go to the same movie. You should then have more to share by letter, phone, or cassette.
- Let your child know you are keeping track of their achievements.

Parents who are part of a parenting coalition encourage their children to keep in touch with an absent parent. When a letter or tape arrives, there is shared excitement, but the child is allowed his or her own privacy in reading or listening to the absent parent's communication. The child is then encouraged to answer by letter or tape. Parents can assist a young child to respond by cutting out a picture from a magazine or mailing a leaf found in the woods. When the child hears one parent encourage him to keep in touch with his other parent miles away, the message is clear. We are still a family even though we live apart with your stepmother or stepfather.

A parenting coalition is also essential in long-distance parenting to ease the child's transition from one home to another. Parting at the end of a summer vacation never stops being painful because the summer visit seems short compared with the long school year. In contrast, when the children arrive from a long summer visit, they may have difficulty settling into their old routine. A vacation routine must be left behind and a school routine resumed. The more connection and consideration the child perceives between the two households, the more easily will the child make the transition. For example, it is advisable at the end of the summer to wind down activities, enforce earlier bedtimes, and make sure the child is as well rested as possible. The transition begun on departure from one home eases the transition on arrival at the other. Parents and children all gain from the mutual consideration and planning.

Enrolling Grandparents in Your Stepfamily

An important part of a parenting coalition is enrolling the support of grandparents and step-grandparents. During the emotional turmoil of divorce, children benefit greatly from the continuity and reassurances provided by one or more grandparent. During and after a remarriage, grandparents can play an equally valuable role if they understand and feel comfortable with how they fit into the new stepfamily. In the rush toward remarriage, however, many remarrieds overlook the feelings, concerns, and discomforts of not only their own parents but their exs' parents as well. The result is often to create another potential source of conflict in the stepfamily rather than to secure another source of emotional (and financial) support.

"The kids adore Grandma Mickie and Grandpa Fritz," explained Arthur about his daughter's and son's feelings toward their natural grandparents. "Just because Marcia left us doesn't mean Natalie and Jamie should lose their grandparents."

"I feel very uncomfortable about Mickie and Fritz," Arthur's second wife Sabrina admitted. "My own parents are dead. Mickie and Fritz live two towns away. They want to see the kids more often than their own mother does. It's as if she's keeping her hold on the family through her parents."

In discussing her feelings about her stepchildren's maternal grandparents, Sabrina revealed that she had yet to make peace with Arthur's ex, Marcia, who had moved to San Francisco, 500 miles away. Arthur and Sabrina had been remarried only two months, so Sabrina's discomfort with Marcia was understandable; they had not yet had the opportunity to establish a parenting coalition. But the issue of how to relate to Marcia's parents was immediate. Mickie and Fritz lived close by, and they adored their grandchildren.

I suggested to Arthur and Sabrina that they might benefit by having a Family Circle with Mickie and Fritz. Arthur, Natalie, Jamie, Mickie, and Fritz all shared preexisting bonds. Sabrina and Arthur also had formed a new bond. To avoid further conflict, the potential triangles in this family needed to be encircled.

In this case, a two-step process was appropriate. Arthur, Sabrina, Mickie, and Fritz held their own Family Circle. Arthur had the opportunity to express how much he valued Mickie and Fritz as part of the family. Sabrina told of her misgivings about friendship with Mickie and Fritz. "It's as if I am stepping into your daughter's shoes," she confided. "It seems very scary." Mickie and Fritz acknowledged their own mixed feelings, but they explained how important their grandchildren were to them. "For our granddaughter and grandson," Mickie explained, "we are ready to accept you as our son-in-law's new wife. I never expected to be saying such a thing, but what could be more right with my daughter off in search of her own dream."

Once Arthur, Sabrina, Mickie, and Fritz had cleared the air, they planned a picnic together with the children. To Sabrina's surprise, her stepchildren seemed to warm to her, and Mickie and Fritz demonstrated their acceptance of her. Mickie and Fritz showed their grandchildren that there was plenty of room in the family for another loving person. It was not lost on the children that if Grandma Mickie and Grandpa Fritz, their own mother's parents, could accept Sabrina, then maybe Sabrina was not so bad after all.

Sometimes grandparents cause conflict with the stepfamily despite their intentions to be supportive. For instance, gift-giving in different amounts to biological vs. nonbiological grandchildren can cause resentment and unhappiness, whereas the grandparent never gave it a second thought. In such cases, a Heart Talk between you and your spouse's parents can be very helpful.

Some stepparents feel uncomfortable about encouraging a bond between their own parents and their stepchildren. The step-grandparent/step-grandchild relationship is unfamiliar. In my own family, I have been delighted to watch the evolution of a very close bond between my mother and my stepsons Damien and Michael. The fact that they thoroughly enjoy their "Oma" helps bond us all as a stepfamily.

Open communication is the best way to enroll your parents and your spouse's parents to support the stepfamily. If tension develops, a Family Circle or a Heart Talk may be very effective. In addition, here are some general guidelines to help enroll grandparents in support of your stepfamily:

- Reassure grandparents and grandchildren that the remarriage will not cut out their relationship.
- Actively encourage grandparents and grandchildren to continue to see one another as in the past.
- Help step-grandparents and step-grandchildren to get to know one another by planning an event, such as a picnic, that everyone will enjoy.
- Once the ice has broken, plan events—whether around holidays, the Super Bowl, or just special family dinners—where you have grandparents, step-grandparents, children, and step-grandchildren. You may not have everyone at every event, but send the invitations and let anyone who could not attend know that they were missed.
- Take pictures at every opportunity with a mix of grandchildren, grandparents, and step-grandparents. Send everyone copies to create their own portfolio on their new extended family.
- Encourage the in-laws to see one another even if they do not share biological children.
- Arrange adult gatherings from time to time where you, your spouse, both your parents, and your ex-spouse's parents can spend time together.
- Avoid pushing any member of the older generation to settle money matters. Better to encourage them to think about their grandchildren and step-grandchildren's futures.
- Do not let tension develop between you and your spouse about one of the parental figures in your lives—whether your own parent, your spouse's parents, or your ex-spouse's par-

ents. Have a Heart Talk to clear the air, and follow up with a Family Circle with the appropriate people involved.

Grandparents and step-grandparents can provide invaluable support to any stepfamily. You will be rewarded manyfold for your efforts in enrolling grandparents and step-grandparents in your parenting coalition.

The New Extended Family

Prior to the ascendance of the isolated nuclear family, kinship provided support for individual family members in times of crisis. The decline of the isolated nuclear family and emergence of the stepfamily may be providing the opportunity for the rebirth of kinship and the emotional support among family members that was once available through the extended family. One of my clients is testimony to the fact that necessity may be the mother of reinvention.

Bruce and Marla are a happily married couple with three children, the oldest of whom is in college. Nevertheless, Bruce came to me for help because he was concerned about a family crisis—in this case, the crisis in his sister's stepfamily. His younger sister Candace had two daughters, ages sixteen and fourteen, by her first husband, an alcoholic whom Bruce thought was a terrible influence on his nieces. Candace and her girls moved into Eugene, her new husband, and his boy's home, and Candace's older daughter had become very difficult.

"Candace says Robin has become impossible," Bruce explained. "She stays out, and she did poorly this year in school and won't listen to anyone. Eugene is trying to crack down, but Candace says it's only making things worse, not only with Robin but between the two of them. Five kids, three teenagers . . . . That's a lot for any parent, much less a new family and new marriage."

Bruce was hesitant to offer to let his niece come live with him and his wife at their beach house for the summer. "Robin (her aunt) and I have had a special relationship ever since she was a little girl," Bruce explained. "Maybe it would take some pressure off her and ease the tension for Candace and Eugene. We want her marriage to make it."

Needless to say, I endorsed Bruce's suggestion. My only advice was to clear the invitation with Candace and Eugene first, and to make arrangements as well for each of the kids, including their new step-nephews, to visit for at least one weekend for the summer.

The fact that Bruce thought he needed counseling to assist his sister and new brother-in-law is testimony to how narrowly we as a society have come to define family. In times past, a brother wouldn't have thought twice about offering to take care of one of the children during a period of crisis. The emergence of the stepfamily is changing that attitude. Your stepfamily is a giant step in discovering what I like to call your godfamily; the people god has surrounded you with that you are meant to learn from, care for, and love.

There is a simple exercise I suggest all my clients try at a Family Circle or family picnic. Each family member should try drawing the stepfamily tree. What children discover through this process is the network of loving adults in their lives—as many as two mothers, two fathers, eight grandparents, and numerous aunts, uncles, step-aunts, and step-uncles, as well as siblings and cousins galore. Typically, you will start with an ordinary piece of paper and start drafting the geneal-ogy only to discover that you need a much bigger piece of paper. Drawing the stepfamily tree creates an immediate sense of connection among all members of the stepfamily. Children (and adults) can see the relationships and appreciate the connections. This exercise is a delightful way to begin appreciating the breadth and depth of your extended family. It is also healing. You cannot forget your ex-spouse and his parents or his siblings. By going through this exercise with your children, they perceive the healing just in the fact that their mom and dad appear near the center of the stepfamily tree.

Proud to Be a Stepfamily

When I give seminars on making peace in stepfamilies, I usually close with a simple message—take pride in your role as a stepparent. Our society is finally recognizing that what defines a family are more the choices people make in caring for one another than genetic chance. To be a biological mother or father requires only a brief encounter. To be a family requires a lifetime of mutual caring, personal growth, and commitment to the welfare of each family member. Bottom line, there is only one family and that's the human family; we are all blood relatives.

The stepfamily was once seen as a broken family. No longer is this view appropriate. In fact, the contrary view is more likely the case. Today's stepfamily is the family repaired and on its way toward creating unique opportunities for the mutual support and personal development of its members. In a stepfamily, you learn to reach beyond yourself in appreciating others, and into yourself in discovering just how much love you have to share.

The isolated nuclear family is rapidly declining as the dominant family unit. Many commentators bemoan its passing, as if the nuclear family represented a hallowed tradition. The fact is that the nuclear family has proven terribly susceptible to isolation and dysfunction. In contrast, ample evidence suggests that stepfamilies are creating kinship networks which have rescued the family from isolation and re-created the extended family with all of its supports.

Yet, to survive and thrive as a stepfamily requires courage and commitment. Having grown up in nuclear families, most of us find the conflicts in the stepfamily to be unfamiliar. Institutions such as schools are still lagging in support of the stepfamily. There is no doubt that stepfamilies are susceptible to a wide array of internal conflicts that require special attention to resolve. What I have found in my own life and in the lives of my clients is that making peace in your stepfamily is worth every bit of effort required.

I have no doubt that I am a better person for having chosen to become a stepfather and having embraced the unexpected challenges in that role. No, it has not always been easy. At times, I was certainly tempted to give up. But what I have gained from my stepfamily is enormous. Most of all, in overcoming our travails as parents and stepparents, I have come to love and appreciate my wife in ways that I had not even known were possible. I have been blessed with the joy of bringing our daughter into the world, and I have also been blessed with the joy of creating a unique parenting bond with my stepsons. I have been forced to examine some of my deepest values, and to learn the real meaning of altruism. For me, my stepfamily has been an incubator of the deepest lessons of living—an adventure of the heart to love and be loved.

Your stepfamily offers you, your spouse, and your children an opportunity to discover and share the deepest joys and satisfactions of a family—a lifelong commitment to caring for one another. Your stepfamily holds promise for the rebirth of family as an extended network of people committed to one another's well-being. The stepfamily teaches us all that, in truth, there is only one type of family—the extended family—of which we all are members. In the eyes of the great religious traditions, we are all family. By embracing your own stepfamily, you walk the living path of these great traditions. I am hopeful that this book serves you in embracing your stepfamily.

$A\ \ p\ \ p\ \ e\ \ n\ \ d\ \ i\ \ x\ \ \ A$

Helpful Books for Parents and Stepparents

Adler, Allen, and Archambault, Christine. *Divorce Recovery.* New York: Bantam, 1992.

Baker, Nancy. *New Lives for Former Wives.* New York: Anchor Press/Doubleday, 1980.

Bayard, Robert, and Bayard, Jean. *How to Deal with Your Acting-Up-Teenager—Practical Self-Help for Desperate Parents.* San Jose, CA: The Accord Press, 1981.

Berger, Stuart. *Divorce Without Victims.* Boston: Houghton Mifflin, 1983.

Berman, Claire. *What Am I Doing In a Stepfamily?* New York: Carol Publishing Co., 1992.

Berman, Claire. *Making It as a Stepparent: New Roles, New Rules.* New York: Harper & Row, 1986.

Bernstein, Anne. *Yours, Mine, and Ours: How Families Change When Remarrieds Have a Child Together.* New York: MacMillan, 1989.

Bloomfield, Harold H., with Felder, Leonard. *Making Peace With Yourself.* New York: Ballantine Books, 1986.

Bloomfield, Harold H., with Felder, Leonard. *Making Peace With Your Parents.* New York: Ballantine Books, 1985.

Bloomfield, Harold H., and Kory, Robert. *Inner Joy.* New York: Jove, 1984.

Bloomfield, Harold H., with poetry by Josefowitz, Natasha. *Love Secrets for a Lasting Relationship.* New York: Bantam Books, 1992.

Bloomfield, Harold H., and Vettese, Sirah, with Kory, Robert. *Lifemates.* New York: Signet, 1991.

Burns, Cherie. *Stepmotherhood: How To Survive Without Feeling Frustrated, Left Out, or Wicked.* New York: Harper & Row, 1986.

Coale, Helen. *All About Families the Second Time Around.* Atlanta: Peachtree Publishing, 1980.

Cohen, Miriam. *Long Distance Parenting: A Guide for Divorced Parents.* New York: New American Library, 1989.

Colgrove, Melba, Bloomfield, Harold H., and McWilliams, Peter. *How to Survive the Loss of a Love.* Los Angeles: Prelude Press, 1992.

Curran, Dolores. *Stress and the Family.* Minneapolis: Winston Press, 1985.

Dodson, Fitzhugh. *How to Discipline with Love.* New York: NAL Dutton, 1987.

Eckler, James. *Step-by-Stepparenting.* Crozet, VA: Betterway Publications, 1988.

Einstein, Elizabeth. *The Stepfamily: Living, Loving and Learning.* New York: MacMillan, 1982.

Espinoza, Renata, and Navaman, Yvonne. *Stepparenting.* DHEW Publication no. ADM 89-579, U.S. Government Printing Office. Washington, DC, 1979.

Frydenger, Tom, and Frydenger, Adrianne. *The Blended Family.* Grand Rapids, MI: Chosen Books, 1984.

Gray, John. *What You Feel, You Can Heal.* Mill Valley, CA: Heart Publishing, 1984.

Issacs, Susan. *Who's In Control? A Parent's Guide to Discipline.* New York: Putnam, 1986.

Keshet, Jamie. *Love and Power in the Stepfamily: A Practical Guide.* New York: McGraw-Hill, 1986.

Kuzma, Kay. *Part-Time Parent.* New York: Wade Publishing, 1980.

Lewis, Helen. *All About Families, The Second Time Around.* Atlanta: Peachtree Publishing, 1980.

Maddox, Brenda. *The Half Parent.* New York: Evans, 1975.

Mala, Burt. *Stepfamilies Stepping Ahead: An Eight-Step Program for Successful Family Living.* Lincoln, NE: Stepfamily Association of America, 1989.

Noble, June, and Noble, William. *How to Live with Other People's Children.* New York: Hawthorne Books, 1977.

Prilik, Pearl. *Stepmothering—Another Kind of Love.* New York: Berkeley, 1990.

Reingold, Carmel Berman. *Remarriage.* New York: Harper & Row, 1976.

Ricci, Isolina. *Mom's House, Dad's House: Making Shared Custody Work.* New York: MacMillan, 1980.

Roosevelt, Ruth, and Lofas, Jeanette. *Living In Step: A Remarriage Manual for Parents and Children.* New York: Stein & Day, 1976.

Savage, Karen, and Adams, Patricia. *The Good Stepmother: A Practical Guide.* New York: Crown, 1988.

Schuster, Sandy, and Palomares, Suzanna. *Family Connections.* Spring Valley, CA: Inner Choice Publishing, 1991.

Visher, Emily, and Visher, John. *How to Win as a Stepfamily.* New York: Brunner & Mazel, 1991.

Visher, Emily, and Visher, John. *Stepfamilies Stepping Ahead.* Lincoln, NE: Stepfamilies Press, 1989.

Visher, Emily, and Visher, John. *Talking About Stepfamilies.* New York: MacMillan, 1990.

A p p e n d i x   B

Helpful Books for Stepchildren (ages 3–9)

Bradley, Buff. *Where Do I Belong? A Kids Guide to Stepfamilies*. Reading, MA: Addison-Wesley, 1982.

Brown, Laurence Krasney, and Brown, Marc. *Dinosaurs Divorce*. New York: Little, Brown & Co., 1988.

Burt, Maria Schuster, and Burt, Roger B. *What's Special About Our Stepfamily: A Participation Book for Children*. New York: Doubleday, 1983.

Byars, Betsy. *The Animal, the Vegetable and John D. Jones*. New York: Delacorte, 1982.

Evans, Marla. *This is Me and My Two Families*. New York: Magination Press, 1988.

Gardner, Richard. *The Boys and Girls Book About Divorce*. New York: Bantam, 1971.

Goff, Beth. *Where Is Daddy: The Story of Divorce*. Boston: Beacon Press, 1978.

Green, Phyllis. *A New Mother for Martha*. New York: Human Science Press, 1978.

Helmering, Doris W. *I Have Two Families*. Nashville: Abingdon, 1981.

Hunter, Evan. *Me and Mr. Stenner*. New York: J.B. Lippincott, 1976.

Jasinek, Doris, and Ryan, Pamela Bell. *A Family is a Circle of People Who Love You*. Minneapolis: CompCare, 1988.

Kremetz, Jill. *How It Feels When a Parent Dies*. New York: Knopf, 1981.

Lewis, Helen. *All About Families: The Second Time Around*. Atlanta: Peachtree Publishing, 1980.

Sobol, Harriet. *My Other Mother, My Other Father*. New York: Macmillan, 1979.

Stenson, Janet. *Now I Have a Stepparent and it's Kind of Confusing*. New York: Avon Press, 1979.

Vigna, Judith. *Grandma Without Me*. Morton Grove, IL: Whitman, Albert, & Co., 1984.

Vigna, Judith. *She's Not My Real Mother*. Morton Grove, IL: Whitman, Albert, & Co., 1980.

Helpful Books for Step-Teens (ages 10–18)

Berger, Terry. *A Friend Can Help*. Milwaukee: Raintree Editions, 1975.

Berman, Claire. *What Am I Doing in a Stepfamily?* New Jersey: Lyle Stuart, 1992.

Craven, Linda. *Stepfamilies: New Patterns in Harmony*. New York: Julian Messner, 1982.

Eichoness, Monte. *Why Can't Anyone Hear Me?* Ventura, CA: Monroe Press, 1989.

Getzoff, Ann, and McClenahan, Carolyn. *Stepkids: A Survival Guide for Teenagers in Stepfamilies*. New York: Walker, 1984.

Hawley, Richard. *The Big Issues in the Adolescent Journey*. New York: Walker, 1988.

Wesson, Carolyn McLenahan. *Teen Troubles: How to Keep Them From Becoming Tragedies*. New York: Walker, 1988.

A p p e n d i x C

Resources for Stepfamilies

ORGANIZATIONS

Stepfamily Association of America
215 Centennial Mall South, Suite 212
Lincoln, Nebraska 68508
(402) 477-STEP

Stepfamily Foundation
333 West End Avenue
New York, New York 10023
(212) 877-3244

Stepfamilies and Beyond
Listening, Inc.
8716 Pine Avenue
Gary, Indiana 46403
(219) 938-6962

HOTLINES

National Runaway Switchboard
(800) 621-4000

Alateen and Al-Anon Family Group Headquarters
(800) 344-2666

Drug Abuse Hotline
(800) 538-4840

Family Guidance Center
(800) 892-5750

A c k n o w l e d g m e n t s

This book is written in the first person singular because so much of it is based on my personal and professional experience, but this should not imply that its writing has throughout been anything less than a collaboration of the highest order. Robert Kory is a superb writer and a brilliant family-conflict mediator without whom I could not have written this book. He combines the skills of a lawyer and personal counselor in ways that should become a model to the profession.

I am deeply grateful to my wife and partner, Sirah Vettese. Her guidance and editorial inputs were invaluable. She taught me what it means to be part of a thriving family through her profound love, wisdom, and loyalty. Special praise to my daughter Shazara and stepsons Damien and Michael for their unconditional love and lessons of the heart.

Special gratitude to my beloved father Max, mother Fridl and sister Nora for their devotion and encouragement.

Special thanks to Phyllis Kory for her editorial assistance and her many contributions. Not only did she work long and hard hours reviewing every word in each draft, but she did more. She added heartfelt inspiration.

I also wish to thank my colleagues in the stepfamily field who have shared their knowledge and inspiration, especially Richard and Patricia Bennett, Claire Berman, Elizabeth Einstein, Tom and Adrianne Frydenger, Jamie Keshet, Isolina Ricci, and most especially Emily and John Visher.

For their input I wish to thank Catie Carpenter, Eleanor Griffith, Marty Kravits, Kenneth Mallory, Harry Pickens, and all the clients that are my privilege to serve in Del Mar, California.

I appreciate the poem and suggestions of my friend and colleague Natasha Josefowitz.

I also wish to thank Khalsa, Marly Meadows, Paul Sanford, and Nora Stern for their help in preparation of the manuscript.

For their friendship and support I wish to thank Robert and Leslie Cooper, Lenny Felder, Mike and Donna Fletcher, Susie Gomez, John·Gray, Christel Hammad, Allen and Maryann Jardine, Arnold Lazarus, Jonathan and Wendy Lazear, Norman and Lyn Lear, Mike Love and Jackie Piesen, Barnet and Jean

Meltzer, Vince and Laura Regalbuto, Bob and Paula Sundquist, Ali and Sybil Rubottom, and Carl and Gina Wilson.

For his suggestion that I do a book on family peacemaking and for his total support and faith in this project, I wish to acknowledge Bob Miller, Publisher of Hyperion. Special thanks to Leslie Wells for her keen intelligence, good taste, and warm friendship in editing this book. Victor Weaver designed a unique, artistic book jacket. For her care as agent for this work, I wish to acknowledge Ellen Levine.

Deep appreciation to the leadership of the Stepfamily Association of America for providing outstanding education and support.

About the Authors

HAROLD H. BLOOMFIELD, M.D., is one of the leading psychological educators of our time. A Yale-trained psychiatrist, Dr. Bloomfield is an adjunct professor of psychology at Union Graduate School. From his first book *TM,* which was a major international bestseller on the *New York Times* list for over six months, to his current bestseller, *How to Survive the Loss of a Love,* which has sold over two million copies, Dr. Bloomfield has proven to be at the forefront of many important and valuable self-help movements worldwide. Along with *Making Peace in Your Stepfamily,* his other bestsellers, *Making Peace with Your Parents* and *Making Peace with Yourself,* introduced personal- and family peacemaking to millions of people. Dr. Bloomfield's books have sold over five million copies and have been translated into twenty-two languages.

Dr. Bloomfield is among the world's most sought-after keynote speakers and seminar leaders for public appearances, educational programs, and conferences. He is a frequent guest on the *Oprah Winfrey, Donohue, Sally Jessy Raphael, Larry King Live,* and *Sonya Live* shows and CNN and ABC News specials. In addition to professional journals, his work and popular articles appear in *USA Today, Newsweek,* Los Angeles *Times,* San Francisco *Examiner, Cosmopolitan, Ladies' Home Journal, New Woman,* and *American Health.*

Dr. Bloomfield is the recipient of the Medical Self-Care Magazine Book of the Year Award, the Golden Apple Award for Outstanding Psychological Educator, and the American Holistic Health Association's Lifetime Achievement Award.

Dr. Bloomfield is an internationally respected family business consultant, who specializes in family therapy, organizational management, and executive coaching. He maintains a private practice of psychiatry, psychotherapy, and family counseling in Del Mar, California. Dr. Bloomfield is a member of the American Psychiatric Association and the San Diego Psychiatric Society. He lives with his wife, Sirah, and their children in Del Mar, California.

Harold H. Bloomfield, M.D., is a much admired keynote speaker and seminar leader for public audiences, corporate programs, and professional conferences. For further information regarding personal appearances and to order audio- and videocassette products, please call or send a self-addressed, stamped envelope to:

Harold H. Bloomfield, M.D.
1011 Camino Del Mar, Suite 234
Del Mar, California 92014
(619) 481-7102

ROBERT KORY is a leader in the emerging field of mediating divorces, custody, and other family conflicts. A summa cum laude graduate of Yale College and the University of Chicago Law School, Mr. Kory practices law in Los Angeles, but regards litigation as destructive and inappropriate to family conflicts. Director of the Family Mediation Center, he applies principles discussed in this book coupled with his legal training to help divorcing couples reach agreements that truly make peace and provide a foundation of support for the divorced family. He is available to speak with groups about family mediation. For further information, Mr. Kory can be reached at:

Robert B. Kory
Family Mediation Center
10960 Wilshire Boulevard, Suite 2224
Los Angeles, California 90024
(310) 473–3316